ROUTLEDGE LIBRARY EDITIONS:
POLICE AND POLICING

Volume 22

SOCIAL CHANGES, CRIME AND POLICE

SOCIAL CHANGES, CRIME AND POLICE

International Conference
June 1– 4, 1992 Budapest, Hungary

Edited by
LOUISE SHELLEY
and
JÓZSEF VIGH

LONDON AND NEW YORK

First published in 1995 by Harwood Academic Publishers

This edition first published in 2023
by Routledge
4 Park Square, Milton Park, Abingdon, Oxon OX14 4RN

and by Routledge
605 Third Avenue, New York, NY 10158

Routledge is an imprint of the Taylor & Francis Group, an informa business

© 1995 by Harwood Academic Publishers GmbH

All rights reserved. No part of this book may be reprinted or reproduced or utilised in any form or by any electronic, mechanical, or other means, now known or hereafter invented, including photocopying and recording, or in any information storage or retrieval system, without permission in writing from the publishers.

Trademark notice: Product or corporate names may be trademarks or registered trademarks, and are used only for identification and explanation without intent to infringe.

British Library Cataloguing in Publication Data
A catalogue record for this book is available from the British Library

ISBN: 978-1-032-41114-9 (Set)
ISBN: 978-1-032-45643-0 (Volume 22) (hbk)
ISBN: 978-1-032-45645-4 (Volume 22) (pbk)
ISBN: 978-1-003-37802-0 (Volume 22) (ebk)

DOI: 10.4324/9781003378020

Publisher's Note
The publisher has gone to great lengths to ensure the quality of this reprint but points out that some imperfections in the original copies may be apparent.

Disclaimer
The publisher has made every effort to trace copyright holders and would welcome correspondence from those they have been unable to trace.

Social Changes, Crime and Police

International Conference
June 1–4, 1992 Budapest, Hungary

Edited by
Louise Shelley and József Vigh

hcap harwood academic publishers
Australia • Austria • Belgium • China • France • Germany • India • Japan • Malaysia
Netherlands • Russia • Singapore • Switzerland • Thailand • United Kingdom • United States

COPYRIGHT © 1995 BY Harwood Academic Publishers GmbH

All rights reserved.

No part of this book may be reproduced or utilized in any form or by any means, electronic or mechanical, including photocopying and recording, or by any information storage or retrieval system, without permission in writing from the publisher. Printed in Singapore.

Harwood Academic Publishers
Poststrasse 22
7000 Chur, Switzerland

BRITISH LIBRARY CATALOGUING IN PUBLICATION DATA

Social Changes, Crime and Police:
International Conference, June 1-4, 1992
Budapest, Hungary
  I. Vigh, József   II. Shelley, Louise I.
364

ISBN 3-7186-5684-1 (HC)
    3-7186-5691-4 (SC)

Contents

Foreword	5
Péter Boross	
Opening Speech	7

Topic I.

József Vigh	
Social Changes, Crime and Police – Introductory Report	11
Robert Reiner	
The British Policing Tradition: Model or Myth?	27
Knut Sveri	
Human Rights and the Right of the Police to Use Physical Force	37

Topic II.

Uwe Ewald	
The Effect of Social Changes Upon Crime	51
Kauko Aromaa	
Emerging Problems of Official Social Control in Finland	62
Sergio Adorno	
Criminal Violence in Modern Brazilian Society	72
Erich Buchholz	
Social Changes, Crime and Police in the Former GDR – Now a Part of the United Germany	83
Ahti Laitinen	
Problems of Controlling Organizational Crime	90

Topic III.

Sándor Pintér	
The Effect of Social Changes on the Police	109
Valér Dános – István Tauber	
Relationship Between the Hungarian Police and Society	118

Jorgen Jepsen
   A Note of Caution on Uncritical Cooperation in the Development of Police 126

Michael Rowe
   The Police and Stereotypes of Ethnic Minorities 130

Philip Rawlings – Betsy Stanko
   Social Change, Police and Protection 144

Topic IV.

Mike King
   Police co-operation and Border Controls in a "New" Europe; an Indication of Trends for Change 149

László Salgó
   The Role of the Police and its Co-operation in Europe 163

Rob I. Mawby
   Changing the Police: Preliminary Thoughts as Eastern Europe Moves West 169

Topic V.

Ferenc Irk
   Transition in Middle-Europe, Questions about Crime-Prevention and Crime Policy 177

Giovanni Battista Traverso
   Social Change and Crime in Italy 184

Josef Zapletal – Mikuláš Tomin
   Attitudes of the Chechoslovak Public towards the Police after 1989 in Light of Empirical Investigations 190

Louise Shelley
   Concluding Remarks 195

   List of Authors 203

   Name Index 205

Foreword

The International Conference on Social Changes, Crime and Police held in Budapest, Hungary on June 1–4, 1992 was organized by the Department of Criminology at Eotvos Loránd University. It was at the initiative of the Criminological Committee of the International Sociological Association (RC29) in professional cooperation with the College of Police Officers' Training, the Research Institute on Policing of the Ministry of Interior and the National Criminological and Criminalistic Institute.

The purpose of the conference was to acquire a better acquaintance with the interrelation of social changes and crime through the introduction of the experiences of different countries, and by knowing them making policing much more effective.

Reports and contributions delivered at the conference were uniform from the point of view that of the changes in crime, its increase was in close interdependence with social changes, and the most effective form of the fight against crime could only be crime prevention. The summaries and contributions delivered at the conference emphasized to a great extent the reinforcement of the relationship between the police and the public.

Of the many subjects discussed, however, one was met with considerably diverse or even opposing opinions.

Specifically, the diversity of attitudes, and the counterposing of opposite viewpoints made the conference so valuable.

The selected material of the conference is published by the Organizing Committee in the hope that not only those who participated at the conference will find this publication beneficial but other specialists as well, and anybody else who happens upon it.

Our thanks to David Levin who helped edit the English version.

Dr Louise Shelley
President RC29, ISA

Dr József Vigh
Chairman of the Organizing Committee

Opening Speech

by
Dr. Péter Boross

I am not the first to state that sharp political and economic agglomerations are to be expected in Europe within the foreseeable future. All this – improbable as it may seem today – will soon put an end to, or at least diminish the "traditional" contradictions among countries in the eastern part of the continent. Having learned about the model of the West European change, we cannot rule out the possibility of the fact that, within a relatively short period of time, such gathering and unification will come into effect in the Eastern part of Europe as well, which is hardly imaginable at present.

One question, however, will surely remain as one of the biggest problems of coexistence; that is the fight between crinie and society.

The fight of society against crime, which is escalating precisely as a result of the political and economic changes of today, expands in space, and thus the fighting sides gain greater possibilities for moving about. We know from our own experience what the previous Soviet-like closure of the frontiers meant from the point of view of law enforcement, but we have already experienced how the democratic opening of the frontiers has created easier conditions for crime.

We are presently facing the basic dilemma – how to find some harmony in the fight against crime – balancing the individual's degree of freedom with the social demands based on individual values. The basic question is what kinds of new concepts will be formulated in this field, and what kinds of new practice will be accepted and used in the next few decades.

It seems to us that in the western part of Europe the activity of policing has become stronger, and its field of action has become wider than many would advocate principles would suggest. We feel that the dynamics, the equipment, and the arsenal used in the fight against crime grows parallel to the threat which is caused by the spread of crime. The growth is parallel even if this has not yet been stated at the level of declared principles, what is more – and it is terrible for me to say this – not even in the formal provision of law! Should I be mistaken in this matter, then please forgive me, since what I have just said is based on impressions only.

Here, in Hungary, we can judge the recent past within the context of a changing society. The previous power, the power which ruled for more than four decades, used the police as a "club". The rule of law was basically of second importance. All this has changed to some extent with the passing of time. In the era of „weakening socialism" while legal security was somewhat stronger, the Hungarian society equalled the police with that power, which this society would not accept as legitimate even some decades later.

In our country, the changing of the political system has come about quickly and peacefully. This change, however, has put the police in a rather difficult position. The administration had to and still has to make great efforts to reform the organisation, the equipment, the number of staff and its field of action, and more generally the significance of the police work within more modern conditions.

People have become frightened of the growth of crime and, as a consequence of this, general public opinion has demanded a more powerful policing. The surface of the political life is affected by debates, which are of different considerations, but this question seems to be resolved in the deeper regions of the society, and thus the Government feels that it has an important task: to try to determine the role of the police in accordance with this social public demand.

Our situation, however, is ambivalent to a certain degree, since at the same time – together with the above mentioned issue – we have to fulfill a freedom ideal as well, which is the principal condition for integration into Europe. Modern rules of law are needed to do this, for instance, the protection of data and the records of data, and generally for the guarantees of the individual's degree of freedom. We have to formulate these rules of law in such a way as to serve the individual's freedom and social peace, both equally and proportionally.

I think that in this case it is very difficult to reach a compromise. It is very difficult to find a common interest, which would fulfill both needs. What the future will bring about is still a question for me, too. If crime continues to increase at the same pace and in technical sophistication, if it can penetrate into the private sphere, then sooner or later society will renounce some of its ideals and it will give priority to the fight against crime. This, however, is only a supposition.

There are several explanations all over the world which are used to explain the growth in crime, and from these reasons I have to mention one factor. In our every day political life people who are engaged in politics often refer to poverty or to impoverishment as causes of the increase in crime. However, according to our observations, a relationship cannot be established between these two phenomena. What is more, in certain countries with a relatively high living standard and with social stability, the rate of crime is astonishingly higher than in our country.

We have to look for the real causes elsewhere. We can look for them, above all, in the universal deterioration of ideals. Perhaps this sounds strange on my part, since I lived through the past forty years here in Hungary. Hungary should not be the first to voice this complaint. I refer to the universal deterioration of those traditional ideals which could influence the society even half a century ago.

The situation today is that – and it is connected to a great extent to the deterioration of ideals – the barrier of law in itself does not mean a moral command, and it does not indicate any models of behaviour. If this view of life changes into a way of life, then, unfortunately, we will not be able to be optimistic about the future rates of crime.

My time is short, thus I would only like to refer to another great problem, the presence of which, I feel, is not only characteristic of Hungary, but can mean a great threat to everybody's future. I refer to tbe widening and strengthening of social confrontations, which are of certain racist character and also to the appearance of such declared principles, which today still come into existence in nationalistic forms, in traditional violent forms of nationalism, in the Eastern part of Europe. At the same time, the fight amid various ethnic groups in Western Europe is also sharpening.

Social eduation, training people to coexist, to find humane forms of coexistence with the descendants of guest workers could be the remedy for this problem. Let us believe in the heavens above and also in the existence of human abilities, which are proven by the ever reviving world, so that in a few decades such fights will not overshadow the European existence. I cannot, however, say that I belong to the most optimistic group of people in this respect.

Public security: the security of the public, the security of the community. It is the task of this conference to reveal methods, to give advice and to provide ideas concerning this issue.

The freedom of the individual and the security of the community. I believe that all this ends in a dilemma, to which a good solution must be found and this is the basic responsibility of those people who are engaged in the professions of academic sciences. The good solutions then must be applied by those who are experts in practice. Thus I look forward to hearing everything which is discussed at this conference about this issue. We must remain open to correct our mistakes by the influence of the scientific and functional system of arguments of a conference. This is why I welcome you all once again and I ask you to help us in solving our dilemmas.

Topic I.

Social Changes, Crime and the Police

– Introductory report –

by
Dr. József Vigh

The eleven subjects of the conference are focused on three essential groups of questions, namely:

1. the relationship of social changes and crime
2. the place and role of the police amidst the changing social conditions and changing crime
3. the reaction of society and the state on the crime problems of our age, or more explicitly the outlines of a criminal policy worthy of imitation.

The title of the conference promises the treatment of the subject on both a general and on an international level. Eastern European problems figure prominently in the discussions because these countries have just started to change their political systems, and are looking for experiences, arguments and counterarguments for the establishment of their future policy.

Social changes

I suppose it would not carry matters to extremes to say that the social changes of our age are mostly determined by the *revolutionary achievements of science and technology.* Results achieved in telecommunciations, traffic facilities, the production of weapons of mass destruction, and the improvement of the means of production require ever newer structural and ideological forms to promote the conditions of human coexistence.

The rapid technological development is changing economic and cultural structures, and creating a temporary instability and difficult conflicting situations. This can be especially well perceived in the ex-socialist countries where the lack of technological development, the low level of labour productivity, and the ideological contradictions have resulted in the change of the system. Within a relatively short period, traditional values and beliefs have changed; whatever was considered an asset is seriously questioned now, and becomes the subject of criticism. Points of view which were previously considered out of date shine with a renewed brilliance, and new ideologies emerge.

Historical experience proves that *the existence of social conflicts and contradictions is regular* and included in the system of general regularities. The recognition of the existence of social regularities means that *we cannot build a society according to our choice, but only one that is related to our past, present, and future possibilities.* This is one of the main lessons we have had to learn from the collapse of the socialist systems. The societies all over the world are very different, therefore the future, especially the near future, cannot be standardized. However, the common criteria, similarities, the basic human rights and responsibilities arising from the phylogenetic development of mankind, can be found.

Remarkable social contradictions are not only characteristic of the ex-socialist countries but they are also more or less concomitant phenomena of the developed capitalist societies, too. *Also in these countries significant forces are trying to break open the present frames, and it can barely be foreseen what kind of changes may occur.*

The full detailed analysis of the concrete social changes cannot be the purpose of the opening lecture. Here we only have an opportunity to emphasize some of the changes that can be considered important from the aspect of crime, police and criminal policy.

a. The nature of crime and police is being significantly transformed by the increasing of inter-relationships among countries. The expansion of international relations and associations, their growing influence on the development of different countries and societies, indicate the integration of mankind. International cooperation and the decisions of international associations are becoming fundamental indicators in more and more issues. This international tendency is a natural consequence of the development of technology and science. Technology enables a quick and continuous establishment of relations, the social sciences recognize the necessity of international cooperation. Thus the national boundaries, the geographical differences and distances, are gradually losing their significance. An increasing part of crime is becoming international, and the fight against it is consequently rising to an international level.

Furthermore, even efficient crime prevention within the national boundary cannot be without international experiences.

The cooperation of the police forces of the European countries is especially important. Already in 1993 the elimination of certain boundaries among the European countries creates an entirely different situation from the point of view of crime and criminal investigation. The cooperation, coordination, and compatibility of the police forces will be more and more essential requirements (European Police Seminar, 1990).

b. In line with the internationalization, we are all witnessing and taking part in the slackening of the centralized state direction and the increasing independence and self-management of peoples, ethnic groups and local communities. From the 1970s onwards, large organizations and communities have been breaking apart into smaller units, and the social and political intertwinements have been fracturing into pieces in the so-called postmodern societies (Soothill, 1992.). *The tendency of polarization increases the responsibility of small communities in the quality of their own conditions of existence, among them in the guarding of a satisfying public order and law and order.* It becomes especially obvious in the period of important social changes that individual countries are not able to protect their citizens from crime on their own. But it is also proven that in the fight against crime and in the prevention of crime, society itself, not these special organs of the state, that is the police, the prosecution, the courts of justice, and the law enforcement bodies can play the most important role. This statement rings true and sounds well, although the self-organization of society may be incidental and a lengthy process, therefore the *direction and support of the state is essential.* The strengthening of social self-management therefore raises the issue of the definition of the role and the function of the state anew. Concerning our own subject matter it means that the specific function of the state police, the private police, the volunteer public order protecting units, and their mutual relationships must be elucidated.

c. Of all the concrete social changes, related to the process of *privatization,* it is worthwhile emphasising that the most important process besides the changing of the political system in the ex-socialist countries it is the splitting up of the state capitalism in the developed capitalist countries. The big state companies split into smaller private or corporate forms of property. Besides the increasing privatization of public health and educational institutions, privatization is being carried out at such places as the big servicing enterprises, i.e. transportation and telecommunications, and the big industrial institutions – mining and metallurgical industries, etc.

This social movement concerns one way or another about more than half of the population in the ex-socialist countries; some are getting new initiatives and propitious perspectives, while others are obliged to carry the burden of an uncertain existence, the threat of unemployment, creating thus an atmosphere of a declining living standard, and fear.

The process of privatization, however, does not only cover the economic life, but also comprises such areas as *the judiciary, police, criminal procedure and the administration of prisons* (Ryan, Ward, 1989). Privatization appears to be a legal response to a crisis in a given area (Matthews, R. (ed.), 1989).

Private police is not a new phenomenon, but the expansion of the private sector necessarily gives rise to the quick-paced development of the privatized police, such as the internal police force at companies (inner surveillance) (South 1988).

The ineffectiveness and crisis of the state panel jurisdiction is prompting us to look for new forms for the establishment of responsibility. Thus new strategies for the establishment of responsibility are coming to the fore, such as the use of mediation, disciplinary responsibility, state administrative and common law responsibility, etc. The procedure of mediation, for example, already exists in many countries, and is perhaps one of the most important additional procedural forms or alternatives to the state penal process (Smith, 1988; Wright-Galaway, 1989).

The idea of *the privatization of some prisons* has intensified with an overwhelming force during the past decade (Weiss, 1989; Taylor-K. Pease, 1989). The privatization of prisons has also been aimed at lessening the crisis of overcrowding of prisons, with the slogan of profiting from it, while at the same time humanizing the prison treatment.

Efforts to privatize jurisdiction may result in giving up significant state monopolies and positions; consequently such issues can be put on the agend as the following:

- To what extent can state direction and support depart from different spheres of social life and what mainly concerns us, criminal justice?
- Upon what kind of new political and criminal-political principles can society build internal reactions to norm violating behaviour?
- How can social control be established under the new circumstances?

d. One of the most significant issues of social problems, and thus that of crime and the reaction to it, is *the issue of social equality-inequality, the issue of social justice and injustice*. The issue wich mainly concerns us is in what direction the changes of our days influence social inequalities, and what effect these tendencies have on crime and the activity of the organs of criminal investigation.

Representatives of the positivist criminology usually consider *social inequalities as one of the essential determinants of crime.* Thus, e.g. in 1985 in Milan at the Crime Prevention Congress of UNO, an unanimous stand was taken concerning the correlation of social inequalities and juvenile delinquency in the section dealing with juvenile delinquency.

The connection, of course, may reveal itself in various ways and forms in various countries. In ours, similar to other ex-socialist countries, during the process of the present great social changes, *as a result of the downfall of the economic situation, social inequality is increasing.* The already poorer part of the population is becoming even poorer, deprivation is affecting an increasing part of society, and the number of unemployed and homeless is also increasing. On the other hand, the social stratum of the rich is forming, and becomes ever richer. According to sociological research, relative to this aspect, between 1989 and 1991 the income of half of the population showed a downward tendency, while in the case of 20 per cent of the adult population there was an upward tendency (Kolozsi-Robert, 1991). According to criminological research it is not so much the low level of social existence, but rather the fall of living standards which contributes to crime. The consciousness of a decline in living standards, and the realization of dim future perspectives diminish many people's respect for dominant norms and consequently lead to their violation. Or quite the contrary, the consciousness of having better conditions of existence today than yesterday or that they will be better tomorrow than they are now may imply one of the most effective means of prevention (Miltényi, 1986, Vigh, 1991).

The increase in social inequality characterizes not only the ex-socialist countries, but can also be found in one or two capitalist countries (Reiner, 1989).

The question, of course, can also be put whether social inequality is the same as social injustice, or the other way around, whether social justice is always included in social inequality. The *experiences of the past decade warn us not to put a sign of equality between social inequalities and social injustices,* because social inequality is not always unjust, while social equality is not always just. The well-known statement 'whereas the use of equal rules of law in the case of inequal persons implies injustice' seems to be true. Anatole France's frequently cited statement that it is equally forbidden for the rich and the poor to sleep under a bridge, to beg in the street, or to steal bread reflects this kind of injustice very vividly.

Social injustice irrefutably manifests itself in the inequality of chances. If either individuals, certain social groups, or social strata, in comparison to others, have unequal chances to develop their potentials, to study and ensure the essential social goods for themselves, then it is undeniable that such inequality also includes injustice.

In this context we can ask with reason whether these injustices can be eliminated at the present level of social development. The answer can be definite in only one respect, that it cannot be completely brought to an end, but in a shorter or longer run a more just society can evolve as a consequence of the development of sciences, especially that of social sciences.

Crime

During this period of change in the social system in the ex-socialist countries, partly as a result of the transitional period, partly because of the crisis and disorder during the past decade, *crime has assumed proportions never previously seen.* In Hungary crime started rising at the begining of the 1980s and since then the pace of this rise has quickened. While in 1980 only 130000 crimes were reported, in 1991 almost half a million more. That is, the number of reported crimes has increased threefold during the past decade. Not only does this largescale increase involve an apparent danger for society, but also a disadvantageous change in the structure of crime. Most significantly, the number of burglaries and robberies has increased dramatically. In line with organized crime, violence against the person have risen, as there are more crimes committed with armed attacks. All these facts force experts and politicans to take the rise in crime seriously, to invest more energy in the prevention of the decline of public law and order, and security.

To a lesser extent, crime is showing an upward tendency in most of the capitalist countries, too (Offe, 1984). In Great Britain, for example, the number of reported crimes as compared to 1990 rose 16 percent, and according to estimates it will reach 6 million this year, almost 10 percent of the population (The Independent, 1992). The Hungarian figures are fortunately only half of this figure. A rise of similar proportions can be seen for example, in Holland, Sweden and Germany.

The large-scale rise in crime and its increasingly dangerous character requires an explanation, a justification. Even at the end of the last century Franz List, an outstanding criminal lawyer and criminologist of his era, one in which there was also a considerable rise in crime, came to the conclusion that *crime was always a regular concomitant of every great social change.* A similar idea is reflected in Durkheim and Merton's theory of anomie, according to which a rise in crime is explained by social disorder, the lack of norms or the slackening respect towards them, the disharmony of socially more correct aims and the means available. All these give a roughly acceptable explanation concerning the situation of crime in the ex-socialist countries; however, the continuous rise in crime in the capitalist countries, showing a relatively undiminished development, cannot be seemingly justified by these statements. *There are criminal experts and politicans who regard welfare, democracy and freedom as the cause of the background and the rise in crime in the developed capitalist countries – according to the concept of the "welfare state", and crime is considered by them as a price paid in exchange for the above mentioned privileges* (Patten, 1991).

They argue that prosperity and the abundance of material goods give better chances to commit crimes: democracy and freedom ensure more freedom to satisfy individual needs. In given cases, these incentives may actually encourage people to commit a crime, but can hardly give an acceptable explanation in general. There is more to the satisfaction of one's conscience and more self-deceit in it than scientifically well-established deduction can explain. According to these views the more prosperity increases in a society, the more democracy accomplishes itself and the less human activity is limited, the more crime will rise.

I think the rise in crime, the expansion of welfare, democracy and freedom does not involve a causality, and we are nearer to reality if we ascribe crime to the injustices committed in social distribution, social disorganization and uncertainty, mistaken ideologies, the lack of appropriate knowledge, genetic and psychic distortions, the escape to the irrational world of beliefs, the abuse of alcohol and other drugs, the lack of well-organized social communities, the insufficiency of the system of law enforcement, crime prevention and the establishment of responsibility (Déri, 1991).

The standpoint concerning the cause of crime to some extent already involves the strategic framework of the fight against crime and its prevention. The theory interpreting crime through welfare, democracy and freedom inevitably focuses its attention on the avoidance of the occasion of crime, on the situation in the field of crime prevention, suggesting we fix our cars to the pavement, guard our material goods behind bars, and avoid those places where we may fall victim to crime (International Conference on Crime Prevention, Budapest, Sept. 1991). Apart from these ideas, or more correctly taking them into consideration, the positivist criminology concentrates on social reforms, the formation of a more just society. Of course, it does not lose sight of the genesis of human nature and the fact that year by year about two-thirds of the perpetrators are convicted for the first time. That is, they come from among us, non-criminals. Perpetrators do not come "from outside", but have been like us, and even the members of our families, our friends, neighbours and close fellow-workers may at one point become perpetrators. Putting it in a different way, there are perpetrators among university lecturers, policemen, politicians, the rich and the poor as well, but not in equal proportion.

When we mention the impact of social conditions on crime we must also talk about the fact that *this mechanism of impact is not unilateral, but mutual.* Crime also has an impact on society, especially in its present heightened form. The large-scale crime of our days evokes fear and terror in people, has a terrible effect on the climate of opinion, results in the diminishing of the authority of the state, and the increase of taking justice into our own hands. The establishment of the perpetrators' responsibility is slowly dwindling.

In our days it is becoming more and more obvious that, besides the state criminal investigation, the crime prevention activity of the local and other communities is an essential factor. At many places *organizations are formed, working at their own initiative.* Still the coordinating function of the state seems to be justified (The Police, 1979).

In our country all the efforts of criminology and those of the criminal experts for almost a decade have not been enough to establish a national organ of crime prevention under state control and coordination. Within the framework of the police there is a network of crime prevention which often fulfills such duties which logically would not even belong to its sphere of authority. Still it cannot replace the manysided system of social crime prevention. I am convinced that as long as in the development of our society reinforces democratic tendencies the building of a system of social crime prevention can be carried out.

The study of the morphology, causality and prevention, of crime makes it possible to recognize its regularities. In the first half of the last century, the founder of criminology, Adolphe Quetelet already realized that there were similar regularities in human behaviour, based seemingly on free will, such as in criminal human behaviour, to the scope of natural phenomena. Using this as a starting point he came to the conclusion that crime, or *criminal human behaviour, could be predicted.* According to him: "Sad condition of humanity! We might even predict annually how many individuals will stain their hands with the blood of their fellowmen" (Quetelet, 1842). Apart from Quetelet, I think that the correlation recognized by him, namely the regularity and predictability of crime as a scientific formula, suggest exactly the optimism concerning the pliability of the future. If we are clever enough and have enough knowledge to recognize their regularities, then the future can be forecast, and accordingly we can make efforts to condition society. The recognition of the regularities in the past and the present depends on our knowledge. On the other hand, the formation of the future is a consequence of a system of action, elaborated and devised on the basis of the appreciation of necessities.

Besides these theoretical theses, which sound so good it seems justified to introduce, at least to the extent of a few sentences, the predictions elaborated about the future development of crime. The *Hungarian predictions* all make a considerable rise likely in the decade ahead of us (Scientific Debate, 1987). According to international criminological findings, almost one-third of the population will have fallen victim to crimes by the end of the century (van Dijk and others, 1990). More concretely in the United States, for example, 83 percent of the now 12 year-old children will fall victim to some kind of a crime in the next 10 years, every thirteenth woman will be raped, and in the next 20 years 87 percent of the population will be repeatedly robbed (mugged), every third household will be broken into and every fifth person's car will be stolen (Dénes Szabó, 1991). During the past four decades crime has risen about 5-6 percent a year in the developed capitalist countries. However, this pace has accelerated during the past years, and in many countries it has risen more than 10 per cent.

In connection with the large-scale expansion of crime many experts ask to what extent crime and the fear of it can keep growing. What kind of freedom is it if one-third or half of the population can fall victim to a crime, where one is free to be scared and free to fall victim (Vigh, 1991). Some experts say that the fear of crime is greater than crime itself (Young, 1990). In other words, do we interpret freedom correctly? Or else could freedom possibly have genetic causes and have we entered the era of a genetic decline (Lorenz, 1989). Or is it perhaps possible that our moral and legal norms are wrong, and human nature can follow them less and less?

The future perspectives of crime are very dismal according to the predictions, and so are the ideas and questions attending them. But as even the most professional prediction can get across under certain conditions and the development of societies settles again for a longer or shorter period after the great changes, and a new era will commence, a new model of a society will be formed and crime will probably be reduced to a bearable level.

Police

The activity of the police belongs to a series of measures embodying the response of the state and the society on crime and the violation of norms. As shown by statistical data and other facts, crime cannot be considered as the act of a few wicked individuals but as a phenomenon that intersperses society more and more. That is why it is so important on what principles, using what means, in what kind of a system of social relationships and how effectively the police do their work (Reiner, 1991).

In our country, just like the other ex-socialist countries, the police face extremely difficult tasks. It is well-known that under socialist circumstances the police exercised relatively great power which consequently created some sort of a feeling of superiority among many policemen. That is why it can be considered natural that during the period of change in the political system, since the 1980s, the police have become, having or not having reasonable ground, the frequent object of criticism for the opposition. This resulted in the fact that after the free elections in 1990, the new government inherited an intimidated, and uncertain police force. But after certain reorganizations. and replacements of staff, the police more and more became themselves again, and can meet the requirements placed on them.

However, the police have undergone a crisis not only in the ex-socialist countries, but a similar evaluation is frequently asserted concerning policing in the developed capitalist countries (Anderson, 1979, Hoogenboom, 1991).

The situation according to Canadian experts, for example, involves a new economic, political, social and cultural menace which is emerging now (Vision, 1990). The state of crisis or at least this stronge climate of crisis which is spreading over the whole of criminal justice justifies the effort to find new solutions in the fight against crime. There are thousands of questions emerging: What kind of a criminal policy should we follow? How to react to crime? What should the proper establishment of responsibility be? What tasks should we expect to fulfill through the police? etc. The slogan of "joining with Europe" is not so unambiguous as many politicans and experts in the ex-socialist countries presume, because there are various concepts in the European countries as well.

It is an essential aim of the present Conference to bring forth all the questions that are expected to be solved in connection with the police, or it should at least outline the guiding line which is in conformity with essential social changes and the rise in crime.

It is difficult to put such issues on the agenda which are equally important for countries, having diverse economic, cultural and ideological problems. Yet I think that the issues, noted in the programme such as the task of the police, their relationship with the population, the press, the cooperation of different police organizations on a national and international level, the training of the police, the role of the police in the support of the victims of crimes and the connection between the police and human rights, are all such questions which can give rise to common interest. To become acquainted with the international tendencies, experiences and strivings may serve as a compass to turn with a steadier hand the helms of their function in the direction of a social development that seems to be the best.

I content myself to introduce a topic of debate which has the following title: "A Vision of the Future of Policing in Canada. Police – Challenge 2000".

This topic of debate was elaborated under the direction of our colleague, Professor Andre Normandeau. For as much as getting acquainted with these visions can be useful, other countries would like or are obliged to follow quite different visions. With my theoretical criminological knowledge I see that the visions are not only Canadian ones but that they will have to be sooner or later universally followed. These visions first of all answer the question as to what kind of public body the police should be developed into in the next few years.

The below listed visions are not to be considered a literal translation and a full text, mostly because of the limitations of the manuscript, but as a summary of it in my own words, emphasizing some important items or visions, such as:

- there will be a full partnership between police and community
- police officers, including local police, should again form a close relationship with the citizens
- police will try to solve local problems with the help of representatives and groups in the neighbourhood (the region), thus preventing crimes from being committed
- up-to date technology will be more emphasized for the sake of a smoother flux of information
- the police will be able to adapt themselves to the constantly changing surroundings and will not be lost in the solution of urgent daily problems
- state police should excel private police
- a senior police officer should only be someone who can be trusted, who is a helpful and cooperative partner of the leader of the community
- a future police officer will not only have to deal with crimes, but must become an integrated part of the community in which he carries out his duties

The above mentioned visions indicate the course the Canadian police wish to take. But they also show what problems we shall have to face sooner or later. The questions are whether the police have to or can serve other interests than the ones of the government, and consequently those of the ruling party or parties. Or else is their service universal, a service to the people? Does not the active participation of the police in the solution of the problems of the community mean a shift from its "guild" towards a body in which they play politics? What kind of a relationship do we expect between state or central and the local or private police, where should the line of competence be drawn? It seems to me that the police in the ex-socialist countries first will have to wrestle with the uncertainty of a change into something else. As the whole country did they will also have to pass through all the advantages and miseries of the change of regime. In line with it they will *permanently have to draw a parallel between their own country and the tendencies in the more developed countries, the national possibilities and the restrictions.* I think one of the aims of the conference to be achieved would be for the participants to receive arguments and counter-arguments to support their ideas, to modify them or perhaps reject them altogether.

There are several problems at issue concerning the future role of the police *but one thing is certain, and it is the necessity of a good relationship between the police and the population.* Police must initiate cooperation with the citizens, and the leaders of the local communities (Hope-Shaw, 1988). Perhaps this may be the starting point, on behalf of the realization of which we must first of all spare no trouble in (Reiner, 1989).

Criminal policy

While discussing the social changes, the issues of crime and the police, we also have to mention those principles that the state and society rely on when responding to crime. The police activity in itself constitutes a part of the social response, and is one of its means as well. The criminal policy of a country considerably influences the nature of both the crime and the police. Although criminal policy is a part of or to some extent depends on the social policy, it also has some autonomy. That is why it is so important to direct and let the inner "self-movement" of the criminal policy get directed into proper channels.

In our country the resocializing penal policy built on prevention which characterized the previous two decades is now being changed into a criminal policy which has set itself the objectives of *classical and neo-classical criminal policies.* Its basic principles are the following: indeterminism, a retributive punishment proportionate with the deed, the exclusion of the perpetrator's education from the circle of criminal justice and the lack of the victim's compensation. In a penal system that is built on retribution this spirit possesses it all and this process is started by the police whether they want to or not. The view that considers only the state courts of justice to be competent to judge a crime – that is the one which thinks that criminal justice is the monopoly of the state courts – also belongs here. According to it there is no diversion, mediation and social justice because it interferes with the principle of strict legality. This principle was included in the constitutional principia when it was last amended (1990).

On the other hand we have the *neopositivist concept* according to which a criminal policy that is built on the laws of causality and the importance of crime, the perpetrator's personality, the victim's interests and the circumstances of the commission of crime are to be followed (Waller, 1989). Hopefully the criminal policy in the near future will rely on the theses of this system of concepts, too.

Amidst the quickly changing conditions of our days it is not easy to determine the direction of a criminal policy to be followed. Thus the concept of a rule of law for example, also became the compass and standard in the criminal policy of the ex-socialist countries, although there are considerable differences in the interpretations of the concept itself (Szabó, 1989, Responsibility, 1989). An example; there are some who interpret a rule of law as a state where the citizen can do whatever he wishes when not forbidden by law. Others, on the other hand, think that this interpretation is wrong and immoral because it leaves the fact out of consideration that a state is built not only on legal norms but also on moral ones (Vigh, 1989). To overemphasize the importance of legal norms leads to the slackening of moral norms, and thus can also be brought into connection with the violation of legal norms. Things stand similarly in the case of human rights when they are overemphasized. What is approriate and desirable is to word individual rights in an exact way, and thus we can protect and create the conditions of their enforcement. But it already belongs to the drawback of society that there is not much said about essential human obligations albeit *the legal norms include not only rights but obligations as well.* There have been propositions which suggest that the essential *human obligations should also be declared internationally as it is done in the case of essential human rights,* and thus the balance that has been upset would be restored, the complete and immediate enforcement of the presumed or real rights would be reduced, and thus the number of norm violating actions would diminish (Vigh, 1990/91).

The re-establishment of the victims' interests is added to the aim of prevention in the neopositivist criminal policy, and such procedures come to the fore when the victim – instead of being a "weak" witness – becomes an important subject of the procedure, and thus the establishment of responsibility for crimes committed will be truly just, or in any case become more just (Williams, 1986).

In the relationship of criminal policy and crime prevention, we must also mention *the prohibition and punishment of norm violating behaviours and the recognition, remuneration and encouragement of norm following behaviours.* Concepts concerning crime prevention are usually aimed at concrete crime preventing measures in the case of norm violating behaviours and the perpetrators' resocialization. *An effective prevention strategy, however, must surpass this and must include the sphere of the encouragement of norm following behaviours, too.* Since the theory of differential associations created by Edwin Sutherland it is frequently said that crime is a learned behaviour. This is in many respects true, but is even truer in the case of the norm following behaviour. The rules of social coexistence must be learnt and must be acquired, they must be internalized. In this process of learning prohibitions, punishments play an important role, but *the most decisive factors are still recognition, remuneration and encouragement.* The so-called positive establishment of responsibility or the remuneration of norm following behaviour is built on the realization of this within the framework of social control (Siófok Conference, 1989). For it is mistaken to presume that to follow norms is an innate human behaviour. Crime is closer to human or primitive human nature. To follow norms requires knowledge, sacrifice, foresight, and rationalism. No wonder that the theory of learning is one of the most comprehensive theories of our day (Akers, 1985).

Out of this theoretical criminal political argument, it follows that we must thoroughly ruminate over the objectives of our criminal policy, the methods of their enforcement because they will have an effect on the nature and formation of crime. The most significant lesson for the police, perhaps, is that a professionally well-trained, thinking, self-confident police force is required which is on friendly terms with the population, protects the rights of citizens, and makes them respect their obligations.

Notes and References

Akers, R. L. (1985): *Deviant Behavior: A Social Learning Approach.* California: Wadsworth Publishing Company Belmont.
Anderson, J. (1979): *Policing Freedom.* London: Macdonald and Evans.
Bűnmegelőzési Nemzetközi Konferencia Budapest, 1991. Sept. (International Conference of Crime Prevention Sept. 1991. Budapest)
Déri, P. (1991): *A magyarországi bűnözés alakulása.* (Development of Criminality in Hungary) Rendészeti Szemle. No. 10.
van Dijk, J.–Mayhew, P.–Killias, M. (1990): *Experience of Crime Across the World:* Key Findings from the 1989 International Statistical Survey.
Európai Rendőri Szeminárium (European Police Seminar) Saint-Pavel-de-Vence Mar. 26-28. 1990.
Hoogenboom, B. (1991): *Grey Policing: A Theoretical Framework.* In: Policing and Society, Vol. 2.

Hope, T.-Shaw, M. (1988): *Communities and Crime Reduction.* HMSQ, London.
The Independent, London. 10. (March 1992.) (Figures showing 16% rise in crime realised early).
Kolozsi, T.-Robert, P. (1991): *A rendszerváltás hatásai* (Effects of Social Changes) Társadalomkutatási Informatikai Egyesület.
Lorenz, K. (1991): *A civilizált emberiség nyolc halálos bűne.* (The Eight Deadly Sins of Mankind) IKVA Könyvkiadó Sopron.
Matthews, R. (ed.) (1989): *Privatizing Criminal Justice.* London: Sage Publications.
Miltényi, K. (1991): *Rendszerváltás és deviancia.* (Social Changes and Deviation) In: Info-Társadalomtudomány No. 14.
Offe, C. (1984): *Contradictions of the Welfare State.* Cambridge, Mass: MIT Press.
Patten, J. (1991): *Fight Against Crime in (the) United Kingdom.* April 24 Lecture in Budapest.
The Police and the Prevention of Crime. Council of Europe Collected Studies in Criminological Research, Strasbourg, 1979.
Quetelet, A. (1842): *A Treatise on Man and the Development of his Facilities.* In: Comparative Statistics in the 19th Century. Godstone: Gregg International Publishers 1973. Limited. (?)
Reiner, R. (1989): *The Politics and Police Research in Britain.* In: Weatheritt, M., Aldershot, Avenury (eds.) Police Research: Some Future Prospects. London.
Reiner, R. (1991): *Policing and Criminal Justice in Great Britain.* Coexistence 28.
Responsibility and Society. (1989.): Responsibility for Crime and Infractions International Conference. Sept. 19-24. 1988. Siófok, Hungary, Budapest,
Ryan, M., Ward, T. (1989): *Privatization and the Penal System.* New York: St. Martin's Press.
Smith, D. et al. (1988): *Mediation in the Shadow of the Law.* In: Matthews R. (ed.) Informal Justice? London: Sage Publications.
Soothill, K. et al. (1992): *New Technology and Practical Police Work* (Manuscript.)
South, N. (1988): *Policing for Profit: The Private Security Sector.* London: Sage Publications.
Szabó, A. (1988): *A büntetőjog reformja - a reform büntető joga* (The Criminal Law of the Reform, the Reform of Criminal Law) Jogtudományi Közlöny 1988. No. 8.
Szabó, D. (1991): *Milyen lesz a bűnözés és az igazságszolgáltatás az ezredfordulón?* Magyar Tudomány 4. sz. (Supposed Crime and Jurisdiction at the Turn of the Century).

Taylor, M., Rease, K. (1989): *Private Prisons and Penal Purpose.* In: Matthews, R. (ed.) Privatizing Criminal Justice. London: Sage Publications.

Tudományos vitaülés, (1987.) Téma: A magyarországi bűnözés várható alakulása az ezredfordulóig, különös tekintettel a személyek javait károsító bűncselekményekről. (Prognosis of Crime at the Turn of Century Concerning Especially Crime Against Private Property) Kriminológiai Közlemények 14.

Vigh, J. (1986): *Causality, Determinism and Prognosis in Criminology.* Budapest: Akadémiai Kiadó.

Vigh J. (1989): *Racionalitás a büntető igazságszolgáltatásban.* (Rationality in Criminal Justice). Belügyi Szemle. 1989 No. 6. sz.

Vigh, J. (1991): *Social Control and Responsibility.* In Chiaers de Defense Sociale. Milano.

Vigh, J. (1991): *Honnan indult el és merre halad a kriminológia?* (Where has the Criminology Started from and where it is Heading?) Magyar Jog. 1991. 9. sz.

A Vision of the Future of Policing in Canada. 1990.: Police Challenge 2000. Solicitor General Canada.

Waller, J. (1989): *Justice Even for the Crime Victims. Implementing International Standards.* In: International Review of Victimology. Vol. 1, No. 1.

Weiss, R. P. (1989): *Private Prisons and the State.* In: R. Matthews (ed.) Privatizing Criminal Jusitce. London: Sage Publications.

William, O. B. (1986): *Criminal Injuries Compensation.* London: Waterlow Publishers.

Wright, M., Galaway, B. (eds.) (1989): *Medition and Criminal Justice. Victims, Offenders, and Community.* London Sage Publications.

Young, J. (1990): *Risk of Crime and Fear of Crime: A Realist Critique of Survey-based Assumption.* In: Crimes and Victim: A New Deal.

The British Policing Tradition: Model or Myth?

by
Robert Reiner

Not long ago an American historian summed up the traditional image of the British police in this way: 'What people in our own age think of when they hear the words "English police" is an unarmed police force of constables who are ordinarily courteous to tourists, patient, and restrained in confronting crowds' (Thurmond Smith, 1985, p. 5). This benign picture of the British police tradition was built up in the first half of this century in a number of celebratory studies which represented the British police as essentially embodying ideals of civility and gentlemanliness (Lee 1901; Reith 1938, 1943, 1956, and many other works). This depiction still has adherents today (Ascoli 1979; Stead 1985), although for the most part is has been called into question by more critical historians (Storch 1975; Brogden 1987; Emsley 1991). This essay will analyze the ingredients of the traditional picture of the British police model, and then assess the extent to which they are still applicable (if they ever were).

The British Police Model: The Ideal

During the first part of the 20th century a particular model of the character of British policing was developed by the historians cited above. It derived ultimately from the principles laid down in 1829 as the ideals by which the new Metropolitan Police should be governed. Its architects were Sir Robert Peel, and the first two Metropolitan Commissioners, Rowan and Mayne. They adopted their strategy in order to win over widespread popular resistance to the early police.

This benign image of the British police became dominant in the 20th century, elevating the police to key symbols of national pride. Often referred to as 'policing by consent' it remains potent as a founding myth of police professional ideology. The model can be analyzed as involving eight elements. (This analysis can be found in more detail in Reiner, 1985, Chap. 2.).

Bureaucratic Organization

'Bureaucracy' is used here in its Weberian sense of an organization in which selection, training and promotion are carried out according to impersonal and objective rules and criteria, not personal connections. At a time when nepotism and corruption were rife in public service, the police were established on a strictly meritocratic basis. Entrance and promotion were governed by relatively stringent tests of fitness for the job. There was an internal disciplinary regime of tight rules, strictly enforced, regulating relations with supervisors and the public (Miller 1977, pp. 26-42; Critchley 1978, pp. 52-5). This contributed to the construction of an image of the police as representatives not of arbitrary or particularistic power, but an impersonal legality.

The Rule of Law

This was further encouraged by the way Parliament and the courts laid down and enforced strict legal constraints for the procedures by which the police were to carry out their duties of law enforcement and order maintenance. The commissioners themselves promulgated rules about how the discretion of constables should be used in stopping, arresting and investigating suspects (Miller op. cit., pp. 4-12, 54-66, 94).

Non-Partisanship

A particular concern of the commissioners was to dispel the fear that the police would be a partisan tool of government. This had been a major factor in the popular opposition to the establishment of the police. The example of the French and other 'police states' had been a particular bete noir in the debates about creating a new police in England. Peel and the commissioners deliberately insulated the police from direct control by government, central and local. They initiated the doctrine of 'constabulary independence', seeing the police as autonomous professional agents of the law not the government.

This was buttressed by regulations prohibiting the police from any form of partisan political involvement. Until 1887 police officers were denied the vote, and they are still not allowed to be members of or affiliate with any political party or trade union.

Accountability

The police were not formally controlled by any agency of government, although they were established by Act of Parliament. However, they were seen as accountable in two ways. First, the legality of their actions was reviewable by the courts, they were accountable to the law. Second, an almost mystical notion of identification with the British people, not the state, developed as a substitute for any tangible control by elected institutions. As Reith put it, 'the police are the public and the public are the police' (Reith 1956, p. 287). This was supported by policies of recruiting police officers primarily from manual working class backgrounds, representative of the mass of the people (Critchley 1978, p. 52). Since the First World War it has been a principle which is supposed to govern even the recruitment of chief police officers, and since the Second World War it has actually done so (Reiner 1991a, Chap. 4).

Minimum Force

Most if not all police forces would claim they use 'minimal force'. Certainly none are proponents of 'maximal force'. What is distinctive in the British tradition is the great concern exhibited by the key policy makers to constrain the use of arms, especially firearms. In the Metropolitan Police from the start the only weapon issued regularly to constables on ordinary patrol was the truncheon. Only on specific dangerous assignments or beats were pistols or cutlasses allowed. Many of the county forces which were created in the mid-19th century at first adopted a much more militaristic model of policing (Steedman 1984, pp. 21-5). But this changed after the Home Office began to exercise more influence on forces throughout the country following the creation of Her Majesty's Inspectorate of Constabulary in the 1856 County and Borough Police Act.

Gradually all forces moved towards a civil model, with weapons other than truncheons being issued only on a tightly regulated basis to selected, trained officers when exceptional emergencies arose. In riot control the military remained the ultimate back-up, but they have never been deployed in a public order role on the mainland since 1919 (paradoxically during the police strike in Liverpool). By the middle of the 20th century the image of the British police as an unarmed force was central to their unique prestige, domestically as well as internationally. This was the celebrated strategy of winning by appearing to lose, as Sir Robert Mark once expressed it. Public sympathy for police vulnerability was a more potent weapon than water cannon or the Colt Magnum.

The Service Role

From the outset the British police have been encouraged by their leaders to be ready to provide a variety of services other than law enforcement or order maintenance to the public in need. This was deliberately cultivated as a means of conveying a benign and friendly rather than oppressive image. Research on police practice in many other countries has revealed that police work involves a service role at least as much as an enforcement role almost everywhere. However, in Britain this was encouraged and emphasised as a key aspect of official policy, although often resented by the rank-and-file as not 'real' police work (Steedman 1984, pp. 53-4).

Preventive Policing

The original formulation of the police mission by Peel in his famous instructions to the new Metropolitan Police in 1829 emphasised the centrality of crime prevention, rather than detection, and made no mention of any political functions. The bedrock of the force has remained uniform patrol. A detective branch came late in the day, and was viewed with great suspicion even by the respectable elite (Miller 1977, pp. 33-4; Baldwin and Kinsey 1982, p. 11). A political police, the Special Branch, had to wait until the 1880s and the excuse provided by Fenian terrorism, by which time the police were already winning the battle for public support (Porter 1987). It remains a pivot of official police ideology that the 'bobby on the beat' is the most important part of the force, even if organizational practice often belies this (Jones 1980).

Police Effectiveness

The final ingredient in the British police model which gained such prestige was the appearance of effectiveness. The spread of policing in the second half of the 19th century coincided with a pacification of British society: a general decline in disorder and lawlessness (Gatrell 1980). The police gained much of the credit for this, although it owed far more to a set of deeper social and cultural changes. Policing is problematically related to levels of crime, as contemporary research shows (Clarke and Hough 1980, 1984).

The result was affection for the 'thin blue line' which, although 'low in numbers, low on power and high on accountability' *(Operarional Policing Review* 1990, p. 4), was a successful shield for the citizen against crime. When crimes were committed, Scotland Yard acquired a reputation second only to the Canadian Mounties for the regularity with which they 'got their man'.

The British model of policing which gained enormous worldwide prestige in the middle of the 20th century thus involved eight elements: high internal discipline and standards of integrity, subordination to the rule of law, non-partisanship, popular accountability, minimal force, a service role, emphasis on crime prevention by uniform patrol, and effective safeguarding of public security. At the time these were seen as virtues of the police themselves. In reality they owed more to deeper structural and cultural changes in British society; the integration of the working class into the dominant political and social order, and the spread of values of citizenship and civility (Marshall 1950; Dharendorf 1958). As these have changed, and inequality and conflict have grown since the early 1970s (and especially the 1980s) so the British police model seems gradually to have crumbled.

The Deconstruction of the British Police Tradition

All the elements of the British police model sketched above have been undermined in the last decade and a half, although not by deliberate design. The changes are the unanticipated consequences of policy shifts, or reactions to the deepening disorder and crime the police face as a result of the increasing inequality and division in British society.

Bureaucratic Organization

The image of the British police as an organization built upon tight internal discipline has been challenged by a variety of scandals about corruption, and by a general relaxation of controls over police officers' private lives. The most damaging blow was struck by the exposure of deep-seated corruption in the Metropolitan Police in the 1970s (Cox et al. 1977), but revelations and allegations have continued to appear regularly since.

The Rule of Law

Concern about police abuse of their legal powers has been growing since the early 1970s. The 1972 Confait case was most significant in which three teenage boys were wrongfully convicted of murder on the basis of false confessions taken in violation of the Judges' Rules then in operation (Maxter and Koffman 1983). This led to the 1979-81 Royal Commission on Criminal Procedure, and ultimately to the 1984 Police and Criminal Evidence Act, which extended police powers but subjected them to a more rigorous system of safeguards (Zander 1991).

Despite these changes, public confidence in the legality of police practice has been undermined seriously by a series of causes célèbres in the late 1980s which revealed or alleged grave miscarriages of justice. These include the cases of the Brimingham Six, the Guildford Four, and the Maguires, all of whom were wrongly convicted of terrorist offenses in the early 1970s. Other serious allegations have been raised about the conviction of the 'Tottenham Three' for the murder of PC Blakelock in the 1985 Broadwater Farm riot, as well as a number of less celebrated cases. Concern about these revelations has prompted the establishment of a new Royal Commission on Criminal Justice, the first Royal Commission to be set up since the Conservatives came to power in 1979.

Non-partisanship

During the late 1970s and early '80s the police appeared to move away from their traditional non-partisanship. Especially during the 1979 General Election and the 1984 miners' strike, their support for the Conservatives both in word and deed reached a high water-mark, for which they were rewarded by generous pay settlements (Reiner 1985).

Since then, the love affair between the police and the conservatives has cooled, as the government's control over public spending has begun to bite on the police. For its part, Labour have tried to repair their relationship with the police. This has not led to a new partisan alignment of Labour and the police. Rather it has restored the previous broad consensus between the parties on law and order. However, the police remain much more prominent in political debate and controversy than at any time this century.

Accountability

In the earlier part of this century the independence of the British police from control by any elected governmental institutions was often seen as a virtue. In the USA, for example, several generations of reformers have regarded the British model of insulation from political reform as a solution to problems of corruption and partisanship (Miller 1977).

As policing has become more controversial in Britain in the last two decades, so the perception of the mechanisms of accountability has changed. Radical critics saw police autonomy as meaning the police were out of control by democratically elected governments, and unresponsive to the popular will. They sought to reform the structure of police governance so as to make police policy-making fully accountable to the electoral process (Reiner 1985, Part III, Lustgarten 1986). These demands have been strongly resisted by the police themselves (Reiner 1991a, Chap. 11).

In addition to overall control of police forces, the question of how individual officers are made accountable through the complaints system has been very controversial, with many critics demanding a fully independent process, a view shared by the Police Federation and a minority of chief constables (Goldsmith 1991). The perceived lack of accountability of the British police has now become an important factor undermining their acceptance. What is clear is that the local accountability of British policing has almost disappeared. What seems to have replaced it is a degree of central control amounting to a de facto national police force (Reiner 1991 a).

Minimum Force

The most celebrated aspect of the British police tradition is their unarmed character. In the last decade, however, this has been departed from to an ever greater extent. Firearms have been issued with increasing frequency, and in the early 1980s there were a series of scandalous shootings in error of innocent people. The procedures for issuing guns have been tightened more recently, and their use restricted to a smaller group of highly trained officers, a policy that appears to have succeeded. Since the mid-1980s most forces have put guns in some high-speed cars, in lockers which can be opened in special emergenices with the approval of headquarters. This is the closest we have come to a regular armed patrol, although a readers' poll in *Police Review* last year found a majority of constables in favour of routine arming.

In riot control situations too the British police have moved in an increasingly militaristic direction, with much of the panoply of riot control available, from Nato helmets to plastic bullets (though these have not yet been used on the mainland). The militaristic strategy is codified in a confidential volume, the Tactical Options Manual, whose existence was revealed only during a trial of miners for riots in 1985 (Northam 1988). There is much debate and concern about these trends. Is militaristic policing a reaction to increasing violence or the cause of it? Does it provoke trouble or is it capable of suppressing it? (Jefferson 1990, Waddington 1991). Whichever interpretation is more valid, there can be no doubt of how militarization has profoundly altered the face of British policing.

The Service Role

Chief constables have advocated a community policing philosophy to an ever greater extent of late, stressing the wide social role of the police (Reiner 199a, Chap. 6). However, this represents a largely futile attempt to counter changes in the organization of routine policing which go in the opposite direction. The move from foot patrol to motorised patrol governed by sophisticated command and control systems has separated the police from the public, and made harder the provision of service functions by ordinary constables. Policing has become what many have called a fire brigade service, concentrating on reactions to emergencies.

This cannot be transformed by the super-imposition of a few community policing specialists.

Preventive Policing

Although lip-service continues to be paid to the paramount importance of the ordinary uniformed constable, in practice organizational trends undermine this (Jones 1980). The main rewards and prestige go to specialist departments, and these have proliferated. The unintended result is that the basic bedrock of preventive patrol work becomes the preserve of the very young or the old, unsuccessful constables. The organizational centre becomes the glamorous but controversial specialist crime investigation department.

Police Effectiveness

Since 1955 there has been a continous tendency for recorded crime rates to rise, and detection rates to fall. This has been particularly marked in the 1980s, and criminologists have spoken of a "hyper-crisis" (Kinsey et. al. 1986). For all the known pitfalls of police crime statistics (Young 1991), these trends are undeniable and are confirmed by victim surveys (Mayhew et. al. 1989). It is likely that the postwar rise in crime owes as little to the police as did the 19th century decline in crime. It owes more to deep-seated cultural and social changes, notably a decline in deference to authority, and a growing underclass as a result of economic polarization (Dahrendorf 1985). However having gained the credit for the earlier fall in crime and disorder, the police are now becoming scape-goats for its rise. They are losing the image of a 'thin blue line' protecting the public effectively, and this is losing them the support of the respectable middle class.

Has the British Police Model a Future?

Since the 1981 Scarman Report there has been a succession of attempts to reform the British police and restore them to the prestige they used to enjoy (Reiner 1991b). Yet crises and scandals have continued to proliferate and the status of the police as measured by opinion polls has continued to fall. The most recent rescue strategy is a combination of managerialism and consumerism as represented by the Operational Policing Review and the Statement of Common Purposes and Values, an unprecedented joint initiative by all three staff associations. (For details of current reform suggestions see the recent special issue of *Policing*, 'The Way Ahead', Autumn 1991). The essence of these efforts is the attempt to redevelop the service role in the face of the developments which have threatened it.

The current ventures, spearheaded by Sir Peter Imbert's 'Plus' programme in the Met, are all laudable in themselves. But they neglect the profound cultural and social changes which underlie the present problems of the police. In the face of these the British model will not regain whatever particularity it may once have had. Instead of being a sacred symbol of British national pride, it will be a mundane instrument of social regulation.

Notes and References

Ascoll, D. (1979): *The Queen's Peace*. London: Hamish Hamilton.
Baldwin, R., Kinsey, R. (1982.): *Police Powers and Politics*. London: Quartet Books.
Baxter, J., Koffman, L. (1983): *The Confait Inheritance: Forgotten Lessons?* Cambrian Law Review.
Brogden, M. (1987): *The Emergence of the Police: The Colonial Dimemsion*. British Journal of Criminology.
Clarke, R., Hough, M. (eds.) (1980): *The Effectiveness of Policing*. Aldershot: Gower
Cox, B., Shirley, J., Short, M. (1977): *The Fall of Scotland Yard*. Penguin: Harmondsworth
Critchley, T. A. (1978): *A History of Police in England and Wales*, 2nd ed. London: Constable.
Dahrendorf, R. (1959): *Class and Class Conflict in Industrial Society*. London: Routledge.
Dahrendorf, R. (1985): *Law and Order*. London: Sweet and Maxwell.
Emsley, C. (1991): *The English Police*. Hemel Hempstead: Wheatsheaf.
Gatrell, V. (1980): *The Decline of Theft and Violence in Victorian and Edwardian England*. In Gatrell, V., Lenman, B., Parker, G. (eds.) Crime and the Law. London: Europe.
Goldsmith, A. (ed.) (1991): *Complaints Against the Police*. Oxford: Oxford University Press.
Jefferson, T. (1990): *The Case Against Paramilitary Policing*. Milton Keynes: Open University Press.
Jones, M. (1980): *Organizational Aspects of Police Behaviour*. Farnborough: Gower.
Kinsey, R., Lea, J., Young, J. (1986): *Losing the Fight Against Crime*. Oxford: Blackwell.
Lee, M. (1991.): *A History of Police in England*. London: Methuen.

Lustgarten, L. (1986): *The Governance of the Police*. London: Sweet and Maxwell.

Marshall, T. H. (1950): *Citizenship and Social Class*. London: Heinemann.

Mayhew, P., Elliott, D., Dowds, L. (1989): T*he 1988 British Crime Survey*. London: HMSO.

Miller, W. (1977): *Cops and Bobbies*. Chicago: Chicago University Press.

Northam, G. (1988): *Shooting in the Dark*. London: Faber.

Porter, B. (1987): *The Origins of the Vigilante State*. London: Weidenfeld.

Reiner, R. (1985): *The Politics of the Police*. (2nd ed. 1992) Brighton: Wheatsheaf.

Reiner, R. (1991): *Chief Constables*. Oxford: Oxford University Press.

Reiner, R. (1992): *Fin de Siecle Blues:* The British Police Face the Millennium. The Policital Quarterly. Vol 63.

Reith, C. (1938): *The Police Idea*. Oxford: Oxford University Press. Hungarian Conference References

Reith, C. (1943.): *British Police and the Democratic Ideal*. Oxford: Oxford University Press.

Reith, C. (1956.): *A New Study of Police History*. London: Oliver and Boyd.

Stead, P. J. (1985): *The Police of Britain*. New York: Macmillan.

Steedman, C. (1984): *Policing the Victorian Community*. London: Routledge.

Storch, R. (1975): *The Plague of Blue Locusts:* Police Reform and Popular Resistance in Northern England, 1940-1857. International Review of Social History.

Thurmond S. P. (1985): *Policing Victorian London*. Westport: Greenwood Press.

Waddington, P. A. J. (1991): *The Strong Arm of the Law*. Oxford: Oxford University Press.

Young, M. (1991): *An Inside Job*. Oxford: Oxford University Press.

Zander, M. (1991): *The Police and (the) Criminal Evidence Act (of) 1984*, 2nd ed. London: Sweet and Maxwell.

Human Rights and the Right of the Police to use Physical Force

by
Knut Sveri

The big dilemma

There may be many attempts to define a "state", but regardless of what definition we prefer, it will always have to include something about *an organization where somebody is able to keep a certain order among the citizens.* If this order is broken – such as it is in Yugoslavia today – there is no meaning to talk about a "state" because there exists no order. In international law this is accepted as a criteria for when a "new state" is born. First when a government has been able to show that it is in its power to keep peace and order within the border of its territory the international community will accept the government as representing "a state".

Earlier days in our history the international community seems to have accepted and erased new states from the map according to what the big powers wanted – but still it was expected that the new states kept order within their territory. The *means* they used were, as the history of Hungary during the last 200 years clearly shows, often violent. Even after the Second World War states did disappear and other were erected depending upon what the powerful nations found to be in their interest. Today, however, it seems to be that the international community not only demands that a government is able to guarantee peace and order, it must also guarantee that those responsible for peace and order are entrusted with this duty as a result of an agreement by the majority of the citizens. In short, we demand that those in charge of the state not only have the power to keep peace and order, but also are *democratically* chosen to do so.

Knowing the situation in the states of this world, where there still are non-democratic societies in many places, we can see that the legal foundation for the police vary greatly, and that the interests which the police are supposed to serve differ very much. Some places, as in South America and Africa, the police are in the hands of corrupt politicians. In others they are serving more as military forces, as in Israel, Lebanon and Burma, or they are trying to establish themselves in new roles, as in many ex-communist states where they earlier were parts of terror regimes and now are trying to gain a new image. And, lastly, we have "our" police – the police of the Western World, ranging from a South-European *gendarme,* a North American *sheriff,* a Canadian Royal Mounted Police, to a German *kriminalkomissar,* an English *Bobby* or a Norwegian *lesnmann.* Although their working conditions, their salaries, their training, and their equipment are very different, they all have one thing in common, namely what the democratic state expects of them, that is: To keep order. They are to use a well known Anglo-American expression, *peace officers.*

However, at the same time we tell them what is expected of them, we also tell them that they are not allowed to do their job in the most effective way. Rather we place a lot of restriction upon them. They have to follow a long row of legal prescriptions, which are set up to safeguard citizens from harassment from the side of the police. Here we most certainly have the biggest dilemma of police work. *On the one hand, the state demands the highest degree of efficiency from its police, but on the other side it places such restrictions upon the activities of the police that it can be foreseen that the efficiency will be fairly low.*

This dilemma is linked to the everlasting problems of *the conflict between "the government" and "the people" of a state.* If we take a look at the history of mankind, we see that those in power – representing "the government" (be it a sovereign, a dictator or a prime minister) – always have a tendency to misuse their power, if they are not checked. Such checks can be either by counterforces or by rules – and here we are only interested in rules, which are the only civilized solution to conflicts. Undoubtedly the most famous of such rules is the English Magna Charta, the "great charter" from 1215 in which the sovereign (King John) was forced by the barons to guarantee the English free men that the King no longer should apprehend people except when they had broken the law of the land and to give people the right to trial by equals. In principle, the King accepted the restriction of his power according to these rules which certainly would make his own rule – as he saw it – less efficient. As far as I understand, the Magna Charta not only has played an important role during the decades in keeping a balance between the English state and its citizens, but it is of importance even today – and not only in England.

However, the basic reason we demand that all governments shall follow rules, comes out of bitter experience. We know that "power corrupts, and that absolute power corrupts absolutely" as it has been said.

We also know that wherever we see this type of moral corruption from the side of those in power, it is the police and the military forces which are used as their means to get what they want. During the terrible years of the Second World War nothing frightened people as much as the word Gestapo and probably GPU, KGB and Stasi have had similar meaning for millions of people in the eastern states. Today we also know that in many states – from Burma, Peru and China to Cuba, Turkey and South Africa – that security police of similar types exist and terrorize people in the same manner as their more well known prototypes.

Knowing all this, the subject of this paper becomes an extremely important one.

Development of the police

The institution of police forces, in the way we know it today, is a fairly recent invention, and the development seems ideologically to have had different starting points. What I have in mind is that I have a feeling the English police had quite a different start than the Continental police, and that these differences, although recently becoming smaller, still are so great that we can talk about two *quite different types of police roles*.

The English police, as we can see them developing in Sir Leon Radzinovicz study on the history of English Criminal Law, started simply by *extending to certain hired persons, later called police officers, the right every English citizen had to arrest and/or charge suspects of criminal offenses before law courts*. Later the local and central authorities also developed an interest in using the police for keeping order and preventing crime, but still one has the feeling that the English police are characterized by having a *civil nature*. It is particularly interesting to notice that, English police forces still lack state control, and that most efforts from the central government to interfere with the administrative decisions of the local chiefs of police have failed (Brewer, p. 14 ff). Running the risk of being accused of idealizing the English police, it has been proved that both corruption, racism and brutality exist. I will still maintain that *the ideal of the English police is to have the role of being servants to serve the law.*

Here on the Continent, and even in Scandinavia, the development has been different, mainly because there has been a concentration of power in the governments of Europe. The emperors – like Napoleon or Franz Joseph or czars like Peter the Great or kings like Sweden's Charles XII – were power builders. *They wanted strong states with obedient, docile subjects,* very much in the same style as Bismarck, Mussolini, Hitler and Stalin. *And I submit to you that the police in states with these ideas were not the servants of the law, but of the state.* While in England the ideal policeman has been a citizen with special duties to keep peace and with a duty to act according to law, a Continental policeman considers himself to be a tool of the state and set to exercise its power.

Although I believe these two models of police roles are the most interesting to discuss, I will not refrain from mentioning that there are others. We have the system in *United States* where the interference of local and central politics have destroyed most of the valuable ideals from England. The fact that some sheriffs and chiefs of police are elected has, in my opinion, been a disaster to the stability and led to moral corruption of the police organization. And we have the increasing number of *private police organizations* which are growing in Western Europe safeguarding rich people's homes, banks, money transports, embassies, state departments, and even police stations. They are obviously functional: they are fulfilling needs not met by the ordinary police. *But what ideals, except profit making for the owners, do the executives of these organizations hold?* Where lie their loyalties? What rights and duties should these guards have in their contact with people? In Sweden our experience with these "security guards" are not positive. Great brutality from the side of guards keeping order at dance halls and rock concerts are reported, and cases of corruption in connection with transport robberies are also known.

The Increased demand for police service.

As I said above, the fact that private police organizations are flourishing is an indication that there is an increased need for services offered by the police. The reason for this is partly that the old duties of the police – to keep order and to catch criminals – have become much more complicated because of urbanization and the increases in traditional crime. But in addition to this, new types of important problems have emerged which have been placed in the hands of the police – such as white collar crime, tax evasion, drugs, immigration and passport control, and pollution problems.

These changes cause many difficulties for any police organization, since it will obviously never have enough resources to do everything properly, and at the same time *the responsible politicians only rarely give a hint of what area of police work should have priority before others*. The result is that the police are easy targets for critics – and rightly so. Perhaps the situation is different in England, where I understand the power structure is not the same as elsewhere. The English chief constables seem to be sovereigns within their own areas and to make their own priorities regardless of what the politicians may want. To what extent the English chief constables' lists of priorities are more aimed at satisfying ordinary people's need for assistance than police organizations governed by politicians would be worth a comparative study.

Another important fact, which emerges out of the expanding roles of the police, is that *the ordinary policemen and the ordinary citizen today meet each other much more often than fifty years ago.* However, these meetings are practically always caused by some minor offense – usually a traffic violation – which has caused the police officer to intervene, or it is a result of a routine traffic control check. When discussing how to improve the relationship between police and citizens, *I suggest that we should not forget these encounters, because it is how the police officers behave in these situarions which more than anything else forms the base for what the single citizen thinks about the police.* It is usually only in such situations that an ordinary citizen meets police officers in their capacity as critic of his/her behaviour.

Police and the use of physical force.

What I have said so far shows, I hope, how different the development, expectations and actual working situations concerning the police are in different states and in different parts of the world. It is then not to be expected that police work is the same everywhere. On the contrary it must be obvious that there are considerable differences. *However, common to all the police forces is the fact that they are given the monopoly of being allowed to use physical force in order to perform their lawful duties.* At least, this is the "normal" situation and in my view there should be no exception to this: to keep order should be the duty of the police, a civil organization. It should never be allowed to call in military forces – the moment we allow military forces to be used against civilians we are in a state of civil war. This is (or was, as may be), in my view, the situation in Northern Ireland, Burma, Thailand, China and other places where guns are fired against civilians.

a) When do the police use physical force?

As far as I know, *no reliable empirical study exists of how, when and how often the police forces in our states use physical force* – or when they threaten to do so. We may, however, try to make a list of the normal situations of ordinary police work where it can be expected that physical force is used.

The most typical stituation, where violence may be used because a person opposes interference, is when a *police officer wants a person to move* – usually to get him to a police station because he is suspected of some offense or because he is drunk or drugged and has to be taken care of. But it may also be to a hospital or even just to get him away from a particular place because his presence causes trouble (part of a group of football hooligans), or because he interferes with important business (such as at a place were there is a traffic accident or a fire). If the person refuses to move, different possibilities may be present for the officer, depending upon the circumstances. He may use verbal arguments, he may call for assistance, he may try to fight the person and to overpower him and he may try to threaten him with a weapon. He may even run away – something which may be quite wise if the person whom the officer wants to arrest is joined by other hooligans. The risk that someone may be physically hurt is actually present in most of these very ordinary situations. A point, which we do not always have in mind when discussing the right behaviour of police officers in these daily situations, is that the officer very often has to make his decision very fast, and usually with little relevant information concerning the person (or persons) involved and about the total situation.

Another common type of situation is when a police officer is entering a place (be it a house, a boat or any other place) *in order to investigate a crime or look for a suspect*. In order to safeguard himself, the officer may take different precautions – usually by having in readiness some kind of weapon. In this situation there is a tangible risk that something, perhaps quite innocent, may happen, which is wrongly interpreted by the police officer and causes him do something which may physically hurt someone.

Next, in this little list of common situations, we have *the handling of crowds*. Even if the aim of the police in any civilized country is to make arrangements so that there will be no violence from either side, it is also obvious that the police in Europe during the last 10 to 15 years have prepared themselves for *direct battles. It seems self-evident that when necessary this means that the police forces are directly preparing to hurt and if necessary kill people.*

The same goes for my last example, namely the fight – and here the word "fight" is not used figuratively – against *terrorists*. Here the aims and measures of the police seem to be more often expressed in military form than in civil language. Personally, from my peaceful corner of the world, I am not convinced that this is the right approach. Among the reasons for this point of view I will only mention one: the risk that our loose definition of "terrorism" one day may be used also against otherwise peaceful persons who wants to protest against something which they consider wrong; the use of dangerous atomic power stations, pollution, death penalty, torture in prisons, killing of rare species.

b) What kind of physical force do the police use?

The most ordinary type of physical force used by police officers certainly is to grab the person and to lead him by use of hands. Use of hands for *fighting* – usually boxing and the more or less expert use of twisting of arms or wrestling the person to the ground. If this is done roughly and the person tries to resist or fight back, there is considerable risk that someone may be hurt. Until about 1960 the Swedish police constables had *sabres* which now have been replaced with fairly long wooden *sticks*. Sticks of different length and material seem to be police officers' standard weapons in most places in the world. Although police officers generally are instructed to use sticks against an opponents body and not direct it against his head and face, we know that this happens – especially since it actually is easier to hit from above than from the side. By the way, a hit from a stick may easily break a leg or a collar bone, if that is what the officer wants. Im my view, we often underestimate the risk of serious damage which may be the result of the use of sticks.

Firearms of different kind have during last 50 years been introduced in most countries as part of the ordinary equipment of ordinary policemen. Although I may be wrongly informed, it is only Norwegian and English police officers who today lack handguns when they are on ordinary beat patrol – and maybe that they are not any worse off for that. I find it a little astonishing that Swedish police officers, seemingly unanimously, claim that they cannot do their work properly without having access to a 9 mm high-velocity gun.

They insist on getting such a heavy gun since bullets from the old 7.65 mm which most of them still have do not stop an antagonist unless it hits in such a way that the person is killed, while the new 9 mm has such power that a bullet throws the person back regardless of where it hits. Personally, I find the acceptance of and interest in firearms among Swedish policemen slightly morbid. If they follow the instructions, it is only under extraordinary circumstances of threat to (their own or other people's) life that they are allowed to use the guns.

I am afraid that the police officers reliance on guns may lead them to unnecessary risks and get them into situations where someone may be seriously hurt.

What I have in mind are situations like the following: A police officer enters a building where a burglary has been reported. Relying upon his gun he does not wait to get assistance – and as a result of this he is attacked by two unarmed burglars scared to death by his gun. Or another situation: A police officer draws his gun when following a teenager who has abandoned a stolen car. The police officer grabs the boy and tries to overthrow him. While doing this the gun fires "by accident" and kills the boy instantly. – In a case now pending before a Swedish criminal court two civil police officers interfered in a small brawl by a hot dog stand. They unfortunately drew their guns when the small crowd started becoming slightly aggressive. The police officers started running followed by some aggressive "hooligans". One officer turned around, shot and hurt one of the antagonists and the other, while running, shot another with a 9 mm Sauger straight through the head from about a 6 meter distance. The fellow who was shot from behind died instantly. The police officer, said to be a well-trained man with many years excellent service and a record as a good shot, claims that he aimed at the legs! (One may wonder what damage a police officer with a normal record might have caused!) – Even worse is the following case: A police officer shows his gun to his 8 year-old son and his friend when a shot goes off and kills the son.

Furthermore, the tendency to militarize the police has increased during the last 20 years. First, the "student opposition", which started in about 1968 influencing both Western Europe and USA and lasting about ten years, then the Bader-Mainhof, the Red Army and other terrorist organizations in Germany, Japan and other places, and even the increased drug problem, all played in the favour of national police forces which claimed that if they should effectively perform their duty to safeguard their nations against threats of international dangerous organizations they needed military strength. What the police demanded to meet these threats with were among other things "special forces" with special training, special equipment, special authorizations, and special stipulations as far as the ordinary criminal procedures were concerned. This simply means that our countries have accepted that police are allowed to use a lot of more of less dangerous equipment, such as tear gas, water guns, plastic bullets (which actually have killed a dozen children in Northern Ireland), and heavy weapons such as machine guns. Adding this together with the shields, visors, flame-secure dresses and gas masks which a "modern police officer" is trained to use, we obviously are a long step away from the ordinary police officer whose duty it is to keep order and arrest criminals. In many countries, among them Norway and Sweden (probably two of the most peaceful countries in the whole world), the police have been able to convince their governments that it is necessary to invest fortunes of the taxpayers money into training and equipping "special forces" of selected policemen who are being trained for killing possible future terrorists.

Most problematic, however, is that the *police demand "introduction of special legislation" in order to solve the big problems which they claim are ahead – which means that they wish the government to let the police have the right to reduce people's rights according to existing laws when they consider this to be convenient for their own purposes.*

Unfortunately, it seems to be that often the politicians will yield to the pressure from the side of the police, mainly because no political party dares in the long run to go against the police. To do so would label the party as being against "crime fighting" that it would "allow the country to be a home for terrorists" or that it would be instrumental in "allowing the next generation of children to die of narcotics".

Human Rights.

The tendency that so many states strengthen their police and give them not only more resources and more "effective" means to fight against criminality, but also take steps to allow the police to use techniques which up to now have been forbidden, *make the international and regional declarations on human rights to be the Magna Charta of our generation.*

When we talk about human rights we are probably mainly thinking of the following documents:

1. From United Nations:

a) *Universal Declaration of Human Rights* – which is a set of principles adopted (unanimously) by the General Assembly on 10 Dec. 1948. This is a set of principles which as such are not binding for the states, but certainly have a great moral impact and have played and are playing an important role in the different states' revisions of their constitutions (where it now is usual to include most of the declaration).
b) *International Covenant on Civil and Political Rights* adopted by the General Assembly in 1966 (together with a Covenant on Economic, Social and Cultural Rights which is of less interest for this presentation) which are legally binding for states after ratification.
c) Of special interest is also a recommendation adopted by the United Nations in 1979 entitled Code of Conduct for Law Enforcement Officials.

2. From the Council of Europe

a) European Convention on Human Rights from 4 November 1950 and in force since 3 September 1953, which also instituted. The European Courts of Human Rights, has shown its usefulness in many respects up to today.
b) In 1979 the Parliamentary Assembly of the Council of Europe accepted a special *Declaration on the Police.* The Declaration – which did not get full support from the Committee of Ministers – is a European equivalent to United Nations Code of Conduct.

What do these documents say about the police and its use of physical force? Neither of the Human Rights charters gives any direct information to what the police, or the executive organs, shall or shall not do. *What they do is to declare what minimum rights people being on the territory of any particular state have,* and from this can be drawn important conclusions as to what the police are *not* allowed to do.

Right to life. Both charters state (UN art. 6, Eur. art. 2) that arbitrary killing is forbidden, and in any civilized society one may think that such a statement is unnecessary. However, as we know, arbitrary killings by police forces do take place, not only in South America and South Africa, but also in Israel, Turkey and perhaps even by British police in Northern Ireland.

Torture and inhuman and degrading treatment. (UN art. 7, Eur. art. 3) This means that a police officer has a duty to treat everyone "with humanity and respect" as it is stated in UN art 10. In a case from 1978 the European court of Human Rights found that British police had violated art. 3 when interrogating suspected IRA terrorists by a) depriving them of food and drink, b) depriving them of sleep, c) placing black hoods over their heads, d) forcing them to lean on their toes and fingers for hours, and e) subjecting them to intensive noise before interrogation.

Right to liberty and security. (UN art. 9, Eur. art. 5). These articles strictly forbid any kind of unlawful arrest – which also means that a police officer is not allowed to use physical violence when apprehending someone unless he has legal grounds for his intervention.

Right to privacy. (UN art. 17, Eur. art. 8). Nown have both relevance for the police practice which consists in stopping and searching people and vehicles. The European charter gives some details about the situations when the police are entitled to use such a procedure. The point is that this type of interference with people's privacy is only allowed when the police officers have a *specific legally* accepted aim for interfering – it is not allowed to do it as routine in order to harass certain groups of people. This reflection goes also for police intervention into "known places of drug addicts" or similarly, where many poliee officers go and "rough up" the persons they find there. Such behaviour from the side of the police is forbidden.

Right to peaceful assembly (UN art. 18, Eur. art. 11) or right to meet publicly and to arrange processions for or against political views, ideologies, religious beliefs etc. is considered to be fundamental for democracies. It is therefore the duty of the police to guarantee that such meetings can take place and stop those who try to interfere.

This duty has also expanded to other areas, such as entertainment like football matches and other such arrangements. It is – as I see it – unfortunate that these two types of public gatherings are considered in the same manner by governments and police chiefs – actually they have nothing in common: Just as important our right to manifest our views and ideals are, just as dispensable are the football matches. From the point of view of police work, the police have certainly no obligation to guard sport events and may do well in saying so instead of risking their lives in trying to keep hooligans away from each other. While it sometimes is so that the police, according to local law, forbid political and other meetings because they believe there may be disturbances, this procedure should certainly also, and often with more relevance, be used against sportsevents.

In addition to this there are in the two other documents – *"The UN Code of Conduct for Law Enforcement Officials"* and *in the Council of Europe "Declaration on the Police"* – which are relevant for the problem of when and to what extent the police may use physical violence. Both declare, that the use of force should be kept at a low level. But they express this slightly differently. In the European declaration it is said that:

> In performing his duties, a police officer shall use all necessary determination to achieve an aim which is legally required or allowed, but he may never use more force than is reasonable.

In the UN Code it is expresked in the following manner:

> Law enforcement officials may use force only when strict, necessary and to the extent required for the performance of their duty.

Furthermore, the UN Code has an interesting and highly relevant commentary to this article. It says that "the use of force by law enforcement officials should be exceptional", and that:

> National law ordinarily restricts the use of force by law enforcement officials in accordance with a principle of proportionality. It is to be understood that such national principles of proportionality are to be respected in the interpretation of this provision.

This is a most important statement. The principle of proportionality simply says that *there must be a reasonable proportionality between the bad behavior of a person and the violence used by the police.* As I see it, it means that it is not allowed for a police officer to endanger a teenager's life by hunting him and shooting at him just because he unlawfully has taken a car and is trying to escape. And it is not allowed for a police officer to start beating an alien applying for asylum with his stick because this alien will not let his fingerprints be taken. Neither should it be allowed for the police to secretly drug people in order to get them to be easier to handle during transport.

Instead of a conclusion

The topic I have tried to cover is a complicated and touchy one. *The police everywhere are a closed official institution and they stand very little criticism.* This raises two very difficult problems.

First, *it makes it extremely difficult to- do reliable empirical studies of how the police actually work.* And this means that the police will not have the advantage of learning from studies made by someone from outside. This is especially unsatisfactory when the studies concern unethical behaviour by the police officers, such as unlawful use of violence.

It is indeed very difficult to perform such a study, mainly because all the dubious cases where the police officer may have used more violence than the situation legally allowed him and all the cases where the victim dares not tell the truth because he is afraid of the police officers' revenge. Any criminologist who has tried to get a bit closer to the truth will know that police officers close ranks against anyone trying to study these phenomena.

An example which may be mentioned is the famous story of police violence in the police district of Bergen on the west-coast of Norway. Two research workers from Bergen University tried to reveal the truth by a most ingenious technique. They went through all the emergency and hospital cases in a certain period and picked out all those where the medical treatment was conducted after the person's arrest – in most cases for drunkenness. They then interviewed the persons trying to find out what had happened and to what extent the violence was within or outside the law. They did find that many of the arrestees claimed that the violent acts had taken place in a lift which the police used to transport the arrested persons. Left with quite a few cases where there seemed to be no other explanation of the injury than police brutality, the research workers published their results. As can be expected, the police and their union protested, a royal commission (consisting of a law professor from Oslo University and a barrister) was sent down and after some time the commission – which also had made its own investigation of police brutality in other police forces in Norway – concluded that the research report was excellent and that the truth in fact was that the police brutality in Bergen was worse than said in the report. The Bergen police – nicely helped by the prosecutors – then started criminal proceedings against the arrested persons, claiming that they had made false statements about state officials – and actually got some of them sent to prison. Furthermore, they have instigated legal processes against the law professor and there is also reason to believe that they have harassed at least one of the research workers by stopping his car repeatedly. Someone also placed drugs in his car. However, he detected it and took precautions before anything happened.

Second, *the closeness of the police leads also to a situation where unlawful violence may continue because nobody is able to get enough evidence to smoke out the bad officers.* I do believe that quite often the colleagues of a police officer who has done something criminal, i.e. beaten up or even killed a person, do commit perjury when they claim to have "seen nothing", and "heard nothing".

How can three police officers, sitting in a van, avoid seeing and hearing that someone is being handled by a colleague in such a manner that he needs weeks of hospital treatment? Studies in Sweden show that in most cases, where someone claims to have been beaten up, this happens at a police station with three police officers present in the same room.

It is obvious that there is a need for both better training and guidelines for the police. And in this connection the continued work of both United Nations and the Council of Europe in elaborating our Human Rights is of the utmost importance.

I will especially recommend that the Council of Europe revise the text of its excellent publication by J. Alderson – in view of recent developments in Europe (there may be new material to be added to the examples given in the text). I furthermore recommend that the book be translated and used as a standard text in all police training institutions.

In the future, when we get a united Europe, one of the most important areas for coordination is to reach one good code for what we shall have the right to expect of those we entrust with the power to keep law and order.

Notes and References

Alderson, J. (1984): *Human Rights and the Police. Directorate of Human Rights.* Strasbourg: Council of Europe,

Benyon, J., Bourn, C. (eds.) (1986): *The Police: Powers, Procedures and Proprieties.* Oxford: Pergamon Press.

Brewer, J. D., Guelke, A., Hume, I., Moxon-Browne, E., Wilford, R. (1988): *The Police, Public Order, and the State.: Policing in Great Britain, Northern Ireland, the Irish Republic, the USA, South Africa and China.* Hongkong: Macmillan Press.

Cowell, D., Jones, T., Zoung, J. (eds.) (1982): *Policing the Riots.* London: Junction Books.

van Dijk, P., van Hoof, G.J.H. (1990): *Theory and Practice of the European Convention on Human Rights.* 2nd ed. Boston: Kluwer-Deventer.

Radzinowicz, Leon (1948): *History of English Criminal Law,* 1938-64. Vol. 5. London: Macmillan.

Topic II.

The Effect of Social Changes upon Crime

by
Uwe Ewald

The Transformation of State Socialism, Crime and Criminalization

Preliminary Remarks

Proceeding from the approach shown above, we see various patterns of explanation and differentiations within the structure of crime and/or criminalization in societies in transition with reference to:

1. crime inherited from state-socialism
2. crime during transformation.

These temporally differing levels of observed crime determine our picture of crime and/or criminalization subsequent to the collapse of authoritarian socialism. With reference to modernization, it is interesting to note that retrospective criminalization (point 1), is involved in the current attempt to deal mainly with political conflicts, namely the repression against democratic movements, using the penal code.[1] This indeed corresponds to the nature of fundamental conflict in these former societies, as well as, to the political power intentions of the new society. By their (negative) evaluation of the past during state-socialism, these political power intentions provide their own position, thus attributing their symbolic meaning to the process of transformation (Bourdieu 1991).

---

[1] The Berlin Senate for Internal Affairs which is responsible for nearly all crimes of unification and governmental crime, lists 8 investigations/indictments involving extortion by GDR organs of the state and 260 investigations/indictments involving attempted or actually committed homicide at the border (Press Release 1992).

The contradictions in unleashing innovative potential and/or its prevention manifested themselves in political conflict, by necessity, within state-socialism.[2] By contrast, in the societies in transition, everyday crime, organized crime and white-collar crime tend to manifest themselves more powerfully. We also confront the criminalization of political conflict, whose significance, however, is of a completely different magnitude.

"Dealing With" State Socialism and Crime

The Macro-Structures of State Socialism and its Criminalization Today

From the description of modernization with its theoretically defined, macro-structurally patterned, fundamental conflicts in state-socialism (see point 2.2.1), we can detect two levels relevant to processes of retroactive criminalization: a) patterns of behavior aimed at monopolizing power and, b) the exclusion of the greater part of society from the process of planning and decision-making in that society as a result of those aims (Ewald, 1992).

The Monopolization of Power

This involves a) the creation of internal power structures and b) the binding of individuals belonging to the power elite to the circle of power.

The former (a) includes the internal power struggles particularly characteristic for the period subsequent to 1945 (Hodos 1990), which differed from country to country. Often it was Communists (in addition to individuals completely uninvolved) attempting to effect a reform of Stalinist policies, who were the victims of this repression. Dealing with this after the collapse involves rehabilitation of the victims as well as criminal prosecution of the formerly powerful and their judicial apparatus (Werkentin 1990).

In addition to the internal power struggle, the former power elite also attempted to create authoritarian power structures ("covert structures"). In the course of such attempts constitutional principles contained in the existing constitutions were often violated. In the new states of the Federal Republic of Germany it is predominantly the activities of the Ministry of State Security (Stasi) which are being scrutinized with reference to possible criminal prosecution. However, to date, criminal proceedings in

---

[2] Of historical interest is the reconstruction of the image of crime during state socialism itself. This image could also be reconstructed using the approach presented in this context, which explains why state socialist and transitional societies' relationships to the evolutionary processes of modern societies were both different and yet also resulted in reciprocal strategies of criminalization in broad areas. I shall not further deal with this question in this connection.

connection with espionage conducted against the (old) Federal Republic of Germany continue to play the central role (Albrecht, Kadelbach 1992). Regarding attempts to prosecute those formerly in positions of political responsibility as well as the activities of "commercial coordination", an area of vast covert economic activity which operated in close coordination with the Ministry of State Security and employed illegal methods and means (Koch 1992), the potential provided by the penal code is obviously limited.

The latter point (b) concerning the linkage of individuals in the circle of power through privileges and corruption, should be viewed in terms of the creation and maintenance of authoritarian power structures (Klemm 1991). Here, criminal proceedings have been completed which have likewise led to criminal convictions.

Exclusion and "De-Subjectification"

Excluding society from significant decision-making processes over development and, thus, preventing innovative change, was achieved at different levels. Particularly during the 40's and 50's, a transformation of the social structure was undertaken in the GDR by means of the penal code. This has been referred to in the literature as homogenization and "de-subjectification" (Adler 1991, p. 157; Meuschel 1991, p. 41). The persecution and often criminal prosecution of owners of private property ultimately led to a leveling of the social structure of the society.

With the heavy-handed transformation of the social structure, the repression and criminalization of democratic reform efforts were also being enforced. It was a direct result of the power theory of state-socialism's leadership, whose "bunker mentality" attempted to prevent not only overt and violent resistance, but nearly all forms of criticism expressed in the public arena. This mistrustfulness of almost every view and opinion, which deviated from current doctrine, led to an extensive system of political control and restraint in which even existing democratic forms became ritualized, and thus stripped of their genuine function. The manipulation of election results is an example of the suppression of democracy, which has already led to the conviction of former political functionaries in the new German federal states. With respect to dealing with political repression in the GDR, this is currently seen in popular discourse as a problem of marginal significance. Yet it was this mistrust of political deviation, which ultimately led to the paranoia of the system, subjecting the whole society to surveillance. This general mistrust of "secondary culture" was manifested most strongly in the institutionalization of the system of informants under the auspices of state security.

It is mainly in these mentioned areas where rehabilitation of those politically persecuted and often criminalized is taking place and where efforts are being concentrated seeking means of subjecting to criminal prosecution those responsible for such political decisions along with those who participated in the political and judicial systems of repression. Concerning the characterization of political crime arising out of state-socialism in the field of political and economic power, it is the criminalization of illegal privileges and corruption, as well as the suppression of attempts to attain democratic rights, which are being given central attention at present.[3]

Criminological study of these processes ultimately leads to an explanation of the structures of authoritarian power making, among other things, the individual's role and potential for action understandable, as well as pointing to the problems of tendentious monopolization of power in non-authoritarian societies.[4]

Everday Crime Prior the Upheaval and Coping Today

The problem of so-called everyday crime or micro-crime "inherited" from the GDR will be dealt with here only marginally, in as much as it is obviously much less extensive and only sporadically significant in terms of the total spectrum of crime in the new states of the republic. Acts which were criminal offenses, both according to the penal code of the GDR and the FRG (theft at the private level, assault and battery, etc.) were reviewed with respect to levels of punishment, if conviction had already taken place according to GDR law. Both as a result of the amnesty proclaimed by the last GDR administration, as well as, the review and revision of sentences to confinement, led to a dramatic reduction of the prison population. In the cases of crimes committed in the former GDR, for which indictments were only pasked down after unification had taken place, convictions were dealt with in accordance with the Unification Accord.

No indictments have been sought for offenses highly typical for the GDR, such as theft from GDR plants. Foregoing prosecution of these

---

[3] Here it is necessary to bear in mind that the criminologically relevant macro-structural phenomena presented in this context are only selective and are being described primarily with reference to internal structure of rule. Other forms such as state-organized damaging of the environment or criminologically relevant arms trading were not further discussed.

[4] Bourdieu raises this question in connection with the retrospective analysis of state socialism in the GDR, "as to whether the difference between major Western parties with their political demonstration fights and their virtual monopolizing of the state in the name of their leaders and the Soviet type parties is merely one of degree, but not of principle". (Bourdieu, 1991, p. 33).

offenses is due to the necessity for the courts to react to current delinquency, a task which is currently overburdening them according to their own statements, as well as, the lack of interest in a penal policy of retroactively pursuing convictions for these offenses. In addition, the privatization of the GDR economy has resulted in the "liquidation" of those entities suffering damage, who would have had an interest in such prosecution.

The Transition Situation and the Criminalization of Social Conflicts

Reorganization of the Macro-Structures and Crime

Using the modernization-theoretical approach briefly presented above, areas of conflict at the macro-structural level are criminologically deserving of closer scrutiny, because they relate negative-destructively to elementary processes of societal self-formation, which were found in two basic processes of reorganization of fundamental social institutions: (a) the transformation of the former political and economic institutions of state-socialism under new conditions (that is continuity and/or discontinuity) and (b) the relationship between (interior) demotic and (superior) exogenous structures (that is, self-formation and/or implantation). Criminologically relevant macro-structural processes should also include (c) forms of organized crime often located on the borderline between micro- and macro-crime, but in terms of their structural and functional characteristics more comparable to forms of macro-crime, since they manifest themselves as expressions of collective structures and reveal less about the conditions of the individual.

a) With respect to the continuity and/or discontinuity of political and economic structures in the new German federal states, special situations arise, because the process of the GDR's joining the (old) FRG led to the implantation of the economic, administrative, and legal systems of the old FRG and the simultaneous dissolution of the corresponding fundamental structures of state-socialism. Yet, despite the predominance of discontinuity, processes can be found which tie down material and/or financial resources, which prevent them from being used for purposes of re-constructing the economy, for example.

---

[5] The press release of the Berlin Senate lists 40 major investigations/indictments in the area of commercial coordination, 30 major investigations/indictments involving fraudulent manipulation of transfer-rubles, 23 investigations/indictments of illegal activites involving pan and/or mass organization assets; charges filed by the Trust Agency, 15 investigations/indictments involving illegal activities in connection with the establishment of the currency union and 26 investigations/indictments involving corruption.

So-called unification crime is the term used to characterize those manipulations subjected to investigation (and criminalization) by the agencies of penal control,[5] which arise from real abuses of the effective control by functionaries of the old economy and/or administration and the party system, over material and financial resources, during the process of creating the currency union (introduction of the D-Mark) and/or privatization of former "people's" property. The Berlin Senate for Internal Affairs estimates the damage at 4.2 billion marks. In this connection it is necessary to study the "old boys' networks", currently characterized as the attempt to preserve the past, and thus, unsuited or hardly suitable structures, with reference to future tasks.[6] Certainly, this situation manifests itself differently in the various states of the former Eastern bloc compared to the situation in the territory of the former GDR. These countries are primarily faced with the task of transforming themselves, since the implantation processes taking place in the new German states are simply not possible.

    b)   The reorganization of the administrative and economic structures in the new German federal states is primarily taking place as a process being performed by outside forces. Both the act of privatization, being performed by the Trust Agency and the influence and expansion of the economic structures of the West into the East of Germany, deserve further study. As does the implantation of West German political structures which produce "external administration". The privatization being performed by the Trust Agency is distinctly oriented to dissolving former GDR structures, as the most recent incidents in connection with the sale of the former GDR news agency "Allgemeiner Deutscher Nachrichtendienst" (ADN) indicates (Spiegel 1992, p. 87). The effect of this strategy will be that ultimately all of the major east German structures are systematically dissolved, and not always in accordance with the rules of economic profit. Even in cases where plants could continue to operate economically with a profit, the search – as far as can be ascertained – for buyers from the West continues. This also includes a willingness to be quite flexible in fulfilling their wishes during negotiations with outside investors (Trust Agency – A Bargain Center?) (Holm 1991; Flug 1992). This makes it impossible for east Germans independently to design complex economic processes.[7] With respect to the expansion particularly of West German economic structures into the territory of the new German

---

    [6] Here, it must be kept in mind that these types of withdrawal of resources were often jointly organized and executed together with western business functionaries.

    [7] Because the activities of the Trust Agency take place behind closed doors it is impossible to make more accurate statements, however the fact that a special group of prosecuting attorneys has been formed to monitor the privatization activities of this agency would tend to indicate that some of its activities give more than reasonable cause for suspicion of criminologically relevant activity.

states, we can safely posit that the East German economy is being subjected to discrimination. Here, too, we can fall back on no larger studies at the moment, but based on information obtained through the media, from police publications and from other experts (Prieve, Hickel 1991), East Germany did not and is not collapsing only because its products no longer had or have a market, or because production was or is too outmoded, but rather because the uninhibited opening of the market was initiated without a sufficient economic concept. There was a firm political intention of establishing the status quo of the old German states. The consequences of this non-design of transition of (usable) economic structures are now manifesting themselves in massive problems in the employment sector, including the continuing exodus of skilled labor into the West, thus causing further structural weakening of the East.

The implantation of political structures – "colonization of East Germany" (Rosenberg 1991) – produces massive outside administration, meaning that in nearly all significant positions within the public sector, administrative officials from the old German states are attempting to organize all complicated processes in the East. In terms of personnel, the intention was and is to install western concepts, values and standards in the reorganization of political and social processes through corresponding staffing practices. The political confrontations in the assembly of the state of Brandenburg (cf. allegations of Stasi-collaboration on the part of the Minister President Stolpe and the resignation of minority leader Diestel) are merely topical and conspicuous examples of such disputes regarding self-formation or alien formation of the processes taking place in the East.

c)   With the background of the transformation and dissolution of macro-structures, the genesis of organized crime appears nearly inevitable. Nevertheless, it is appropriate to deal with the problem of organized crime in the context of transformation, because, independent of the structural and functional implications, from the vantage point of the new federal states, organized crime is as much an implanted phenomena as all of the other implanted phenomena. What this means is that the collapse of formal and to a certain extent informal control has generated a structure of opportunity for organized crime which remained nearly totally "unused" by the citizens of the former GDR, but which was obviously attractive to outsiders. This type of organized crime (as alien crime) appeared immediately after the "change" particularly in those areas where it was possible to take advantage of the gullibility of the East Germans with respect to the new structures. Surreptitious economic consultants caused businesses and plants to behave in a manner calculated not to put them on sound footing, but rather to cause their downfall and the enrichment of the "economic consultants". East German banks granted credit lines to fly-by-night and other slick operators. Major theft operations (for example, widespread cattle and livestock theft) were only possible due to insufficient security measures on the part of the businesses. Among the popular targets of organized breaking and entering and theft were museums, churches, even banks and savings and loan association offices. It is worthy to note that to date no significant trafficking of illegal drugs has been reported or recorded. By contrast, according to police reports, car theft has become a serious problem.

Everyday Crime in the Transition Situation[8]

To the extent that crime is individual behavior reflecting the state of the individual, explanations which interpret crime as an expression of a lack of opportunity to adequately develop one's personality will also be useful in the transition situation. Social-psychological models, such as this one, often proceed from the assumption that existing interest or need structures can only be fulfilled to a limited degree if at all. This postponement of need fulfillment or the loss of needs can be amplified in transition situations, thus providing an explanation for deviant behavior. Such an understanding also permits the integration of classic theories of anomie and/or strain, as well as, theories of social disorganization seen as patterns capable of partially explaining delinquent behavior in the transition situation. Generally speaking, everyday crime (that is, traditional crime) in the transition situation can be conceived of as individual coping with social conflicts in the process of societal transformation. Using such an approach, it will become necessary, on the one hand, to study objective conflict situations and, on the other, the subjective potential for coping with such situations, while pursuing one's own interests more intensively (Hradil 1992, p. 185; Hanak, Stehr, Steiner p. 7). Such an analysis of living patterns and opportunities for action on the part of the individual, ultimately lead to the question of the real increase in personal freedom for the individual effected by the transformation.

The first findings from studies[9] of unreported and/or unrecorded crime provide a general picture of the development and structure of (traditional) crime in the new federal states. The information available to

---

[8] Normally it is precisely the area of everyday crime and its criminalization which is presented as the real crime problem. This at least holds true for the larger research projects in Germany. That the media direct nearly all of their attention to these types of crime which generate the greatest fears and anxieties in the general public is well known. But it is precisely the inordinately broad coverage in terms of the social significance of the problem with reference to the social transformation taking place which raises the question as to the function of such one-sided presentation of the problem of crime. The processes of scandalization deserve further study.

[9] cf. footnote 2

date on the appearance of crime after the "change" indicates that, in comparison with the GDR, the number of crimes committed is on the rise. Yet, this increase can be termed quite modest in the face of the deep societal dissolution taking place. This still holds true even if we keep in mind that a number of serious types of crime, as already mentioned in connection with organized crime (organized car-theft, slave-trade of women and bank robbery), were essentially imported into the new federal states from the outside, and thus were not "produced" within the GDR population by the conditions of transition as such. It is, however, precisely this implanted crime which is being given great coverage in the media's presentation of crime in the East of Germany.

With respect to the structure of crime, it is possible to make two general statements based on the first results of the mentioned quantitative studies: Firstly, the general structure of crime in the new federal states is relatively similar to the structure in the old German states. This refers both to the relative proportional amount of specific types of crime (the ratio of property crimes to crimes of violence to sex-related crimes) and to the quantitative levels of such crimes which, for all of their obviously apparent differences, nevertheless reveal remarkable similarities. Secondly, the differences clearly point to certain peculiarities with respect to the areas of conflict in the new federal states. If we compare Kury's presentation of victimization in the new and old German states in terms of the period before and after the "change", then it is (at least hypothetically) possible to interpret the differences we find, which correspond to different conflict situations in the East and the West. Whereas we observe higher rates of bicycle theft, burglary, and assault in the old German states for the period since "die Wende", that is after 9 November 1989, the converse holds true in the new German states with respect to theft of cars, theft from cars, vandalism to cars, motorcycle theft, robbery(!), theft of personal property and sex-related crimes. In one respect, the total of seven crime groups included in the study (compared to three groups for the old German states), whose ratios since the and of 1989 are higher than in the old federal states, indicates that social conditions in the new German states are more subject to the turbulence of transition than in the old ones. In another respect, the types of crime contained in the group of seven indicate that particularly those types of behavior have become more prevalent which can be exhibited by youth and young male adults in the anonymity of the public sphere. Particularly conspicuous is the fact that robbery plays a significant role in the new federal states.

In general, the situation in the new federal states cannot be characterized as dramatic despite its scandalized illustration in the media. This does not deny that serious levels of crimes of violence can indeed be observed. This is particularly true for crimes of violence with a right-wing extremist background. Results of an offender interview survey indicate that delinquency involving violence is typical of structurally weak areas. This refers to areas of the former GDR which provide no or hardly any opportunities for spare time recreational activities. Initial assumptions that violent crime is particularly related to social insecurity found no corroboration for any of the crimes of violence included in the study.[10]

Tentative Conclusions

The effects of social change on crime and criminalization in the transitional societies as viewed from the vantage point of the new German states, using the perspective developed above can be summed in the following three points:

1. The radicality and all-pervasiveness of the social change taking place calls for an expansion of the perspective of criminology in order for it to be able to describe the social fields of conflict and analogous processes of criminalization. Of key importance in this context is concentration on the processes of securing and releasing evolutionary potential significant to the development of modern society in the former state-socialist countries.

2. With respect to the comparative study of crime incidence and change in the control of crime during social transformation in the countries of Central and Eastern Europe, it is possible to define various contexts whose similarities and differences provide us with explanations of the differing pictures of crime and crime control within these countries.

- The basic structure of social conflicts is dependent on the specific initial situations and national peculiarities in the respective countries. The pre-requisites for completing the transition to a modern society in the territory of the former GDR and the CSFR, Poland and Hungary or the CIS, Bulgaria or Romania, differ from country to country. It might be, for example, that conditions in the new states of Germany or the CSFR are more advantageous than in, for example, the CIS, Bulgaria or Romania.In this context it must be pointed out that variously intense conflicts between various nationalities play a key role in these processes.
- With respect to the transition situations - the new states of the FRG enjoy a special status with respect to their unification with the FRG,

---

[10.] Cf. the initial findings of a self-report survey (part of the DFG-study; see footnote 2) (Ewald 1991).

which is, as far as can be ascertained, singular among these countries. This status can be characterized, albeit slightly exaggeratedly, as caught up in the ambivalence of outside domination (that is, determination of the significant processes by West Germans) and alimentation (that is, provision of a higher standard of living through participation of Western affluence). Both aspects are directly connected to the development of crime and crime control.

3. Information about the development of crime in the individual countries makes it possible to formulate propositions about the connection between social change and crime. The transitional situation obviously leads to a rise in recorded crime in all of the countries discussed. Here it should not be forgotten, however, that changes of the control systems have also led to changes in the strategies of criminalization. In addition to the removal of sections of the respective penal codes, the areas being criminalized have also been expanded. This alone leads to a rise in recorded crime. On the other hand, selective criminal prosecution directs police attention toward certain areas, such as crimes of violence and organized crime, while directing relatively less attention to other areas such as white-collar crime.

Existing differences in the extent of increases in crime and in the structure of crime obviously correlate with the differences in the various initial situations and the transitions to be made which have been described in the foregoing. The special situation of the new states of Germany results in part because the collapse of the GDR was experienced as an act of liberation, the initial phase in the organization of new social structures and the initial acceptance of West German structures were also, for the most part, perceived as securing and expanding the standard of living.

By contrast, in the other countries an economic crisis due to the perception of need and scarcity in the elementary sectors of everyday life was a determining factor which not only could not be eliminated after the political collapse, it continued to become even more acute. Here, high levels of disorientation and scarcity continue to be characteristic.

Emerging Problems of Official Social Control in Finland

by
Kauko Aromaa,

Introduction

European integration being basically an economic affair, its possible consequences in the field of criminality and crime control have begun to be dealt with only rather recently (cf. Heidensohn & Farrell 1991). Integration does, however, probably have many unwanted and unforeseen side-effects on the incidence of crime, the structure of criminality, and also on the numbers and kinds of people to be subjected to crime, and, on the other hand, to repressive crime control measures.

Simultaneously, the emerging social changes, together with formal integration, create both possibilities and pressures concerning police powers and police cooperation in Europe. This development also produces new problems of protective measures obviously needed for the local population facing the prospect of a new "Euro-police."

Examples of official concern

Such problems come forth in all countries concerned. In the case of Finland, not (yet) an EC member state, very little preparatory work to deal with them has as yet been undertaken. Some ideas have, however, been presented by leading politicians and officials. For example, the Finnish prime minister has recently pointed out that the rights of individual citizens must with great care be protected against actions from the future "Big Brother Euro-police."

Also, the chief of the Finnish security police has claimed that changes in laws concerning police powers and other legislation are needed in order to cope with the extensive social changes expected. His concerns were, among others, that the Foreigner Act is too liberal and the existing asylum rules need to be adapted to the new situation, particularly because of the flow of migration from the area of the former Soviet Union. Additionally, he wanted to have telephone surveillance legalized, referring to the example in Sweden where a court-granted right to tap telephones in specified cases proved to be useful even for the Finnish police (the recent war in Iraq was given as an example; the Swedish police could, on the basis of information gained by telephone surveillance, give the Finnish police a warning of terrorist operations in progress against Scandinavian, and also assumedly Finnish, targets). At the level of international police cooperation, the chief of the security police stated that new forms of direct cooperation between national police forces need to replace or supplement the traditional, Interpol-based cooperation. In this context, he also spoke of cooperation in the exchange of information contained in police registers in different countries.

Some basic concepts

My central concern being crime as part of everyday life, I have chosen to sketch some forthcoming social changes that are going to influence future criminality.

In this exercise, I rely on a logical model of crime, useful when trying to sort out crime-changing aspects of some interesting social processes. It is a simple model of the basic logical elements of crime and has resemblances with Marcus Felson's analytical tools (cf. e.g. Cohen & Felson 1979, Felson 1986, 1987). It does not say what is considered to be criminal behavior, i.e., it only operates within a given definition of crime. I shall return briefly to the subject of crime definitions at the end of this paper.

Figure 1.

The logical elements of criminal events

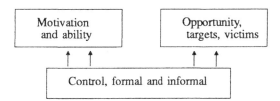

According to the model (see Figure 1.), for a criminal event to take place, it requires a motivated and competent offender, a suitable target opportunity (situation), and insufficient control.

If we look back, increases in property crimes in the few past decades, for example, have very much depended on the opportunity element that has grown dramatically. The changes I have located in the following presentation have connections to all three elements.

The social changes that I have sketched in this scenario are in one way or another connected with the three elements of the model. I have, in a somewhat arbitrary manner, picked out seven different dimensions of change by "translating" certain characteristics of the integration development to a crime-relevant terminology.

An attempt to sketch some of the emerging social, crime-related problems in greater detail; dimensions of change

Primarily, integration means free movement of labor and people in general between the countries. When the EC is concerned, this is expressly the case. But the same holds true, to a certain extent, also in the other European countries. I have translated this development into five crime-producing dimensions that mainly depend on the integration pressure. These five are:

1. *The "home-base effect"*
2. *The deterioration of local networks that are responsible for informal social control*
3. Improved *possibilities for organized and organizational crimes*
4. *The emergence of "imported", earlier (locally) unknown crime techniques and types of crime*
5. *The changes in criminality* that appear as *the old underworld* and the outside underworlds try to sort out their conflict concerning the crime market, and to integrate, as well.

Additionally, a sixth and seventh dimension of change are pinpointed. These two seem to be of a local character, and seem to be found only in Finland and only today. These, too, would seem to be effected by integration and the EC membership. They are:

6. *the urbanization development* that now noticeably accelerates through the EC memberships
7. a polarization development of the standard of living of the local population, a development that must be expected to create pressure towards increasing crime.

The "home-base effect"

Free movement of labor and people means larger migrant populations, in particular people who are prepared to take over low-paid work requiring realtively little special skills. These are also people who are more able than average to commit many kinds of traditional crime. However, they need not be particularly criminal populations, and they often are not (cf. Albrecht 1991). Regardless of this, they create "home-bases" for criminally active elements moving from place to place, finding improved possibilities to come and go and stay undetected with their own people, protected against outsider interventions. Such home-bases also provide members of the criminal underworld with local know-how, local networks of information that also are useful in criminal operations. Thus, social conditions favoring the mobile racketeer are being improved. An earlier example of this process may be found very near us in Sweden in the 1960s, when very large numbers of Finns migrated over I have been informed from Estonian sources that a similar pheomenon, the "home base effect", may be responsible for some present-day crime problems in Estonia, in particular in larger cities that have a large proportion of Russian population. Russian racketeers are believed to be able to operate rather safely under such circumstances. For Finland, representing an unusually uni-national culture for the time being (cf. Jaakkola 1991), this is going to be a new experience.

Deteriorating social control

Another likely consequence of such changes, is to create conditions similar to the U.S. Local informal social control networks are going to weaken, with large parts of local populations remaining relatively unknown to each other. The creation and maintenance of local control and support networks will be hampered by a very transient population. If this means an increasing anonymity, it also may mean an increasing violence level, in particular if it goes together with an increased level of alcohol consumption (cf. Tigerstedt 1990), likely to result from breaking the state alcohol monopoly together with falling alcohol prices.

The increasingly free flow of economic transactions

The increasingly free flow of economic transactions similarly improves the structural conditions in which economic and/or organizational crime is committed. Already today, economic transactions, in particular those involving participants from several nations, are often so invisible and complicated that they are able to conceal almost any amount of illegal activities. This characteristic of economic transactions will grow even stronger. In this realm, crimes against EC regulations represent a whole new problem area for control agencies.

The present-day political program, introducing deregulation and privatization of the economy (a sort of latter-day Thatcherism) in increasing degrees, is going to have unplanned side-effects in regards to organizational crime likely to flourish under these circumstances. When speaking of crime, a peculiar trait of this type of activity is that they tend to slip away from being defined as crimes however unethical they may be considered.

This development presents many new problems to the control system. In the present context, I cannot develop this line of problems any further. Undoubtedly, this should be considered as being a major area of concern.

The emergence of imported (foreign) criminal techniques and patterns

As foreign practices become familiar to the local populations, a structural change in traditional criminality will become visible, meaning that "imported" elements gain space. Narcotics offences provide an obvious example. The Finnish narcotics market is as yet probably the smallest in Europe, relatively speaking. This need not remain this way, considering the changing living conditions of the new generations.

Organizational crimes, if profitable, are likely to flourish. After the economic boom of the mid and late 1980s, the country has considerably more potential for such crimes than before that period. The boom created a large number of new entrepreneurial potential, partly of a speculative character, that now is in great difficulties and rather likely to resort to any profitable racket, including the narcotics branch. Foreign forces, as well as the native ones, may also grow more interested in the Finnish narcotics market.

Another example, perhaps arbitrary, but nevertheless illustrative of the point, is the recent appearance of cases of extorting protection money from shopkeepers in Helsinki. This concrete form of crime being practically unknown in Finland until now, has entered a virginal market, as yet rather unable to cope with it; a foreign practice finds a local vacuum where it, at least temporarily, is able to thrive. I shall not try to suggest here what is going to happen to this innovation over the course of time.

Criminal underworlds merge

The local criminal underworlds begin to merge in part with imported underworlds, primarily, in today's experience, from the Russian and

Estonian cultures. Borders still being relatively closed to the East, this pressure is not very marked but, however, already clearly discernible. A small but prosperous country in the immediate neighborhood of an economic catastrophe such as the former Soviet Union may develop into a highly attractive target for the most mobile and able elements of the Eastern underworld. How the local and the foreign underworlds are going to sort the market out among themselves remains to be seen. Violent showdowns are not excluded.

The ongoing urbanization

Finland is still, compared to most Western European countries, in the process of urbanization. This urbanization is forcefully accelerated through very recent political decisions, the objective of which is to harmonize the price level and the production structure of Finnish agricultural products with Western European standards. Simultaneously, these trends mean that, as the degree of urbanization still continues to grow, (traditional) criminality will also increase. Recent comparative European victimization surveys (van Dijk et al. 1990) may be interpreted as supporting this conclusion.

Local populations become more criminal as a consequence of a polarizarion development and a declining economy

Locally, looking at the situation of Finland, the most direct and immediate development in this context has to do with the likelihood that the local populations become more criminal, committing more crime of traditional, maybe also of a new, character. Whether also the heavily criminal populations are going to increase or not depends to a great extent on whether the future social development results in a further polarization of the population into those in the center and those in the margin (we sometimes also speak of A and B citizens).

Traditional crime and criminals increase, it is assumed, due to the large-scale changes of the everyday life of the local populations to the worse. At present, Finland seems to be facing a permanent economic decline of its living-standard, creating extensive economic problems for large parts of the population. This "revision" of living is almost directly "translated" into crimes of the traditional type, resorted to also by others than those thought of as criminals in the past. These crimes share the common trait that you can make some extra money on them. It may sometimes be theft, but it may as well or even more likely be many other things: insurance frauds, credit card frauds, bankruptcy crimes – activities resorted to by more or less ordinary people facing a situation of an increased criminal motivation. Recent experience shows, as an extreme example of the meaning of such a change, that even bank robberies are undergoing a dramatic change in this country today involving people who often have no previous criminal background, but instead have drifted into a catastrophical economical situation. Such bank-robbers were practically unknown until only a couple of years ago.

Such changes in the motivation element of the commission of crimes primarily concerns those who already are "in the market." The future generations, then, face a new situation with a future worse than ours was. Future prospects are often stated to influence criminal choices to a rather great extent, pointing out that people with little or nothing to lose have less reason than others to follow general social conventions, including avoidance of criminal behavior.

Consequences of the crime changes

How dramatic, large and fast such developments are actually going to be is, of course, unknown. What is cleaner is that formal control agencies, in particular the police force, should be making preparations to meet with them. Police control would seem to be the obvious element in need of adjustment:

- For example, as national borders disappear, external boundaries are reinforced to improve protection against intrusion from outside nations. In this situation, police resources, local and international powers and techniques, international cooperation and information exchange are all likely to be revised.
- Informal control elements are also in need of adjustment. This need hardly be said but with a weakening potential of informal control, police may again have to be resorted to even more strongly, at least in a short time-perspective.
- Parallel to police repression, activities designed to improve crime prevention must gain greatly in importance. This is a very important area of measures. Police should, by law or otherwise, be made to concentrate great effort on crime prevention. As an example of such policy change, I could give the Norwegian model – to take one from Scandinavia – where a training project has been launched with the objective of training all members of the police force to also apply a crime prevention perspective in their everyday work. Most crimes remaining undetected or unsolved, as is known, it is sensible to expect preventive efforts to yield an equally important contribution to crime control as does the traditional repression and re-integration of known criminals, necessary as these are, too.

If the social changes come to a society unprepared, the likelihood to meet them with (massive) repression is great, other means typically require more time for preparation.

A few final remarks

I have been visualizing a near future of an increasingly repressive formal control. The general ideological prerequisites for such a trend are also good. We have often found that the control climate grows tougher in economically hard times, and easier in better times. Good times support tendencies to integrate and reintegrate marginal people, criminals, and other representatives of problem populations such as immigrants or local social minorities; bad times tend to cut down on resources available for integration, leaving bare repression.

Such ideological pressure is also supported by the increasing flow of foreign people seeking work or asylum, and actually representing an additional, probably objectively marginal but subjectively very visible threat to the everyday life of the local people.

Popular feelings of insecurity and rapid social change go together. This brings up a separate emerging problem regarding crime policy: fear of crime, reflected in calls for more police and more repression. Such climate changes create increased pressures favoring private security developments, available for the affluent, and contributing to trends that direct crime will increasingly be suffered by the less affluent parts of the population, and by individuals rather than organizations. Private security is a growth business.

A declining economy also means that, in the sphere of crime control, new or experimental ways of operation loose their funding, and planning and research activities are paralyzed, being considered as luxuries in hard times.

The old, traditional elements of the control system are less flexible, and less vulnerable to saving efforts, whereas innovative work, planning, research and development work typically function on funding that is relatively easier to cut if necessary. The short time-span of political decision-making supports this paradoxical tendency of saving; savings must be concentrated in areas where they can be made without delay. Savings expected after a delay of two, five, or ten years are, in such a situation, less attractive.

This presentation was primarily a problem inventory. Legislative and other policy measures that could contribute to their "solution" are at this point not suggested. Taking into account the nature of many of the problems sketched in this analysis, quick solutions are not likely to be found.

The changes and developments suggested are, for the most part, and at least initially, marginal and slow – they are not the whole world. They do, however, represent real and serious problems. I have no great faith in our decision-making bodies as to believing they are going to tackle these problems successfully. The low awareness concerning these problems does not promise very elegant solutions.

There is, thus, the tendency of perhaps having a future of increasing repression to be expected. This development would place a particularly heavy burden on those parts of the population who are coming or have recently come from areas worse off than Finland.

It may seem striking that I have not mentioned any processes that might be seen to counteract the crime-increasing pressures. Some, at least, may indeed be pinpointed. One is the *"graying"* of the population that is going on in most western countries. *This process counteracts the tendencies to an overall increase in crime rates.* However, we must not be deceived in believing that an old population is not a problematic population crime-policy-wise. It does, for example, have an influence on the crime policy climate, likely to produce increasing pressures for law-abiding behavior and repression of even rather unimportant deviants. Elderly people become, already through their sheer numbers, an inceasingly powerful force influencing the crime policy atmosphere. Also, although this is hardly a matter of immediate concern we must not believe that elderly people are incapable of crime. They are less capable of crimes typical for juvenile parts of population, but they also present an increasing potential for many types of crimes, traditional or other. If they are going to face a seriously deteriorating future due to the social changes we are facing there is no guarantee that all of them will remain in the weak and harmless mass of depressed pensionists they are now. Also, their quickly increasing numbers may eventually create a new situation where behavior frequent among the elderly may be redefined as being crime problems.

A second rather important force counteracting some of the forces I described as favoring increasing crime rates is the declining economy. This development makes Finland a less attractive market for many types of rackets. Affluence still remains high, however. This means that Finland is likely to become less attractive for most intruders from Western Europe, but it still will remain very attractive for those, in particular, coming from the Estonian and St. Petersburg area that are very near our country, and also for people of other poverty-ridden areas.

Notes and References

Hans-Jörg A. (1991): *Ethnic minorities: Crime and criminal justice in Europe.* In Heidensohn, Frances & Martin Farrell (eds.): Crime in Europe. London and New York: Routledge.

Benyon, J. (1991): *La coopération de la police en Europe.* Iki: IHESI: Les Cahiers de la Sécurité Intérieure. Polices en Europe. Paris: La Documentation Francaise, p. 137-165.

Cohen, Lawrence E. & Marcus Felson (1979): *Social change and crime rate trends: a routine activity approach.* American Sociological Review, Vol. 44 (August): 588-608.

van Dijk, Jan J. M., Mayhew P. & Killias M. (1990): *Experiences of crime across the world.* Key findings from the 1989 International Crime Survey. Deventer-Boston: Kluwer Law and Taxation Publishers.

van Dijk, Jan & Jaap de Waard (1991): *A Two-Dimensional Typology of Crime Prevention Projects.* With a Bibliography. Criminal Justice Abstracts, Vol. 23 (3, September 1991), 483-503.

Felson, M. (1986): *Linking Criminal Choices, Routine Activities, Informal Control, and Criminal Outcomes.* In Cornish, Derek B. & Ronald V. Clarke (eds.): The Reasoning Criminal. Rational Choice Perspectives on Offending. New York, Berlin, Heidelberg, Tokyo: Springer-Verlag, 1986, 119-128.

Felson, M. (1987): *Routine activities and crime prevention in the developing metropolis.* Criminology, 25 (November).

Gahrton, P. (1990): *I Stället för EG.* Stockholm: Ordfronts förlag.

Graham, J. (1990): *Crime Prevention Strategies in Europe and North America.* HEUNI – Helsinki Institute for Crime Prevention and Control, affiliated with the United Nations. No 18. Helsinki, Finland.

Heidensohn, F. & Farrell M. (eds.) (1991): *Crime in Europe.* London and New York: Routledge.

Jaakkola, M. (1992): *Suomen ulkomaalaiset.* Perhe, työ ja tulot. Työministeriö työpoliittisia tutkimuksia. Helsinki: VAPK-kustannus,1991. Keskusrikospoliisin vuosikertomus 1991 (Annual Report of the Central Criminal Police of Finland 1991). Helsinki, 1992. Rikspolisstyrelsen: Europeiskt polissamarbete efter 1992. Stockholm: Rikspolisstyrelsen, 1990.

Simpura, J. & Tigersted Chr. (eds.) (1991): *Social Problems Around the Baltic Sea.* Report from the Baltica Study. Helsinki: NAD Publication No. 21.

Takala, H. (1991): *Rikollisuus ja kansainvälistyvä Suomi.* Uusi Kriminaalihuolto, 8 (3), 4-9.

Tigersted, Chr. (ed.) (1990): *EG, Alkohol och Norden,* NAD-publikation nr 19. Helsingfors: Nordiska nämnden för alkohol-och drogforskning (NAD).

Törnudd, P. (1990): *En otacksam uppgift.* In Wiklund, Gunilla (Ed.): Nordiska Kriminologere om 90-talets kriminalpolitik. Stockholm: Sober Förlags AB. Wie Dr. No. Der Spiegel 2/1992, p. 125-125.

Criminal Violence in Modern Brazilian Society
The Case of the State of São Paolo[1]

by
Sergio Adorno

Introduction

Over the past twenty years, the public administrations of large Brazilian cities have shown themselves incapable of overcoming their principal problems. These problems refer not only to the populace's disbelief in the ability of political authorities, elected by universal suffrage, to administer socio-economic programs adequate and effective for the scope of urban problems, but also – above all – to a pattern of insecurity, be it experienced in its collective or subjective dimensions.

The feeling of fear and insecurity has become widespread due to the expectation, ever more probable, that any person, regardless of race, class, culture, creed, or ethnic or regional origin, will become the victim of a criminal offense. This sentiment does not seem unfounded. Official crime statistics show the growth of all types of criminal offenses, with violent crimes growing most rapidly.

In this text I will deal with the increase in violent urban crime's impact on the criminal justice system. I will attempt to present the strategies adopted by law enforcement agencies in order to combat that increase. I will describe the general directives contained in public penal policies, implemented particularly in the 1970s and 1980s. I will identify some of the reasons explaining these policies' failure, pointing out the impasses and dilemmas in democratic control of criminal violence.

The Growth of Violent Urban Crime

In the municipality and the region of Greater São Paulo[2] the number of violent crimes[3] in the toal of reported crimes wavered around 20 percent in the early eighties. By the end of the decade that rate had grown to 30 percent. That fact, however, must be compared with data showing urban demographic growth. In the case of the city of São Paulo, that relation shows surprising results. In the intervals of 1982-1983 and 1983-1984, the indices of crime per 100,000 inhabitants rose. In the following periods, these indices systematically tended to decline. Even so, for 1987 that index was on the order of 747 violent crimes per 100,000 inhabitants, higher than the 1981 index (685,6).

In disaggregated terms, burglary and assault are the most prevalent types of violent crimes. Since 1983, burglaries have begun to represent around 50 percent of the total of those crimes, as its behavior greatly influences the variations of violent crime. Murders and attempted murders show elevated rates of growth during the 1982-1983 period (48 percent in the municipality of São Paulo), with no negative rates of percentile variation per 100,000 inhabitants. These facts tend to be more surprising if we consider only murders, excluding attempted murders. In this case, the rate rose to 53.8 percent.

Rapes and attempted rapes oscillate greatly. Considering the period as a whole, there were negative rates of growth. We should add data indicating slayings by the police, particularly those by the Military Police,[4] which represented 23.3 percent of total registered homicides in 1992 and 14.9 percent in 1985, according to the Americas Watch Committee (1987).[5] According to research conducted by the Núcleo de Estudos da Violência (Nucleus for the Study of Violence), from 1983 to 1987 "more than 3,900 people (were) killed, counting police and civilians, and more than 5,500 wounded, according to data from the Military Police. The number of deaths reached an average of 1.2 deaths per day in this period, with a maximum of 1.6 in 1985. The totals of deaths in confrontations with the police in the state of São Paulo are extremely high, even when compared with other countries. In comparison, Australia, with a population of nearly 17 million, slightly less than the region of Greater São Paulo, 49 people and 21 police officers were killed from 1974 to 1988, or, in other words, forty-six times fewer".[6]

Incidents related to drug use and trafficking demonstrate irregular behavior, growing throughout the 1981–1985 period and rising notably in 1988 in the metropolitan area. These oscilliations can more likely be explained due to the police forces: behavior in the repression of this type of offense rather than by changes in the movement of traffic or in users' behavior. Finally, we should point out that the pronounced growth in irregular possession of weapons, notably in the 1981–1985 period, was stabilized in the following years.[7]

In the general calculation, considering all violent crimes committed in the metropolitan region of São Paulo between 1980 and 1987, amost 30 percent of that total were turned into police inquests.[8] Crimes with the highest incidence are those which show the least tendency to cause a police inquest. Thus, for example, in 1985 crimes against property represented 65.42 percent of incidents. Of that proportion, only 36.98 percent became police inquests. Therefore, we can assert that the growth in crimes was not accompanied by a proportional elevation in the number of inquests instituted.

As for the inquest-penal process segment, 1970-1982 data for the state of São Paulo indicates that, in relation to the general total of inquests arbitrated, inquests grew 191.4 percent, penal actions grew 148.5 percent and deferred inquests[9] grew 326.2 percent. Those values mean that deferred inquests grew 43.3 percent more than inquests arbitrated, while penal actions increased 14.7 percent compared to inquests arbitrated.

The growth in processes is greater than the growth in accusations which, in turn, is greater than convictions. In 1970, 75 percent of people processed were accused; 27 percent, convicted; and 48 percent, acquitted. In 1982, a decade later, those proportions were reduced to 63.22, and 43 percent, respectively. In compensation, the extinction of punishability,[10] on the order of 3.4 percent in 1970, rose to 6.3 percent by the end of the period. Thus, the percentage of condemnations declined in that period and, consequently, acquittals rose. These data suggest, accordingly, the relative fall of principal judicial activities. Reflected in another component of the criminal justice system – prisons.[11]

In the country as a whole, the total number of prisoners represents about 1.8 prisoners per thousand inhabitants, a coefficient paradoxically low when compared to that of other societies. In the United States, for example, it is on the order of 3.7/thousand inhabitants.[12] In spite of that coefficient, in the state of São Paulo during the 1983-1989 period, there was a 62.4 percent growth in imprisonments for murder, followed by a 32.4 percent growth for burglary and extortion, and 17.2 percent for drug trafficking. Conversely, there was a decrease in the rates of imprisonments for other crimes. Nevertheless, we must point out that the majority of these imprisonments do not effectively correspond to people prosecuted and condemned. Thus, in 1982, in the metropolitan region of Greater São Paulo, of the total of 4,274 prisoners prosecuted for crimes against the person, 33 percent were condemned. In the case of crimes against property, that proportion is even smaller. Of the total of 20,564 prisoners held responsible for those crimes, only 28 percent were sentenced.[13]

Overcrowding is a reality in the majority of Brazilian prisons. Though not a recent phenomenon, as it appears to be endemic,[14] and the general situation has been aggravated year after year. Data collected by the Ministry of Justice's Secretariat of Justice and Security in 1988 indicate the existence of a prison population of 88,041 prisoners, distributed among 43,345 spaces, consequently leaving a deficit of 44,696 spaces. One must further consider the existence that year of 267,6767 arrest warrants not executed, corresponding to an estimated 67,000 people sentenced to prison terms, though not placed in penal institutions.[15] Prisons in São Paulo are no exception. Remember that the state concentrates 36 percent of the country's and 60 percent of the southeast's prison population. Data available for the same year show a deficit of 19,900 spaces and 30,000 people with outstanding arrest warrants.

Everything seems to demonstrate that, in its functioning, the system for administering criminal justice takes on the shape of a funnel. Wide at its base – criminal occurrences – it narrows at its neck, when considering the defendants, convicted and placed in prisons. That funnel arises, in part, from the imbalance between the "potential" for crime within the populace and the criminal justice system's effective capacity for taking in those sentenced to prison terms.

Impact on Law Enforcement Agencies

The increase in violent urban crime throughout the 1980s had a definite impact on law enforcement agencies. That impact caused pressure to expand police, vigilance, and judicial services, altering consolidated routines, making the agents inclined to seek alternative expedients and transitory arrangements, treating stressing the immediate need for the reallocation of material and human resources, the result of which seems to have affected and influenced, at least early in the decade, the operationalization of security and justice policies. Demands, not unfounded, for the rationalization and re-equipping of police agencies were constant. That pressure on police agencies tended to be transmitted in a chain-reaction, in the form of increased arrests and processes begun, to the judicial and penal agencies, which were forced to review their rules of operation.

We can evaluate the results of that impact. On one hand, there is an increase in arbitrary police action. This agency, pressured by the scarceness of resources, tends to become ever more selective in producing inquests, reserving them for what they consider the most "serious" and "important" crimes. Proceeding thus, it expands the informal mechanisms of police activities. Relegating legal formalities to a second plane, it transforms certain occurrences into the privileged area of attention and, consequently, of conflicting interests, sharpening struggles for power both among different law enforcement agents and between them and those involved in crime, particularly aggressors and victims.[16]

On the other hand, as the judiciary's capacity tends to be equally exhausted it is inclined to be more rigorous in ascertaining criminal acts. In determined situations, it has sought to demand greater formal rigor from the police, refusing inquests prepared sloppily due to the nonobservance of legal requirements. In other circumstances, it has become equally selective. It has softened penal sanctions in cases considered "less serious" or irrelevant in order to avoid putting pressure on the penitentiary system, overloaded by overcrowding. At the same time, it has been less indulgent with crimes considered "serious" from the magistracy's perspective and, above all, with those committed by repeat offenders. Be what these strategies may, the penitentiary system is necessarily the tributary for the failure to control crime. Its basic unit – the prison – persists in deserving the label of "crime school", due to the conditions of life reigning therein.[17]

Public Penal Policies: The State's Response

Here we should ask, what have public authorities done to contain this situation of "functional anomie?" The State has responded with changes in penal legislation, modernizing and re-equipping the police, and with more spaces in the prison system. Between 1964 and 1985 we can see that changes in penal legislation responded to two stimuli. On one hand, they were motivated by questions of a formal nature, tending to perfect and rationalize penal procedures. On the other, there were legislative changes intended to produce true reforms in penal policies. These changes intervene in the philosophy of sentencing, regimes of execution, the categorization of criminalizing behavior, in the interdiction of rights, and in the types of social and judicial assistance to those condemned by the criminal justice system (Federal Laws number 7209/84 and 7210/84).

In spite of the effort undertaken in the reform of penal legislation, normative precepts tend not to be fulfilled. They are worn down within the law enforcement agencies, when not instigating conflicts that can, at their limits, stimulate collective manifestations of revolt and resistance, such as the extreme cases represented by riots.[18] This exhaustion occurred above all when the tribunals themselves hesitated to apply the legal benefits because they recognized, though in a veiled manner, that the criminal justice system was not equipped to implement the innovations introduced by legislation, such as, alternative sentences to imprisonment.

Analysis of the legislation consequently points out a flagrant divergence between the legislative innovations and their impact on the criminal justice system. Everything seems to indicate that those innovations did not contribute to altering the imbalance between the growth in crime – especially so-called violent urban crime – and criminal justice rates of production, which are always subordinated to prison occurrences and overcrowding.

Alongside those innovations, since the forties, especially when police efforts prioritized repressing political militancy, the modernization of Public Security consisted of a deliberate project of initiatives that included physical expansion through the construction of new installations and increasing the size of the police force, broadening the radius of police action, rationing services and institutional organizations, renovating the fleet of vehicles and the communications system, professionalizing the force through human resources perfecting and training in specialized courses, and computerizing police investigative services.

Nevertheless, the directives orienting public security and justice policies have not been able to repress or restrict violent practices for repressing crime and protecting judicial order. In fact, extensive police rounds with their spectacular demonstrations of police abuse of authority, as well as brutality against criminals or people suspected of engaging in criminal activity, persist alongside greater technical implementations. The paradoxes in judicial action that favor condemnation for crimes against property over crimes against the person remain. Life remains full of conflicts in the prisons, where disorder, violence, and disrespect for rights are the tonic of the day.[19]

As for the prison system, government policy has consisted of increasing the number of spaces available by building new establishments. This is a narrow policy which has been unable to overcome the situation of privation in the São Paulo state prison system, represented by the predominant living conditions there: "overpopulation; rudimentary sanitary conditions; deteriorated food; precarious medical, legal, social, educational, and professional assistance; unrestrained violence permeating relations among prisoners, between prisoners and the agents of social control, and among the institution's very agents; incommensurable arbitrary punishment."[20]

The Fragility of the Legal Order

Certainly, there are more than a few reasons for this ongoing situation. Two should be pointed out. First, we must consider the impact of local organizations. It results from a complex of circumstances and causes: law enforcement agencies' historic tradition; organized groups' influence on constituted authorities; the imposition of private orders over public order; predomination of the supply of knowledge accumulated from concrete experience – in short, organizational culture – prejudicial to respect for the law and bureaucratic formalities; "arrangements" between criminals and police agents – a phenomenon which can have a greater or lesser connotation depending on the greater or lesser presence of the state bureaucratic apparatus;[21] and the appropriation of the material means of administration as if they were private resources; precarious professionalization of agents commissioned precisely with providing security for the populace.[22] Be what those hypothetical considerations may, common citizens certainly do not receive the constitutional guarantees of equality before the law. Specifically workers with low incomes, who as a rule do not know their rights, are the segments of the population most vulnerable to legal agents' arbitrariness.

Secondly, we must consequently consider the fragility of legal order. From the point of view of the agents reponsible for justice and security policies, the perception and uses they make of the law demonstrate a hardly uniform understanding of what judicial order means. For some, the law hinders fighting crime more than it helps. For them, the "law" is a repertory of lines of action acquired from institutional practice. The criteria for conducting investigations, for the penal characterization of criminal acts, for imputing criminal responsibilities, for concluding cases, for elaborating reports and official documents, such as bulletins of occurrence, are taken from this repertory. We do not have to be meticulous to argue that "subjectivity" in the fulfillment of public functions frequently results in arbitrary actions mostly affecting the poorest and blacks.[23]

Others, however, appeal to the law, interpreting it as the guiding principle for institutional action. They recognize the justness of judicial order, though they call for the periodic need to make changes and adjustments in the principal texts and public institutions. Those, not rare, individuals who behave in this manner, appeal to the laws' universal nature, regardless of the social and cultural context in which legal precepts tend to be applied. They express a narrow understanding of the multiple factors which compete for the diffusion of behaviors divergent from what is recognized as legitimate judicial order. In order to explain the growth in crime and public authority's failure to contain crime, they resort to worn out notions of moral responsibility, free will, and habitual criminality, written into a liberal judicial culture that is not the least bit competitive with the force of local organizational culture.[24]

Conclusions

In Brazil the reconstruction of a democratic society and State, after twenty years of authoritarian regime (1964-1984), has not been vigorous enough to contain the arbitrariness of agencies responsible for public order. Notwithstanding the growth in urban crime and diversification of patterns of violent behavior, the public penal policies implemented by the new democratic governments, elected by universal suffrage, differ little from those adopted by the authoritarian regime. As in the recent past, on one hand, everything takes place as if just and perfect laws were enough to make the criminal justice system function as intended, that is, to be able to satisfactorily attend the impact that the growth in crime causes on law enforcement agencies, as well as be able to respond, readily and immediately, to the pressure of public opinion. On the other, it is believed that this effective control can be reached through "militarizing" public security, in other words, by massive police presence in the streets, the suspension of legal guarantees, greater freedom of action for police agents, harsher treatment of criminals in prison, and the death penalty.

In either case, the result is frustrating in the best of cases because the problem is not attacked at its roots. The bottle-necks and zones of tension that fragment the criminal justice system into discontinuous areas of competence – fragilely integrated with one and another, only capable of offering insecurity to the populace instead of security – remain untouched. As we sought to illustrate, the roots of administrative, bureaucratic, or technical administration do not explain public penal policies' failure, even though they may have their share of responsibility. Those reasons barely alter the division of labor and power among law enforcement agencies, the foundation sustaining the fragility of the lines of institutional action and conflictive relations among organizational culture and public authority.

Notes and References

1/ Paper prepared for the plenary session "Effects of Social Changes on Crime and Criminal Policy." Version based on Sérgio Adorno and collaborators, *O Sisrerna de Administraço da Justiça Criminal (Fragmenraço e Conflito no Caso Paulista)*, Research Reports (São Paulo: Núcleo de Estudos da Violência, 1991), mimeographed, (Ford Fouondation, Secretaria de Ciência e Technolgoia do Estado de São Paulo, and CNPq).

2/ Brazil is a federative republic governed by the Constitution promulgated on 5 October 1988. The political system is presidential. Executive power is exercised by the president of the republic who occupies the positions of chief of state and head of the government, and is elected for a five-year term in a two-phase, direct election. The seats of state government are located in the state capitals. In a territory of 8,511,966.3. km, there are 150,367,841 people, with 74,992,111 males and 75,375,730 females (1990). The majority of this population is concentrated on the Atlantic coast, especially in the southeast, where the state of São Paulo, the federation's richest, is located. São Paulo holds fifty-one percent of the gross national product, has nearly 33 million inhabitants and 80,000 police agents. Its capital, the municipality of São Paulo, is the largest, most populated, and most industrialized city in Latin America.

3/ The following are considered violent crimes: murder (crime against the person); burglary, burglary followed by death, extortion through kidnapping (crimes against property); rape (crime against honor); drug trafficking (crime against public health).

4/ In Brazil, vigilance and the repression of crime are conducted by the Military Police, distinct from the army though organized along military lines. Criminal investigations are the responsibility of the Civil Police, a non-militarized public organization. See: H.

Fermandes, *Política e segurança* (São Paulo: Alfa-Omega, 1973). See also: Paulo S. Pinheiro, Polícia e Crise Política, in the collectane *A Violêncie Brasileira*(São Paulo: Brasiliense, 1982).

5/ The report cited summarizes analysis found in Brant et al, *Trabalhar e Viver* (São Paulo: Brasiliense, 1989, 151-167). See also Americas Watch Committeee, *Police Abuse in Brazil: Summary Executions and Torture in São Paulo and in Rio de Janeiro* (New York: Americas Watch Committee, 1987).

6/ See Pinheiro, et. al., Violência Fatal: Conflitos Policiais em São Paulo (81-89), *Revista USP* 9 (March/May 1991) 95-112.

7/ According to all indications, that growth in crime and the pattern of criminal organization are not specific to Brazilian society, having been observed in the United States in the 1920s and 1930s, as well as in recent periods. See: H.M. Enzenberger, *Polirique et Crime* (Paris: Gallimard, 1967); J.F. Short, Jr., ed., *Delinquency, Crime and Society* (Chicago: Unviersity of Chicago Press, 1976); L.A. Curtis, ed., *American Violence and Public Police* (New Haven: Yale University Press, 1985); K.N. Wright, *The Great American Crime Myth* (New York: Praeger, 1987); Ph. Robert, org., *Les poliriques de prévention de la délinquance a l'aune de la recherche* (Paris: L'Harmattan, 1991).

8/ In Brazil, a criminal act discovered by the Military Police or reported to civil police authorities results in a register called a bulletin of criminal occurrence. Legally, every register must be followed by a police inquest in which an investigation, properly speaking, is conducted. That investigation is made up of field investigations, expert reports, and depositions by victims, assailants, and witnesses. Once an investigation is concluded, the inquest is forwarded to the judicial authority who, in turn, sends it to the Public Ministry. In this organ, the prosecutor, if convinced that in fact a crime did take place and of the existence of a possible perpetrator, presents the accusation. Once the accusation is accepted by the judicial authority, the police inquest becomes a penal process. Thus, the citizen, cited in the police inquest as being under investigation, successively is accused and becomes a defendant. After the procedures have been completed, the judicial authority issues a final sentence (which can be conviction, acquittal, extinction of punishability, or dismissal of the case). In cases of murder, the jury trial has competence. Roughly speaking, it can be said that in the first instance the criminal justice system functions in the following segmentation: occurrence-inquest-accusation-(indictment, in cases tried by jury)- final sentence.

9/ When the Public Ministry believes there are insufficient elements for proceeding with penal action, he proposes to the magistrate that the police inquest be deferred. The extinction of punishability occurs when, due to the time period between the criminal occurrence and penal action, the public authority finds itself impeded from issuing a sentence of condemnation (Please note that, though similar, this is not the statute of limitations found in United States jurisprudence. The latter is a statute limiting the period in which legal action can be taken in a given matter).

10-11/ The unavailability of data for the following period (1983-1990) makes it impossible to evaluate that tendency's behavior throughout the 1980s.

12/ Americas Watch Committee, *Prison Conditions in Brazil*. (New York: Americas Watch Committee, 1989).

13/ Similar conclusions may be found in Sérgio Adorno and E. Bordini, Reincidência e reincidentes penitenciários em São Paulo, 1974-1985, *Revista Brasileira de Ciências Sociais* 9(3) (February 1989): 70-94.

14/ In fact, the majority of institutional reforms implemented by different state governments have been stimulated by preeminent problems arising from prison overcrowding. This is especially corroborated in Rio de Janeiro and São Paulo at the very beginning of the republican regime (1889). In 1955 the São Paulo state government undertook substantive reforms in the penitentiary system, planning an expansion of spaces for the following two decades, a project implemented in the following administrations which included the construction of a new prison. A few years later, there were visible signs of the depletion of spaces available, and problems arising from prison overcrowding persisted. See: Sérgio Adorno and R.M. Fischer, *Análise do sistema penitenciário do Estado de São Paulo: O gerenciamento da maginalidade social* (São Paulo: CODEC, 1987), mimeographed.

15/ See S. do A. Faria and collaborators, Sistema Carcerário Nacional: perspectivas para a década dos 90, *Fundaço para o Desenvolvimento Administrativo,* Documentos de trabalho, DT/QS, Assistência Social, Sistema Carcerário (São Paulo: FUNDAP, 1991, 9-41).

16/ An interesting analysis of these confrontations may be found in R. M. Fischer, *O direito de populaço à segurança* (São Paulo: CODEC, Vozes, 1985). See particularly chapter 2, 17-60.

17/ See V. Coelho, A administraço da justiça criminal no Rio de Janeiro 1942-1967, *Dados, REvista de Ciências Sociais* 29(1) (1986): 61-81.

18/ As of 1985, a change in penal legislation affected decisive aspects of the philosophy of sentencing and its execution. The changes introduced sought to make punitive sentences harsher for violent crimes, while simultaneously applying alternative sentences, rather than imprisonment, for crimes considered less serious and committed by first-offenders. The riots in the São Paulo prison system between 1982 and 1987 were provoked directly by judicial and prison authorities' nonfulfillment of benefits conceded by the law. See E. Goes, A recusa das grades: Rebelies nos presídios paulistas, 1988-1986 (Master's thesis, Faculdade de Ciência e Letras de Assis, UNESP, 1991).

19/ See H. Fermandes, Rondas à cidade: uma coreografia do poder, *Tempo Social, Revista de Sociologia da USP* 1(2) (1989): 121-34; E. Bordini and S. Abreu, Estimativa da reincidência criminal: variaçes segundo estratos ocupacionais e categorias criminais, *Temas IMESC, Soc. Dor. Saúde* 2(1) (1985): 11-29.

20/ See Sérgio Adorno, Sistema penitenciário no Brasil: Prolemas e desafios, *Revista USP* 9(March/May 1991): 65-78. See also M.M.P. de Castro, Ciranda do medo: Controle e dominaço no cotidiano da priso, *Revista USP* 9(March/May 1991): 57-64.

21/ The integration between *jogo do bicho* bankers and local political elites in the city of Rio de Janeiro illustrates this phenomenon. See J.M. Carvalho, *Os bestializados: O Rio de Janeiro e a república que no foi* (São Paulo: Companhia das Letras, 1987); M.A.R. de Carvalho, "O jogo e a cidabe" (Master's thesis in Social History, PUC-RJ, 1991), mimeographed; Roberto da Matta, *Malandros, carnavais e heróis: Para uma sociolgia do dilam brasileiro* (Rio de Janeiro: Zahar, 2979) (The *jogo do bicho* is a game of chance somewhat similar to the numbers game found in New York City and other major urban areas in the United States – Trans.)

22/ Certainly, not all of these circumstances have an equal impact on the agencies considered. Judicial tribunals are possibly more exempt from these external influences. Nevertheless, this does not mean they are exempt from their contribution to the fragmentation of the criminal justice system, expecially since they demonstrate little capacity to be integrated into the whole of the system and because they enjoy autonomy in the sense of traditional, patrimonial-type administration.

23/ An admirable description of the phenomenon of arbitrariness may be found in A.L. Paixo, A organizaço policial numa área metropolitana, *"Dados: Revista de Ciências Sociais* 25(1) (Rio de Janeiro: 1982): 63-85. See also A.L. Paixo, Crime, controle social e sonsolidaço da democracia, in *A democracia no Brasil: Dilemas e perspectivas,* G. O'Donnell and F.W. Reis, org. (São Paulo: Vértice, 1989); *Revista do Tribunais,* 168-199; a. Zaluar, A polícia e a comunidade: paradoxos da (in) conveniência, *Presença Revista de Cultura e Política* 13 (May 1989): 144-153.

24/ See Sérgio Adorno, Criminal Justice, Urban Violence and the Social Organization of Crime, paper presented at the Twelfth World Congress of Sociology, Madrid, 9-13 July 1990, mimeographed. See *Sociological Abstracts,* International Sociological Association, 90521889/ISA/1990/5571,5.

Social Changes, Crime and Police in the Former German Democratic Republic

by
Erich Buchholz

The subject we have to deal with is, I believe, unique in the history of crime and criminal prosecution. There is no other example of such large and deep social changes in the lives of people in the former socialist countries with such emormous consequences for the dynamics, structure, and the phenomena of crime and for the activities and possibilities of the police, too, as we find it now in these countries.

I believe my experience as a scientist in the former GDR might be interesting for you, because the former socialist GDR is now a part of a large and important western country, of the now even greater Germany. Here we find the breakdown and destruction of what was called real existing socialism in the eastern part of Germany, immediately connected with the integration (or unification) into or with the Federal Republic of Germany, a country based on capitalistic economic order, as we understood it.

On 3 October 1990, the legislation of the FRG was enforced, became obligatory and binding on the people of the former GDR; the whole state system of the FRG was etended to this part of Germany, while the influence and consequences of the West German economy had already started in the middle of this year, by means of the so-called currency-union (Währungsunion) on July 1.

Such a situation existed neither in Hungary, Poland, nor in Czechoslovakia, and of course not at all in the former Soviet Union. German unification is a very special development, different from that of all other East European countries.

We all know that in any criminological theory or understanding, if we would follow a crimino-sociological concept from a strictly materialistic or economic standpoint or take a more socio-psychological approach, or in some aspects a crimino-biological one, there is a distinct connection between the changes in society and the dynamics, structures and phenomena of crime.

The former GDR, was faced all the years with another great socio-historical experiment (like a great socio-historical laboratory) on the reality and on the proof of the reality of the existence of this connection and influence. After World War II we had generally the same situation concerning delinquency in the whole of Germany for some years: the unusually high figures of reported delinquency in the statistics immediately after the war were very rapidly replaced by lower ones in the eastern as well as in the western parts of Germany. The everyday life of the people became better and better, need and hunger, homelessness and unemployment were overcome. The people became more and more hopeful, they began to look forward to the next day, to tomorrow; the psychological situation of the people became normal and better.

However, beginning in 1952, the statistical data gave evidence of a different stituation: according to statistics the crime rate in West Germany was rising again, the crime rate in East Germany was falling. In the following years, in general, the rate of crime in the west was several times higher than in the east. In spite of any political views and trust in the statistics (we all knew very well, that the statistical figures on delinquency are quite different from the reality of crime, i.e. because of the great number of undetected cases), there was a common understanding among criminologists of the different countries, and even in reports under UNO-sponsorship, that delinquency in the GDR was on a low level, and the crime rate of the FRG on a higher one. Some people argued or explained this phenomenon as the consequence of a strict system of social control ruling in the GDR, while on the other hand the higher crime rate in the FRG was the price (or tribute) of freedom. This was also the general everyday experience of the people. They were not in a situation to be afraid of criminals, not in fear of delinquency. (This was also the individual experience of travellers visiting the East and the West.)

Therefore the criminologists in the East and the West were sure that after the unification of Germany the delinquency in the East would rise within a very short time; among other, things they assumed that drug-crimes would find their place in the east of Germany, in the so-called new federal states.

Indeed, beginning from 1990 in this region, delinquency was rising especially among youngsters. The crime stiuation became more and more critical, explosive. The chiefs of the interior and the police were over and over again deliberating on the new situation. Today, it is too early to bring actual and informative figures. Besides that, as the detection rate of crimes, due to several reasons, decreased at the same time, more than in former times, the statistical data cannot give a real insight into the crime situation in the eastern part of Germany. Even more important is the change in the structure of crime, the kinds of criminal acts committed, and the psychological situation among the people. The fear of crime is now, after the general problems of unemployment fear of an uncertain future, and social unsecurity, one of the most important feelings and thoughts of the people.

Actual delinquency in the east of Germany might be divided into three groups:
1. traditional delinquency
2. new kinds of delinquency, mostly coming from outside of the eastern part of Germany
3. delinquency in connection with the unification of Germany, above all its economic unification

1. Traditional delinquency increased in nearly all important categories of crime: theft, fraud, robbery, murder (homicides generally), rape. New in this field is the amount and expansion of violence, of power, especially in the streets, in the metro and on other means of public transport. What is new is the use of firearms, which are now available to any one who is interested in getting them, without any difficulties. What is new is the robbery of banks and similar institutions where you can find money. In some areas nearly every institution was burglarized and robbed.

The speaker of the Berlin union of criminal investigators gave information on some figures in Berlin: Compared with the first months of 1990, in the beginning of 1991 the number of robberies increased from 3300 to 5600; the number of shopbreakings from 2300 to 6000; the number of thefts of cars from 4400 to 9700. Above all there was a rise in those crimes committed in juvenile gangs: in the first 6 months of 1991 there were 2691 of such crimes reported in Berlin; this is the figure of the whole of the year before. In 1991 the police – as it was stated by the Chief of the Police in Berlin, Mr. Schertz – reported half a million crimes in Berlin. This was the figure of all reported crimes in the whole of East Germany in 1946! Compared to 1990 this constitutes an increase of 42%. Generally speaking, according to the statistical average of the East German states, in every minute a crime will be committed. Altogether 500,000 crimes – this is the figure of 1946! Compared to the last years before the end of the GDR, experts of the police considered the increase rate to be 400%.

In the whole of 1991 nearly 500,000 crimes were registered. In the first 3 months of this year more than 140,000 crimes have already been registered; this is more than all the crimes registered in the last 30 years or the average of all the crimes, registered for a year in the whole of the former GDR.

The sum of all crimes registered in Berlin amounts to:
every 3 days a case of murder
every day a rape case
80 thefts of cars
130 burglaries
100 cases of violence

Especially important is the number of street crimes. About 40% of these crimes in Berlin were committed by youngsters, persons under 21 years. In this year there will be expected in Berlin about 600,000 reported crimes. When we regard all the so-called "new-states" (the eastern counties of Germany), the general crime rate (for 100,000 inhabitants) amounts to a figure between 3000 in the south (Thüringia and Saxonia) and 5000 in the north (Mecklenburg-Vorpommern), where we find the highest rate of unemployment.

2. The second group of crimes, the newly introduced ones, are crimes in connection with drugs, smuggling, especially of cars, and environmental (ecological) crimes. Concerning drug-crimes in 1991, in Germany the figures continued to increase. But the prediction that in the so-called new federal states drug consunption would reach an explosive level has not yet become true. It seems, that in this regard we can be glad of the delay in this dangerous development. Also the direct invasion of organized crime into the eastern states of Germany seems to be delayed longer than expected.

A very dangerous phenomenon is violence against foreigners. In the GDR there lived, worked, and learned or studied for years many thousands of, in general, young foreign people from Vietnam, Cuba, Mozambique, and other countries, mostly of the Third World. These people very often worked and learned in places like state owned factories, at schools or universities. Their lives were of course under some social control and safeguard. The contacts with the population were not very strong. Now they have lost their jobs, and the financial resources for their studies have come to an end. To return to their home countries is often very difficult or even dangerous. Thus they are now in a very new situation, characterized especially by contrast to and even competition with the German people. There arose hatred from the Germans toward the foreigners: Germany for the Germans is the new political slogan shouted by some new-racist or new-fascist groups. Mass-actions against foreign people have occurred.

3. A very new phenomenon is the so-called "Vereinigungskriminalität", crimes committed in the course of unification. I would like to mention in this connection first crimes in the economic field, a very large and not clearly defined phenomenon. They were caused especially by the following specific economic situation in 1990: the former great state owned enterprises, great trusts with many thousands of workers, which were concentrated under the management of ministers, and thus under the direction of the government, had to be changed and transformed into economic units adequate to the capitalistic system of market economy.

They had to be split into several smaller firms especially in the form of Private Limited Companies (PLC). Very often the directors (managers) of the former state-enterprises made themselves the representative managers of the new firm and took the money or other (economic) values of the former state-enterprise and invested in the new firms. Very often this economic transformation took place through the assistance or influence of West German managers.

I can not explain in detail the different forms of such economic transformations, but what is important here, is that in this change process, the difference between legal and normal transformation on the one hand and illegal and criminal forms on the other hand is quite difficult to recognize – the so called grey-zone is very large.

In the process of such transformations several people tried to make money, to get personal extraordinary profits of millions of Deutsch marks. The damage of all these crimes is enormous, many many billions.

To discover these kinds of crime is rather difficult and happens very seldom. There is no individual victim, all participants are usually winners of such manipulations and therefore interested that these manipulations will not be detected. Only by mere chance can the police and prosecutors while studying the book-keeping papers, under certain circumstances find some illegal transaction.

Another category of unification criminality covers the large number of crimes, especially sorts of fraud (cheating), committed by people coming from the West, at the expense of people living in the East. Exploiting their ignorance and their lack of experience in capitalistic methods of money-making, some West Germans committed fraud (cheating), against East Germans. Because the offenders very often were unknown in the area or had given a wrong name and a wrong address, a cover-name and cover-address, prosecution was not possible or the people were ashamed to confess that they had become the foolish victims of swindlers.

All this shows that police and prosecutors are faced with an enormous mass of crime, and I have not yet mentioned the so-called "Regierungskriminalität" the political or economic-political crimes in the former GDR, committed by the officials themselves, even by members of the government. Crimes whose discovery and examination need very great powers and activities by the police and the judicial organs. Therefore police, prosecutors and judges are overburdened. It is nearly impossible for them to manage, to administer, to control the increasing delinquency rate in East Germany.

In addition, the East German police-system and management is under transformation, too. As the former police (Volkspolizei) served as one of the most important instruments of state power, of governing the country, there arose an interest to destroy this instrument. But in order to protect the public and to safeguard common security it was necessary to maintain, and use this apparatus. This unclear and contradictory situation hindered and stopped the activity of the policemen. Many of them did not know how to deal with delinquency today, or how to keep contact with the people. Many former policemen were afraid to be too strict against the people and therefore, often "looked the other uzy." In Berlin, therefore, we are sometimes faced with the fact that the policemen from the West are sometimes stricter and more rigorous then the policemen from the East, and it happened that people said or cried "They are worse than our policemen!"

What I should like to express here is, that the relation between the people and the police currently quite often is not a very good one. In a high degree, the police lost the trust of the people. Some people have a somewhat reserved attitude towards the police, and some of them do not report crimes, which have been committed in their house or neighbourhood. They pretend that nothing happens because the proceedings take such a long time, many months or even a year.

In Berlin, e.g. 85% of all inhabitants believe that the police is overburdened in controlling crime (some years ago in the western part of Berlin this figure was under 60%!). About 60% of Berlin citizens, especially older ones and youngsters, are in great fright to walk in the streets in the evening or to go out after dark. On the other hand the policemen in the East are in a very complicated personal situation, too. Many do not know if they will be dismissed, and they are afraid of unemployment; many have been demoted. Usually their salary is less than the salary of their western colleagues, even if they have the same job, and they are doing the same police-work (e.g. car patrols, policing buildings etc).

Therefore there is a need for policemen. Furthermore their technical equipment generally is very bad. There is a lack of modern technical means, especially in the field of communications. A consequence of this, the job of the policemen today is a very, very hard one. It is therefore not surprising, that in connection with the increase of offences the rate of detected crimes decreased to about 30%; especially the rate of detected thefts, which is extraordinary low.

Therefore people do not trust in the preventive activity and efficiency of the police. Less than 10% of the population believe that the police is able to protect them.

Besides that, many people do no not like to serve as witnesses because they fear attacks and violence by the criminals, by the accused or his friends.

It is to be noted, last but not least, that in this situation a number of criminals from the western part of Germany came into the eastern part because they believe that the police will not be able to detect and find them, to fight them successfully.

In great contrast to the difficult situation we very often hear from politicians the same false and only politically motivated slogans – as we were used to bearing in former times: "A strict fight against crime and delinquency is necessary! Severe and harsh penalties are necessary! Penal law should be more harsh and sharp! More policemen and a greater competence even in the control of predelinquent activities, control of everybody by the police, by undercover agents use when necessary and so on!". But, as it was in former times, these politicians ignore and refuse a realistic analysis of the real sources, conditions and causes of the increase in crime and delinguency in general, and especially in the new federal states in East Germany.

You do not need great intelligence to see and to recognize that an important cause of the increase in crime and delinquency in East Germany are the new social conditions and their socio-psychological consequences. Above all is the enormous expansion of unemployment, homelessness (throughout Germany there exists nearly one million homeless people!), the great – in former times unknown – social insecurity and uncertainty, the fear of the next day, of the future especially among young people.

As a criminologist I feel there is a lack of interest among politicians to learn about and understand the real situation of delinquency. Among other facts this lack of interest is proven, too, by the fact that the very small, scientific capacity in the field of criminology in East Germany, in the former GDR, has now nearly been completely destroyed at the universities as well as at the two academies.

Therefore I have no reason to be optimistic. On the contrary, I am sure the peak of delinquency and crime is still awaiting us, and this peak will be a very high one. The psychological working up of the new social situation by the people in East Germany and their future behavior, dictated by their socio-psychological feelings and conditions, will bring us a lot of nihilistic individual actions, as well as even more suicides, drug addicts and more crime, even among the youngsters and children.

Indeed, we seem to be facing a rather dark future!

The Problems of Controlling Organizational Crime

by
Ahti Laitinen

Introduction

In this presentation I will use the term *organizational crime* as practically synonymous with the concept of corporate crime. These usage by me may not the most common in this field. Traditionally the concept of white collar crime has been used. Only in 1979 was corporate crime separated clearly from the concept of *white collar crime* in *Clinard's* report (Young 1989, 257). I, too, will make a strict distinction between organizational/corporate crime and white collar crime.

Organizational crime is a form of criminality that is possible only in connection with an organization. It is a form of criminality which is bound up with the operation of the structures of society. Organizational crimes are not necessarily individual actions; herein lies the difference between white collar crime as such. A typical example of organizational crime is environmental crime; in this the actor may well be an industrial company.

The harm caused by organizational crimes is also different in kind from the harm created by individual crimes. This is true in cases of financial or physical loss as well as for the harm done to society's moral climate.

In many analyses, making special references to my own country, Finland, I am examining the structure of society at two levels: the organizational level and the level of civil society. The essential elements of the organizational level consist of different power institutions, which comprise, for example, administrative machinery, economic institutions, (e.g. the executives of) trade unions, political parties and parliament.

The distinction can also be seen as different types of interaction between persons and corporate actors. The types of interactions are between: (1) Person and person, (2) person and corporate actor and (3) corporate actor and corporate actor.

Table 1. **Types of relations between actors**

		OBJECT OF ACTION	
		Person	Corporate actor
SUBJECT OF ACTION	Person	1	2a
	Corporate actor	2b	3

(Coleman 1990, 546-552)

As shown in Table 1. it can be realized that corporate or organizational crime is typically a phenomenon of a type 2b or type 3-interaction. This is why it is a mistake to reduce illegal corporate action to the level of citizens, in other words, to an interaction of types 1 or 2a. According to the criminal law of most non-common law countries such a reduction is still a prevailing practice.

On this basis Coleman argues that corporate actors have a will, interests and goals of their own. These are not necessarily reducible to the will, interests and goals of the individual members of the organization in question. If the above-mentioned argument is valid, it leads to important conclusions: (1) corporations (collective actors) and their offenses must be dealt with as categories of their own, (2) in the non-common-law countries like Finland, it is no longer possible to deny the principle of corporate criminal responsibility by appealing to the hypothesis that only individual persons could have a will, interests and goals of their own. This latter assumption has been one of the leading legal principles of Finnish criminal law.

One further remark must be made. Recognition of corporations as independent subjects cannot be a valid means for denying the personal responsibility of the members of an organization. Especially where the corporate criminal responsibility is unknown, it is easy to make organizations a scapegoat. (See Broms & Paavola 1961, 66). It might be said, for instance, that the offending agent is a poor communication system, not a person whose duty is to deliver information. In this way it might also be possible to utilize collective actors in the watering down of an evident, personal individual responsibility.

The above-mentioned differences between corporate and individual action are reflected also in the disclosure and investigation of the organizational crime. One reason for the difficulties in dealing with this kind of criminality is the collective nature of the action. Later on in this presentation I shall refer to these.

A small capitalist country like Finland is perhaps not the best possible target for research, the purpose of which is to study the characteristics of organizational crime and to produce generalizations in this field. On the other hand, comparative material, coming from Finland, might sometimes reveal important matters. For example, our rules over bank secrecy are lenient. When the corresponding regulations are tightened up in other countries, certain illegal activities and international corporate criminality begin to move from these countries to the countries of lenient control, like Finland. Money laundering is one concrete example. This is big problem for the controlling authorities, whose resources, experiences – and sometimes also skills – are limited in regard to organizational/corporate crime.

Further, by developing new control-mechanisms against organizational crime, the Finnish experiences, or at least our social situation might offer something. For example, we have an experience of state owned industrial firms and other state companies in a market economy. Sometimes it has been suggested that state ownership or state controlled management of private firms could be one means of exerting control over organizational crime. According to my research findings this will, however, produce new kinds of problems, and, now and then, other forms of illegalities.

Harms and damages caused by organizational crime

I will present only a few brief examples showing the extent and nature of the harms caused by organizational crime.

A comparison of individual or traditional crime with organizational crime reveals some important differences in respect to the advantages, profits and costs of the crimes.

1) Financial harm. According to a study made by the Finnish Ministry of Justice *(Committee Report* 1983:7) the value in monetary terms of the financial harm of organizational crimes in 1978 was some 7.6% of the gross national product, which is about 2 billion US dollars.

We shall try to make a rough, corresponding estimate for traditional, individual crimes. In 1987 the monetary value of compensation in cases of damage to property was some $500 per case. In cases of personal injuries the value of the compensation was about $1800 per case. (See *Rikollissustifanne* 1987, 131). If we consider the *total* figures of individual crimes, however, we find that the financial costs of traditional crimes are under 5% of those of organizational crimes.

According to Finnish (Lehtonen 1986) as well as to Swedish (Magnusson 1981, 1985 and 1987) research findings, the differences between individual and organizational tax offenses are very wide, too. The average monetary value of an individual tax offense is only a few hundred US dollars. In the case of an organizational tax offense the average value varies from 250,000 to 500,000 dollars per case.

In (West) Germany the losses caused by the evasion of property taxes and the evasion of other taxes amounted to approximately 1.5 billion DM in 1983. The value of tax audits in business was around 7 billion DM (Liebl 1985, 1988). According to another German study the financial costs of organizational crime totalled from 130 billion to 170 billion DM during the 1980's. (v. Weinhofer & Schöler 1986).

It has been estimated that in the United States the monetary costs of organizational crime range from $174 to $231 billion. (Simon & Eitzen 1986). The financial cost of "street crime" has been estimated to be only 1.7-2.3% of that of organizational crime in the USA.

I admit that my own Finnish estimations are only approximate and partly derived from studies made a few years ago, but they are nevertheless very similar to estimates from other countries. They also show that the financial harm from organizational criminality constitutes a totally different dimension from that of traditional, individual criminality.

2) Social costs of organizational crime. When people think of the "costs of crime", they often think of losing property or of sustaining bodily harm. Yet crime also exacts social costs in the sense that it weakens the social order and detracts from the quality of the life that people might otherwise enjoy. Organizational crime damages the social fabric covertly. It has the capacity to erode public confidence in the social and economic system and to threaten the moral foundations of our society. (Cullen, Maakestad & Cavender 1987, 64-65).

According to Simon and Eitzen (1986, 29) public confidence in the economic and political elite of society has drastically declined as revelations of organizational crimes have occurred. In addition, many criminologists believe that organizational criminality provides either motivation or rationalization for individuals to commit profit-oriented "conventional" crimes. Researchers have shown that *organizational* crime has been an important cause of the persistence and growth of *organized* crime in the United States. This assistance has been provided by both economic and political elites.

3) Physical harm. The physical injuries caused by individual and organizational crimes are very different. A typical example of the physical harm arising from an individual crime is the injury to a person's body. By contrast, a typical example of an organizational crime is the damage to our environment. Unfortunately, we have no objective means of measuring damages like these. Every productive activity must always take into account some risks. The definition of an acceptable risk is a matter of social and political agreements.

If we consider workers as victims of organizational crime, consumers as victims and the public as victims, the difference between individual and organizational crime is really very wide. I will take only one example. The average number of violent (individual) crimes known to the police in Finland has been about 6,000 in the 1980s. The average number of accidents causing at least three days disability from work has been about 110,000 a year. All accidents are not caused by labor crime, but a considerably significant share are so caused. (STVK 1980-1990, Työmarkkinat 1989:23, Rikollisuustilanne 1988). Organizational crime has become a profitable form of criminality without effective control.

Contemporary reactions against organizational crime

It appeared from my figures that the financial as well as other harm caused by organizational crime is large in kind and covers many aspects of society. Now I first want to give some figures from my own research describing the reactions against organizational crime.

I have analyzed 23 cases of organizational crime which comprised a total number of 167 accused persons and 891 charges. The proceedings in 5 cases took place in the fifties, in one case in the sixties and the trials of the remaining cases in the seventies or eighties. The final outcome in the trials of 124 accused persons (75% of all the accused) took place in the eighties.

In general, it is impossible either to comprehend the totality of a crime by reducing the act merely to the behavior of the individual law-breakers or by summarizing the individual acts. The totality of an organizational crime is qualitatively different from the sum of its parts. Seen as separate acts, the crime might seem very innocent, while the criminal processes – the totality – created by these individual acts could be very serious. The economic losses in some Finnish cases like these run into millions of US dollars.

The actual spectrum of the different crimes linked with the network of many power institutions is somewhat narrow.

Without exception the *status* of the accused persons has been very high. This is evident, because the offenses in question presuppose certain powers and rights to make important decisions. The accused persons coming from enterprises are mostly (90%) management leaders, financial leaders and corresponding persons, and persons coming from the administration are at least heads of divisions (80%).

The state of affairs is different among the accused coming from political parties of which we have many in Finland and a concomitant complex system of consensus politics. Sometimes these people were simply loyal to their parties without any personal advantages. In general, the accused were composed of the financial and other personnel in the offices and organizations of political parties. Although, most probably, the political leaders have been conscious of the illegal activities, they have also permitted these activities of their staffs and even encouraged them. Very few top political leaders – let us say at the ministerial level – have been accused and convicted. I found only 12 such persons in the whole group of the 167 accused. An interesting feature is that the conviction has been no obstacle for the career of the person in question. For example, some convicted persons have later became ministers, and many persons have continued in and improved on their political career, and even one convicted person has afterward been appointed Minister of Justice. I emphasize, however, again that my main goal is to study organizational crime, not to search for the guilty individuals.

When I am presenting in the following paragraphs research findings concerning economic losses and the consequences of the crimes as well as the sentences given by courts, it must be borne in mind that the courts deal with these cases only at the individual level. Damages are measured according to individual behavior, sentences are given to individual persons, and so on.

In 35% of all the cases, the courts have been able to make some monetary calculation in respect to the advantages afforded by the crime to the accused person. The average number of personal advantages for 91% of the accused has been estimated at 5,000 US dollars. Taking all the accused together the average value of the advantages gained was about 24,000 USD. The value is linked to the social status of the person in question; the higher the status, the greater is the monetary advantage.

The advantages for enterprises and other organizations appeared to be more difficult to define. But in some cases the courts presented rough estimations, and they amounted to millions of marks. The means of gaining advantages are limited, but they vary considerably. Examples: the creation of monopolies on the market, different tax frauds, the misuse of public assets and the transfer of these monies to private enterprises, the allowance of favorable loan conditions for enterprises, etc.

A total of 69% of the convicted persons whose illegal advantage as a result of the crime was proved in their trial has been ordered by the court to pay monetary damages. For this group of convicted persons the average value of damages has amounted to 2,800 US dollars. The average amount of all compensations was 1,200 US dollars. As we can see, this is only a half of the amount of the advantage (on average). Furthermore, some persons were ordered to pay joint and several compensations by the courts. The average amount of these was 2,200 US dollars.

In my study (Laitinen 1989) the percentage share of a convicted person (of the accused) was 67,7. This is much lower than in general in Finland. During the period 1976-1986, the percentage of all convicted persons varied from 97,6% to 98,0% of the accused. Can it not be assumed therefore that the accused with high status and high social ranking are sentenced less frequently than "ordinary" people?

The most usual sentence is a fine. The average number (median) of day-fines[1] – as they are called in Finland – was 5. If we suppose that the monthly salary of a person is 20,000 FMK (around $ 5,000), the monetary value of 50 day-fines is 11,000 FMK (around $ 2,750). In comparison with these 50 day-fines, we can take the minimum number of day-fines for aggravated drunken driving. It is 60 day-fines.

Table 2.

Decisions of the courts according to the status of accused

Status of accused	Number of cases	Percentage of sentenced	The punishment cases to be in force	Statute-barred offense etc.
Highest level	61	60.0	36.7	3.3
Middle level	42	76.2	19.4	4.8
Lowest level	43	73.6	23.5	2.9
Politicians	30	63.4	13.3	23.3

The crimes examined in this study (see Table 2) have been undertaken on average 4 years before the trial. The duration of the legal proceedings has been 1 year and 7 months. The length of the whole proceeding (calculated from the beginning of the crime to the decision of the court) has been approximately 6 years. The length of the whole proceeding has continually increased, particularly in the eighties.

Research findings in other countries confirm my results. One of the many examples is *Wheeler's* and *Rothman's* study in the USA. According to the study, the duration of organizational crimes (35.7 months) is longer than that of individual crimes (22,0 months). Only 5.6% of individual crimes covered the whole country, whereas 31.9% of organizational crimes were wide in range. Although the number of organizational crimes (221) studied was smaller than the number of individual crimes, the economic losses caused by the former ($1,077,432) were ten times bigger than those of individual crimes ($74,585).

---

[1] One day-fine is equal to a person's monthly income divided by 90. According to the Decree of Day-Fines (Nr 789/1985) the minimum amount of one day-fine is 20 FMK (around 5 US dollars).

Wheeler and *Rothman* reported that the educational level of persons accused of organizational crimes was higher than the level of those who had committed individual crimes. In spite of the seriousness of organizational crimes, the number of suspected law-breakers arrested for the investigations into these crimes was not more than the number of those arrested for individual offenses (46% vs. 48%). (Wheller and Rothman 1982).

In Finland Posio and Vähätalo (1987) have studied labor offenses. Their conclusion is that sentences are lenient, confiscations have been used too rarely and the economic value of the confiscations has been too small. They conclude that labor crimes are profitable in Finland. Träskman (manuscript 1990) has found that the probability of being accused of environmental crimes is very low in Finland and the sentences have been lenient and without relation to the damage caused. Environmental offenses are, also, profitable for the enterprises, although not necessarily for the individual decision-makers.

It is possible to present a ratio of "fines/losses" of the crime. It is in my study 0,11 without confiscations and compensations, with these the ratio is 0.22. In the cases of conventional theft the ratio in Finland has been 1.75 if we suppose that the average value of the financial harm is about 400 FMK (around $100) per case, the average number daily fines is 35 and the value of one daily fine is smallest possible, 20 FMK (around $5).

In the United States the ratio has varied among organizational crimes from 0.05 to 0.19 without compensations and confiscations. With these it has been 0.26-0.63. The ratio of theft with compensations has been 1.00 (Cohen 1989).

A United Nations congress reported ten years ago that until recently, the main focus of criminologists, national authorities and the international criminal justice community, which shares the same priorities, has been the control of so-called "street crime". Occasional attempts to take up matters of increasing concern, such as corruption, were deemed risky and unlikely to yield fruitful results. (UN, 1980).

Problems in the control of organizational crime

There are some difficult obstacles in developing more effective controls over organizational crime. The obstacles can be classified as follows: *(Cullen, Maakestad & Cavender* 1987, 319-334).

(1) Ideological obstacles
(2) Legal obstacles
(3) Structural obstacles

(1) Ideological obstacles to the development of controls affect our thinking about crime. It is not so easy to envisage organizational/corporate offenses as conventional crimes. Because of the tight relationships between the power institutions of society, it is difficult to define unethical corporate behavior as illegal. This is especially so because the definers themselves are located at the organizational level of society and they are also the (potential) objects of these definitions. It is understandable but not acceptable that decision-makers are unwilling to create any threat to their own power and positions.

Organizational crime is not a good social enemy against which an attack can easily be made (see Christie & Bruun 1986). It is easier to recognize individual offenders than the corporate state. Organizations are strong and they are able to resist the powers and controls of the state. Besides, the state is dependent on economic enterprises and organizations. It must take into account their reactions. Finally we must remember the multi-roles of decision-makers in different power institutions. In Finland more than 80% of the ministers during 1950-1986 (Laitinen 1989) were also members of the board of some enterprise. All this makes it much easier to direct public concern on to street crime rather than face the problems of corporate crimes.

(2) In respect to the legal obstacles, I only want to mention some of the most important points from the perspective of my own country. A favorable social atmosphere is a necessary but not sufficient condition for developing controls in this field. It is self-evident that the wielders of power can form public opinion by their own behavior, decisions, announcements, etc.

In countries like Finland, the successful control of organizational crime has been difficult because of the lack of full corporate responsibility in criminal law. Only changes on the individual level have been possible.

If that distinction is not made, the court decisions of criminal cases are based on the behavior of individuals without depending on the collective nature of the action in question. The situation does not become better with the increase of legal rules. A good example is that of crimes against the environment. The number of laws criminalizing actions against the environment has increased in European countries. At the same time the number of lapsed environmental prosecutions has also increased (Beck 1990, 191-193). The politicians in Finland have indeed told us that we have more environmental laws than ever and therefore more effective control over environmental (in general, organizational) crime. But in legal practice very little has happened. Empirical research findings (Forurensning 1991, 133-156) confirm this conclusion. It can be said that political decision makers are exercising some kind of symbolic legal policy.

One reason for the situation described above is the stability of principles and definitions created a long time ago. In those days the main problems were individual offenses, individual behavior and relationships between individuals. That is why the legislation itself is a problem. It does not very easily touch collective actions, and organizational crime cannot be proved by using individual arguments.

The basis of the legal responsibility of our system is a structure made up of simple cases, of violent individual crimes, of damages to property done by individuals, etc. The elements of that structure are clearly defined unambiguous events and the parties to these are clearly defined individuals or groups of individuals. That is why the two basic functions of legislation, the regulation of harmful activities and compensating the harm done to the victims, have lost much of their original meaning in the field of organizational/corporate crime. Unfortunately the real offenders, viz. corporate actors, are seldom regarded as responsible for the damages of their law-breaking. The costs of the crime have been transferred to the individual members of the organization, or the individual victims of the crime of the state. (See Ritter 1987, 935).

(3) The following structural features weaken opportunities to control organizational crime

A. Compared with individual offenses, organizational crime is difficult to reveal and investigate. Some of the difficulties are very practical. According to the Finnish Central Criminal Police, the following problems are most evident:[2] (1) The difficulties of understanding the professional language, (2) the difficulties of utilizing circumstantial (indirect) evidence – this is common in the cases we are now talking about, (3) the long duration and multi-dimensionality of the cases, (4) the different skills and backgrounds of the parties in the cases, (5) the unique juridical features of many cases, (6) the difficulties caused by the large amount of work in proving the crime – this is a difficulty because of the perennial problem of limited resources, (7) the high probability of falling under the statute of limitations and (8) the difficulties of handling a large number of documents.

There are also other problems, for example, that of training the judge. It is usual for judges and other lawyers not to be able to understand the language used in different financial documents, for instance, in audit reports.

---

[2] Note that according to our legal principles the investigation of organizational crime concerns the behaviour of individuals.

B. Often it is difficult to define who will be prosecuted because usually the cases are wide and multi-dimensional. Sometimes statements are required from other branches of the administration. It is also possible for security regulations to prevent depositions which could be important for the prosecutors.

C. Like any defendant, corporate offenders are reluctant to cooperate with their prosecutor. But in contrast to street criminals, who have little control over the evidence that comes to the attention of enforcement officials, the organizational position of corporate executives gives them the opportunity to obfuscate evidence or to reveal it selectively. As a result, they exert considerable control over both the degree and kind of information that prosecutors are able to ferret out. Moreover, their attorneys help them to deflect prosecutorial attempts to secure incriminating evidence.

D. Bringing the defendant to trial is often a real problem. The time between an organization's indictment and the trial can determine the character and perhaps the very survival of a case. In my study the average time between the revelation of the offense and trial is 4 years. According to Finnish law the period of limitation of most offenses is either 5 or 10 years.

It is typical that corporate offenders try to neutralize their guilt by different means. These means are seldom – in a real sense – available for individual law-breakers. The following means are used (Hills [ed.] 1987. 194-200):

Denial of responsibility. A distinguishing characteristic of large-scale organizations is the fragmentation of responsibilities. In a hierarchical labyrinth of specialized tasks and segmented organizational units, employees can easily evade any sense of personal responsibility for the ultimate consequences of their actions. In a bureaucratic organization, most employees see only a small part of the whole corporate enterprise and can conveniently ignore – or choose not to see – the larger implications of their occupational decisions. Bureaucracies depersonalize, and corporate officials rarely confront the victims of their organizational crimes.

Denial of injury. Another social-psychological device to avoid moral responsibility and alleviate feelings of guilt is to define what occurs as an unfortunate "accident" or the hazards inherent in dangerous work. For example, managers can suppress medical data and reports of injuries or hazardous conditions and contend that they are acting in the best interest ot their company. Speeding up production, taking shortcuts on product safety, falsifying lab tests, refusing to recall defective products or implement costly safety measures in the workrooms - all are being done, it can be rationalized, to enhance the company profits. Although the consequences may be viewed as unfortunate, the insistence that there is no intention to harm (despite deliberate violations of safety and heath regulations) takes the offender off the moral hook.

Denial of the victim. One way to neutralize the moral implications of one's actions is to blame the victim for the harm. For example, a producer could argue that the products are not unsafe, but that bad conditions and irresponsible consumers are the problem. Another way organizational officials can neutralize their guilt is to deny the victim full human status. Anonymous victims, often of other races, from impoverished Third World nations, may help business managers avoid confronting their own qualms about dumping carcinogenic garments, dangerous drugs, highly toxic pesticides, or other products banned or under strict controls in this country.

Condemning the condemners. A technique by which corporate officials may neutralize the moral weight of the law is to deny its legitimacy and not only condemn it, but also those government regulatory agencies that are enforcing such "unfair laws."

Appealing to higher loyalties. Corporate managers may rationalize their evasions of laws and ethical constraints by appealing to a "morally superior" set of business ethics to justify their actions. I do not want to deny the importance of ethical discussion and principles. It is, however, possible that an actual discussion about business ethics may help frustrate the development of more effective controls; it can then be argued that because we have good ethical principles already we do not need more legal regulations.

On the means of controlling organizational crime

In this presentation I have dealt with some aspects of the social and theoretical background of organizational crime. It is obvious that this form of criminality is tightly related to the structural features of society. I also pointed out three categories of obstacles which at least in some degree prevent the development of rational legal-political solutions. I have, however, said nothing about solutions applied or planned in the fight against crime in different countries.

We know many types of alternatives to traditional sanctions in the cases of organizational/corporate crime; they have been either planned and suggested or applied (See, for example, Braithwaite 1982, Fisse & Braithwaite 1983, Fisse 1985, 141-152 and Shipp 1987). In Finland only two types of corporate punishments have been suggested, a corporate fine and the order of publicity. Here I do not want to repeat different plans and proposals. Instead I will comment on a some legal-political principles and their role in developing more effective control over organizational crime. When I am speaking about the matter, we should always keep in mind the international surroundings to the problems. The national legislation of each country is more or less linked with the internationalization of the economy and criminality. It is easy for "dirty money" to move from one country to the country of more lenient rules, as I have already stated.

1. More rules and more severe punishments?

The increase in legal rules and the decrease in crime rates have very little to do with each other. The Finnish example shows an increase in the number of laws and orders after the Second World War, but during the same period the number of crimes also increased. Of course I do not want to argue that there is a causal connection between the two trends. I have sometimes said that the creation of new laws is only a means for politicians to show their supporters how active they are; it is a kind of symbolic legislation and policy-making. Some researchers (see, for example, Clinard 1979) have regarded severer punishments as an effective means of preventing organizational crime. At least in countries without full corporate responsibility the significance of strengthening punishments is very limited. I only want to point out a couple of facts. Most organizations operate according to the cost – *profit* – principle. Punishments present only one type of cost for the organization. If the profit is constantly bigger than the costs, organizations are tempted to continue their illegal activities. Individual punishments alone are not effective. It is not difficult to get a replacement if the managing director, for instance, is sentenced to imprisonment.

In general, under legal systems where corporate criminal responsibility is unknown, punishments affect only the individual members of an organization, not the organization itself. In addition, the forces influencing the content of corporate legislation are those which are the potential objects of this legislation.

2. The role of the state and public power

In Clinard's report (1979) public ownership and a management appointed by the state organs have been recommended as one means of controlling corporations and organizational crime. The proposal sounds good, but the question is how it will operate in practice.

In Finland, for decades, large state-owned firms have existed especially in the fields of wood and metal industry. The members of the administrative boards of these enterprises have been appointed parliamentarily. There has been also a system of administrative boards in large private firms, including banks, insurance companies and so on.

Gradually membership of the boards of state-oned firms has become some kind of political reward. Political parties share these positions, which offer large substantial financial remunerations and other material advantages. According to interview data, members know very little or nothing about the activities of their firms.

Private firms are willing to appoint top politicians, ministers,[3] members of parliament, and civil servants as members of their boards. They offer, if possible, better advantages than state-owned firms do. The result has been a tight network of relationships between enterprises and top political and administrative leaders. For firms, the system has been, among other things, a means of influencing the content of the legislation they are interested in. For politicians and civil servants, as well as for political organizations, the system has given monetary support. This has also created a basis for corruption and organizational crime. During the last fifteen years many big criminal cases linked with this system have emerged in Finland.

The system has become so corrupt that serious consideration has been given to abandonikig the whole apparatus. A weakening in the network of relationships between the power institutions of society bas been especially demanded by researchers, not by the top executives themselves.

3. The change in certain legal and structural principles

Previously I have mentioned the problems caused by the lack of corporate criminal responsibility. This lack is based on the idea that only individual human beings have intentions and goals of their own; organizations and corporations have, correspondingly, no independent conscious goals and interests. That is why, in the light of this thinking, it has been found logically necessary to reduce organizational crime to the level of individual, conscious behavior. If we want to develop a more rational policy against organizational crime, we must drop that principle. Coleman, as mentioned above, has confirmed that there are not theoretical obstacles preventing this change.

Another firm and traditional legal principle has been that the prosecutor must prove the guilt of the suspect (individual or organization). The purpose of the principle is to guarantee the rights of the aecused and prevent arbitrary decisions. Unfortunately this reasonable principle does not operate very well in the field of organizational crime. It is difficult to find unambiguous evidence to prove illegal organizational acitivity. That

---

[3] According to my study more than 60% of the Finnish ministers have been members of the administrative board of some private enterprise; when you include estate owned firms the percentage is more than 80%.

is why the adoption of the principle of the reversed burden of proof has been suggested.(Salminen 1991, 11). This would mean that the suspect has to prove absence of guilt.[4]

Parallel principles to the above-mentioned proposal have been adopted in Japan when courts deal with environmental crime - these latter are the most typical examples of organizational crimes. The courts have no longer required negligence and intent as necessary bases of the sentence. According to the new procedure, it has been enough to prove the probable connection between the damage and the activities of the suspect (Beck 199U, 196-197).

On the practical level there have been several proposals for improving the liability of organizations and their structure. Coleman (1990, 553-578) has suggested that the representative of the employees and adjacent interest groups should be present in corporations. Their duty would be (1) to supervise the legality of the corporate behavior and (2) to show, and request the corporation to consider, the direct and indirect consequences of its activities.

A second means suggested by Coleman is the directing and controlling of corporations and other organizations by using taxation. Here possibilities may be limited.

Thirdly, Coleman sees that individual members of an organization must not be held responsible for illegal corporate activity solely as an employee of the organization, but also as an individual. This means that we must take into account two types of liability: personal and corporate liability.

Some researchers (e.g. Young, 1990) have argued that the market economy itself produces organizational/corporate crime. This argument embraces the idea that another type of industrial, post-industrial or information society does not produce similar crime. Unfortunately we have very few alternatives for comparison. One was the socialist system of the Soviet Union and the Eastern European countries. Now the results are well known. This system has produced, according to Lirhanov and Belyh (1990), if possible, more organizational crime than the market economy has. The content of the crime has, however, been different from that in Western countries. It is another thing that the changes in former socialist countries will cause much organized and organizational/corporate crime. The cause of this is not the market economy, but rather the lack of sufficient regulation machinery.

---

[4] The Supreme Court of Finland has applied this principle (KKO 11.4. 1990, 1019, R 88/585), and this is very unique. A firm (in practice the managing director and owner of the firm) was sentenced, because it was not able to show that the poisoning of the wells of the resort was not caused by it.

A concluding remark

Most radical and most effective means of controlling organizational crime are structural in nature. This means changes in the power structures of society (See e.g. Simon & Eitzen 1986). The changes required are very difficult to make. We can, however, consider partial changes. Among these, would be an attempt to make the activities of economic enterprises and other organizations open and more public. This would require the breaking-down of bank-secrecy regulations and the abandonment of the strong protection hitherto given to information about the ownership of firms, their administration and so forth.

Whatever we are planning or doing for the improvement of the command of organizational crime, a couple of things are evident. First, organizational/corporate crime is much more harmful for society than traditional individual offenses are. Secondly, the contemporary crime-fighting solutions on the level of civil society only serve to cover over the real nature of the whole problem.

Notes and References

Beck, U.: (1990): *Riskiyhteiskunnan vastamyrkyt* (Die Organisierte Unverantworlichkeit). Vastapaino, Tampere 1990.
Braithwaite, J.: (1982.): *Enforced Self-Regulation:* A New Strategy for Corporate Crime Control. Michigan Law Review, 80 (1982), No 7, 1466-1507.
Broms, H. & Paavola, V.: T*raokkijohtaminen* (Management by Tarot Cards). WSOY, Juva 1991.
Christie, N. & Bruun, K.: *Hyvä vihollinen* (A Good Enemy). Weilin & Göös, Espoo 1986.
Clinard, M. B.: *Illegal Corporate Behavior.* Washington D.C., U.S. Department of Justice, 1979.
Cohen, M. A.: *Corporate Crime and Punishment:* A Study of Social Harmony and Sentencing Practice in the Federal Courts, 1984-1987. American Criminal Law Review 26 (1989), 605-660.
Coleman, J.: *Foundation of Social Theory.* The Belknap Press of Harvard University Press, 1990.
Committee Report 1983:7. Taloudellisen rikollisuuden selvitystyöryhmän mietintö. (A Report of the Working-Group investigating Economic Crimes). Oikeusministeriön lainvalmisteluosaston julkaisu (A Publication of the Law Drafting Department of the Minsitry of Justice). Helsinki 1983.

Cullen, Francis T., Maakestad, W. J. & Cavender, G.: *Corporate Crime under Attack.* Anderson Publishing Co., Ohio 1987.
Fisse, B. & Braithwaite, J.: *The Impact of Publicity on Corporate Offenders.* State University of New York Press, 1983.
Fisse, B. L.: *Sanctions against Corporations: The Limitations of Fines and the Enterprise of Creating Alternatives.* In Fisse, Brent & French, Peter A. (eds.): Corrigible Corporations and Unruly Law. Trinity University Press, San Antonio 1985.
Forurensning og straff – et nordisk studium. Nord 1991.2. Nordist Ministerrå, Kbenhavn 1991.
Hilis, S. L. (ed.): *Corporate Violence.* Rowman & Littlefield Publishers, Inc. Maryland 1987.
Laitinen, A.: *Vallan rikokset* (The Crimes of Power). Lakimiesliiton kustannus, Jyväskylä 1989.
Lehtonen, A.: *Veropetoksesta* (On Tax Fraud). Jyväskylä 1986.
Liebl, K.: *Developing Trends in Economic Crime in The Federal Republic of Germany.* Police Studies 1985:8/3, 149-162.
Lirhanov, D. & Belyh, V.: *Toveri kummisetä. Rikollisuus Neuvostoliitossa* (Comrade Godfather. Crime in the Soviet Union). Orient Press, Helsinki 1990.
Magnusson, D.: *Ekonomisk brottslighet vid import och export* (Economic Crime in Imports and Exports). Brottsförebyggande rådet (The Council of Crime Prevention). Rapport 1981:2. Stockholm 1981.
Magnusson, D.: *Företagskonkurser och ekonomisk brottsligheten. Forskning in ekonomisk brottslighet* (Bankrupties and Economic Crime. Studies in Economic Crime), 1985:1. Stockholm 1985.
Magnusson, Dan: *Fel och oegentligheter i tulldeklarationer. Forskning in ekonomisk brottslighet* (Mistakes and Impropieties spelling in Customs Declaration. Studies in Economic Crime), 1987:2, Stockholm 1987.
Posio, A. & Vähätalo, T.: *Näkökohtia taloudellisen hyödyn konfiskoinnista työrikoksissa* (The Confiscation of the Economic Profit in Labor Offenses). Oikeus 16 (1987), 350-353.
Rikollisuustilanne 1987 (Criminality in Finland 1987). A Publication of the National Research Institute of Legal Policy. Helsinki 1987.
Rikollisuustilanne 1988 (Criminality in Finland 1988). A Publication of the National Research Institute of Legal Policy. Helsinki 1989.
Ritter, E.-J.: *Umweltpolitik und Rechtsentwicklung* (Environment Policy and the Development of Law). Neue zeitschrift für Verwaltungsrecht, heft 11, 1987, 929-938.
Salminen, M.: *Erään tutkimuksen anatomia* (The Anatomy of a Police Investigation). Unpublished manuscript, 1991.

Shipp, S.: *Modified Vendettas.* Journal of Business Ethics 6 (1987), 603-612.
Simon, D. R. & Eitzen, S. D.: *Elite Deviance.* Allen & Bacon, 1986.
STVK (suomen tilatollinen vuosikirja, Statistical Year Book of Finland), Years 1980-1990.
Työmarkkinat (Labor Markets) 1989.29. Helsinki 1989. UN, Sixth UN Congress on the Prevention of Crime and the Treatment of Offenders. Caracas, Venezuela, 25 Aug to S Sept 1980. (A/Conf. 87/6 22 July 1980, s. 3).
v. Weinhofer, K. & Schöler, U.: *Die Spitze des Eisberge* (The Tip of the Iceberg. WSI Mitteilungern Nr 1/1986, 40-51.
Wheeler, S. & Rothman, M. L.: *The Organization as Weapon in White-Collar Crime.* Michigan Law Review, 80 (1982), 1403-1426.
Young, T. R.: *Corporate Crime: A Critique of the Clinard Report.* In Timer, Doug a. & Eitzen, D. Stanley (eds.): Crime in the Streets and Crime in the Suites. Alley and Bacon, 1989.

Topic III.
The Effect of Social Changes on the Police

by
Dr. Sándor Pintér,

In order to be able to demonstrate the impact of social changes on the Hungarian police after the change of regime in 1990. I must give a short resume of the events leading up to it.

Two years have passed since the Hungarian society broke the back of the task of changing the regime in a peaceful way, although this process was clogged by many conflicts, before it could start on the road towards democratic development. I do not wish to give a detailed survey of this process of social transformation.

I would like to start my evaluation with the social conditions. What conditions confronted the Hungarian police before the changes of 1990? What changes have occurred in this respect and what effects have hit us?

Previously our borders were closed down, and there was free passage for the citizens only towards the so-called socialist countries. In relation to the Western states there was an obligatory visa system. This obligatory system worked as a strong filter in the sense that only those persons could enter the country who were preferred by the society or by the political leadership of that time. There was a strong personal, social, and cultural control. People were checked out, certain parts of social and cultural life were under the party's control. Standards of socialist morality were being introduced, in an attempt to replace religion and morals that had been customary in other societies. At the beginning of the changes frontiers collapsed, and this meant not only advantages but that such persons were able to enter the country who were not desirable from the point of view of public order. International adventurers appeared; about 500,000 to 600,000 people entered the country, tailing fluxes of migration. Most of them had no proper financial background, and tried to make ends meet by committing minor offences. It increased our surveillance of foreigners, yet up to the present day we have no law covering this field. To set this right it has come under the auspices of the police, but they have a no solid legal background behind them. Among moral standards, religious values have also come to the fore again, but because of a confessional division and the backwardness of social standards, not even religion is able to substitute the existing shortcomings.

Previously the stability of law and order was maintained, although it was by all means a very peculiar sort of law and order. At present we have a changing law and order, in which a part of the citizens cannot find their places. Democracy is mixed up with anarchy, and in case of personal interests, duties are neglected and only rights are taken into consideration. There is a different social expectation towards the police. Before the change of the regime it conveyed the political expectations, coming to the police from a party directive. On the other hand, members of the police felt secure, because if they met the requirements of the party polities, they could feel a safe background behind them. The press did not attack the police. However, relations with the population were developing in a specific way. A considerable part of the citizens accepted policemen, less held them in contempt, and Hungary was a place where the greatest number of jokes concerning policemen were made up per year, in which policemen always played a negative part. The police reacted in a special way – by feeling superior which, combined with a non - satisfying level of training, further increased the citizens' antipathy.

Therefore during the changes the police became the No.1 target of those forces which required a democratic change. They looked upon the police as the pillar of the former regime, and felt that they must be attacked in every respect. The police were attacked politically, through the press. After the change they realized that the police are a necessary organization, but they could prove their necessity only by remaining party-neutral. The "ars poetica" of the present police directive is also to establish a party-neutral police force, one that is independent to a required extent and is subjected only to the law. I will later return to the subject of the control of such a police force.

The different attacks made the police and their leadership very unsure of themselves. This uncertainty was reflected in the measures taken. Policemen did not take such measures, the legal background of which they were unsure of. But they did not initiate such steps which might have led to personal attacks against them. Thus it became obvious that public law and order worsened during the period of transition.

This is slowly beginning to change. We and the press are becoming partners. The press is still our fierce critic; in a certain respect we are grateful for this as its aim is no longer to annul the police but to lead them on the right path.

Our relations with the public have also changed. The police are more and more accepted by the citizens. People have understood that the police are needed. Its clearest evidence is the Day of the Police, first organized on 24th April this year, which attracted 40,000 visitors, creating a May Day feel in the capital. This acceptance is felt not only here, but in the relations between societal organizations and the police, but let me return to this subject somewhat later.

The policeman is always an integral part of the community, and there is a change in this respect, too. The policeman has become an equal partner in society now, and this state has been achieved not by trying to prove his superiority but by accepting the fact that a policeman must serve the citizens and the society. This service has certainly improved the image of the police which is becoming better and better.

As I have mentioned before the directive of the organization was mostly under Party control, and only in the second place under government control. It must also be stated here that in Hungary there is a unified police force which means that there is no constabulary or other forces besides us. After we escaped Party control there was a change in the control of the organization. Through regulations the Home Office supervises the National Police Office in a normative way, so the national Chief Commissioner of Police is subjected only to the laws. This enables the police to serve the interests of society and to stay neutral in battles of Party politics. The new leadership has resulted in organizational changes. Previously the state security organization was a part of the police and frequently worked under police cover. In many cases this provoked a strong aversion in society.

The so-called "Danubegate"-scandal, the case of the 3/3 Department is well-known for all the Hungarian participants; actually, it was initiated by the state security organization as part of the police, so by this scandal they damaged not only their own image but that of the police as well. In consequence of the changes, the state security department left the police force and became independent, so now the National Police Office only deals with cases covering public law and order, criminal investigation and administration. Organizational changes include the dissolution of the voluntary police force which formerly also belonged functionally to the police. Concerning voluntary policemen it must said that different civilians, working as voluntary policemen, got official authority. They could stop and demand other people's papers and could even inform against them as acting policemen. This service ended in December 1991.

Relating to the organizational changes, it must also be mentioned that the Hungarian police did all the security tasks by themselves. They had no such support as the private security services which can assist the police in the field of the protection of property. There are not and never have been private police forces in Hungary. The lack of voluntary policemen had to be supplied somehow, so we created the civil guard. (I would like to return to the subject of the situation concerning the number of our work force). This is a completely voluntary organization; it is up to the citizens' decision whether they join it or not. In comparison to the voluntary police force the biggest difference is that there is no official authority. It means a civilian grouping, such an organization which fulfills well-known, so-called "neighbourhood watch" tasks that are already common in the Western democracies.

The number of our staff has shown a specific development. The closed borders, the great social control were taken into consideration. There was a considerable check-up and muster-role in 1972. Then there were about 80,000 crimes committed in the country. We worked with the then established index-numbers until 1980 when there were already 130,000 crimes. The number of the work force was increased by 20 per cent in 1980. Subsequently there was no considerable staff increase until 1991. At the same time the number of crimes, as a result of the social changes and the democratization, showed an increase to 430,000. It is evident that such a police staff cannot meet these demands. We have sized up our staff condition and have done a European comparison, and as a result it has been proven that there are about 40 per cent fewer policemen in Hungary than required compared to the European average police staff number. We have also taken into consideration that in Western Europe 240-260-270 citizens fall to one policeman. In Hungary, however, he keeps watch over the security of 460-480 citizens, and he cannot meet this requirement. Realizing this, the Home Office, taking into consideration the suggestions of the National Police Headquarters, achieved a staff increase of 3,000 in Parliament in 1991. This staff increase of 3,000 will come into force in the second half of 1992, and thus right now it does not help the maintenance of public law and order, does not manifest itself in everyday work, as we are speaking of untrained and ill-equipped policemen at the time of entry into service.

A few thoughts must also be mentioned concerning the changes of the permanent staff. First let us see the considerations of selection. The most important consideration was reliability, meaning a reliability not of the police profession, but in any case of a political aspect. It is commonly known that those who had relatives in Western Europe or overseas became unreliable and could not become policemen. Academic qualifications were of secondary importance. A considerable part of the policemen joining the force finished only eight forms of the comprehensive school. Training was not considered important; the average training period up to last year was six, then eleven months, but even without training a policeman could start patrolling, he could get a gun, a uniform, official papers; he was then attached for service to another, more experienced policeman. This was also changed. First the most important consideration of selection changed; it has become training. It is training and knowledge that determine who can become a policeman and who can be assigned to which post.

Following the social changes almost 9,000 persons got discharged in the past two years. One part of them left the force when they had to swear an oath on the new constitution. Many of them did not take this upon themselves and left. Besides there were tremendous changes in the leading staff, in their composition. The Ministry of Interior invited applications for different posts, and this meant that one had to meet certain requirements if he wanted to be a chief again. Thus such persons occupy the posts of national chief commissioner of police, country chief commissioner of police and municipal commissioner of police who were appointed by competition, conducted partly by involving the local governments. Academic qualifications also became more important. It is our aim to have only high-school graduates as policemen, and nobody can patrol the streets who has no special training, or has not graduated from a police academy.

During the period of transition applicants will have to attend and graduate from a school, receive a training of a minimum eleven months and maximum two years until 1995. From 1995 on, this term will only be two years. Training will also include a knowledge of data processing and language skills.

Police techniques must be separately mentioned. Our motor-pool is absolutely out-of-date and extremely scarse. Our telecommunication equipment does not meet the requirements of the age and not every policeman has them. To control deployment was an unknown concept in Hungary in 1992, for the Hungarian police and computer techniques play a minor role only, except in police registers and record systems. Therefore the leaders' aim is to attain the European average. The first steps have already been taken. First of all, substantial amounts were allocated for retooling. This means that in 1992 we spent Ft 229 million on cars of a medium category represent the highest technical standards.

Telecommunications and the control of deployment will be a joint undertaking. It is commonly known that the National Police Office has called for tenders in this respect, the judgement of which is just in process. One billion forints will be allotted to this purpose in the next two years, which would mean that in Hungary the capital would first get such a deployment controlling centre which could track, by means of computers, events in the street and thus it would multiply the reaction time and ability of the police. The present 15-20 minute reaction time – and this is by far a very good time! – would be improved to a 2-3 minute reaction time.

Criminal techniques must also be separately mentioned. They show an ambivalent, controversial picture. In certain fields they are at a very high level, in others they are at a Stone-Age level. Shortfalls are especially frequent in the peripheries and in regional organizations. We would like to solve this by meeting the technical requirements of our colleagues by the establishment of new microcentres with German help in 1993-1994. These microcentres will have such equipment that they can accomplish tasks out of turn in their vicinity.

Computer techniques, I think, would deserve a separate paper. We cannot talk about notable computer techniques in Hungary except for record systems. Following the change of regime different sorts of criminal record systems were introduced in the second half of 1991, but so far this does not mean that the regional police force can get in touch with the central police registers.

In everyday work, in leading, in control, in the reduction of different written materials and that of the paperwork we have no electronic equipment. We are still considering different ways of solving this problem, although our financial means have our hands tied in terms of how to realize this. However, one thing is sure: according to the intentions of the National Police Headquarters there will be local networks of computers functioning in every police station; this will be achieved by 31st December 1992. The efficiency of this computer network depends a lot on how much our software experts will produce until this deadline. Technology also includes the following: I think Hungary is the only European country which has no monodactyloscopic police registers. The lack of this monodactyloscopic registers is acutely felt. We have neither manual, nor data processing registers, although I think that it will be supplied in the first quarter of 1993. This way it will also be possible for us to get into contact with the European data processing system in this field, too.

Some of our concerns relating to international crime must also be mentioned. We have no adequate technical equipment, devices for detecting crimes. Our Western European colleagues have promised much help in this respect, but nothing has been accomplished so far. We have been quite successful in the field of drug-related crimes as we are able to collar small-time pushers or dealers; however, on the other hand we are able to collect and gather information concerning the big transit routes from the briefing of our foreign colleagues. In spite of this I am delighted to say that is was exactly last week that we nabbed 28 kg of heroin on the Hungarian border and could prevent its being distributed in Western Europe. Raw material starts its long way from Afgani territory and the transit route goes across the Balkans to Western Europe. Pre-packed drugs then come from the direction of Western Europe, mostly from German and Dutch territories. Arrested dealers usually get drugs in Western European countries. Our cooperation with the police of these countries is good, and I think that it is growing deeper and deeper. And if we are talking about international cooperation, then I must also add that Hungary was a member of Interpol before 1990 as well, so our international cooperation has a past of almost ten years.

Interpol membership has made it possible for us to get an inside view of criminal investigation activity of different countries, and so in many respects we have got some help from them. Interpol membership has also made it possible to apprehend persons wanted by the Hungarian police. Suspects accused of serious crimes are caught and transported back to Hungary. There has been no decided change in this since 1990, unfortunately; for different political considerations, economic and other – for us hardly understandable – reasons, we are shut out from the Sengen Treaty. We do not even know how to join the Trevi Treaty or the Europol. These shuttings out are not considered by criminals. They cross the borders freely, they do not care which country has joined the Sengen Treaty. They care only how many advantages they can turn to profit and how they can wriggle out of police tracking. We must at all costs advance in these fields and must attempt – perhaps even before economic cooperation – to establish such a cooperation of the police forces that prevents criminals from carrying on their activities.

International cooperation also includes the drawing up of bilateral contracts. The Hungarian police insist on and prepare such contracts after the Minister for Home Affairs has entered into his agreements. First we have started negotiations with Western Europe. We have valid agreements with many countries of Europe. I feel that these bilateral contracts help our work, but cannot substitute for our absence from the European police associations and they cannot replace our joining forces with these treaties.

Finally I want to talk about two things. About the change of attitude within the police and the change of social recognition.

The change of attitude is tangible. Police distinctly concentrate their efforts on criminal investigation and crime prevention activity, on public law and order. Accordingly – I think, for the first time in Europe – success and efficiency have been attempted to be measured exactly.

Therefore since 1991 we have been keeping continuous record, of how many crimes are detected by each police station. We have been keeping track of how many crimes are committed in the territory of each police force. We exhibit how many crimes fall on one detective, one policeman, one investigator, and what is the clearance rate, and how many criminals are caught by a policeman on duty in a public place during his time of service. These surveys are done with no wanton purposes. I think that if a spirit of competition is to be created relating to where the perpetrator of crimes against life is caught quicker and sooner – I need hardly to say that strictly by respecting the law – then it will be possible for the police to take the necessary steps more quickly and more efficiently. It will also be possible for the citizens to recognize this ability to react. Naturally, by increasing efficiency prevention is enhanced, because if we catch the perpetrator, then he will not commit another crime for a certain time. The data in question are processed by a computer program at the National Police Headquarters, and the results are published. Our colleagues are informed about how many crimes have been committed and how successful their detection has been; this briefing is done every quarter of a year, every month. I think this is an initiative from which no immediate conclusions of effectiveness should be derived, although after some time, half a year or a year, it can be determined whether this experiment is the most adequate way or not, whether such methods can be used for measuring police performance or not.

In conclusion let me talk about social recognition. We feel that citizens more and more focus their eyes on the police with the worsening of security and order. The worse public order gets, the more they need police presence. If citizens feel that public law and order is getting better, then they show their appreciation to the police. In each residential area they require the deployment of a police station; they want the policeman to be in a public place in a given spot at a given time. The population always wants to know where a policeman can be found. The other side of appreciation is that there is a lack of due payment of a policeman's services at the moment. The financial aspect of a police force's recognition so far has remained on the level preceding the nineties. Police pay is near average salaries, but it is much more below them than above them. I hope that the discernment, namely that society needs a Hungarian police force, later will result in a not only moral but financial recognition. Their income will be boosted above average pay. It will be appreciated that a policeman risks his life, takes the burden of danger on his shoulders when he is on duty. A changed way of looking at things is needed to achieve this, even in the case of police chiefs, and among the management of the police.

This has no tradition in Hungary. Policemen have worked, society has recognized us in a way. The essence of management is that society is well aware of what efforts the policeman makes, what he risks while on duty. The public must be aware of the fact that the average age of policemen is not higher than sixty years, and from this a policeman's service is fifty-five years. That state of stress must also be shown which is shouldered by the policeman, and the public must be informed about this. Probably it will not be enough to tell once; it will not be sufficient to tell twice, and it must be supported by concrete programs. The other part of management is the management of the organization. To awake the consciousness of its being worthwhile to join the force because it serves society.

Finally, reverting back to the thoughts mentioned in the introduction I would like to repeat that I have on purpose neglected the abstractions of a scientific paper, and relied only on concrete facts: I have expounded how the chief of the National Police Headquarters sees the effects of social changes on the Hungarian police.

Relationship Between the Hungarian Police and Society

by
Valér Dános

Challenge and Response

Perhaps the motto could apply that "law enforcement agencies will never enjoy popularity." Food for thought that should be investigated further.

As it is a well-known fact that a peculiar culture, set of values and traditions had evolved in Central Eastern Europe in the last 1000 years or so, specific to the region that include expectations that constitute traditional sets of values applicable to the rest of Europe also. Undoubtedly, this region tends towards adopting traditional Western European values somewhat out of phase in time with Western Europe. The revolutionary, philosophical ideas of the bourgeois middle classes were adopted in this region with some delay, while some ideas are yet to be adopted and applied in the region.

It is also a well-known fact that this country "was forced" to traverse a peculiar development path during the past four and a half decades; the development path of socialism. Yet, this country, even in this period of time, had preserved certain values "specific" to the country.

In many countries around the world, including Hungary, the police are not really popular. Why is this so? Several answers may be provided to explain this phenomenon, such as:

- This is the very organization that, in certain circumstances, may be empowered by the political system to restrict some of the most fundamental human rights of the ordinary citizen
- The same applies to causing bodily harm in circumstances quite legal
- May represent the arm of subversive political power
- Many may think that "even my own behavior is not above board in all circumstances", "I am also guilty" or have grave reservations, or even aversion to any and all law-enforcement organizations or agencies.

There is no end to empirically derived examples and motivations to fortify the above argument.

Apart from the above other serious problems will have to be tackled. Crime rates are on the increase everywhere, particularly serious, capital crime.

In addition, due consideration needs to be paid to the fact that until recent times, the law-enforcement agencies of Central and Eastern Europe were viewed as the very agents of a totalitarian, dictatorial state. Let us examine this latter aspect:

1. One of the characteristic features of a totalitarian system is an obsession with control over its citizens. Application led to an abnormally large police organization with an increased number of tasks assigned.
2. Expertise and police skills were devalued due to the authoritarian philosophy and anti-democratic principles employed. Yet, these do not necessarily mean that excellent experts and talented persons were excluded from the force. Admittedly few reached a position commensurate with their skills, particularly management skills, since skills and excellence were of secondary importance ranking behind political considerations in terms of promotion.
3. Some of the tasks regularly assigned to the police would have been regarded as quite nonsensical in a democratic framework of European values and cultural background.
4. The biggest drawback of the system proved the lack of democratic principles and an almost complete disregard of democratic principles, where the most fundamental human and citizen rights were ignored or pushed into the background. Yet, this had nothing to do with the law-enforcement agencies as such. This all stemmed from the totalitarian, Stalinist principles of political considerations and the political system prevailed at the time.
5. Quite contrary to the democratic principles of Western Europe the communist dictatorship was obsessed with so-called national security as its top priority concern.

It can be empirically proven that some of the actions and methodology applied by the police, even in these circumstances, were "sympathetic" to the population. Thus, these dual, often contradictory aspects of the work of the police must be taken into account combined together in order to have an inkling of the situation in a totalitarian political system. Thus, it appears important to find out and to describe what made the Hungarian police "sympathetic" and "antipathetic" in the eyes of the population at the same time.

The majority of Hungarians detested the police:

- because the police seemed to have failed to comply with basic human rights and basic European democratic values
- because it often applied brutal force even in instances when application of brutal force was not warranted at all
- because the citizens of the country were viewed as subjugated human beings
- because the police force was involved in politics as well as involved in criminal matters
- because that segment of the police force that came in daily contact with the population was, by and large, basically unskilled from the point of view of human endeavors and police work.

The police enjoyed popularity in the eyes of the average Hungarian:

- because the police tended to be determined and well disciplined when required in action
- because the police controlled crime well by apprehending 70-80% of those who committed a criminal act
- because the police were quick on the scene when called to deal with a (justified) "problem"
- because many still retain respect for rank and file police personnel, a still decreasing number today, while some of the rank retained respect by the rank and file of police personnel as well.
-

The reason behind describing the above line of thoughts was to demonstrate that even in a totalitarian system the Force may acquire both favorable and unfavorable impressions and projections from the population at large.

Let us examine current trends and changes that are taking place in the police force today. These are:

- The totalitarian system of the past has gone once and for all. The so-called communist bloc has disintegrated: Hungary makes colossal efforts to build a democratic state based on democratic principles and traditions of Western Europe and to extend democratic principles to the entirety of Eastern Central Europe. For this reason, the entire government apparatus was reorganized, or is in the process of re-organization, including the police force.
- Some of the tasks that were previously assigned to the Hungarian police force such as government security, were assigned to other government organizations directly controlled by the government and

government organizations. This, now, makes it possible for the force to be cleansed of past unfavorable images and to seek the support of the population when needed and appropriate.

Introduction of these changes are being carried out in conjunction with some negative processes that hinder these developments. These may be:

- The entire economy of the country is in the process of reconstruction, one of the results of which is that many thousands of companies go broke these days. The rate of unemployment is unprecedented.
- The long lasting and long drawn out economic, social and moral crises that hit the country favor deviant behavior and crime; both are on the increase.
- The courts of law are over-burdened and are operating under an archaic system. For example, the most recent restructuring of the police force in Hungary took effect in the 1960's and the 1970's. In these years some 110,000 – 120,000 criminal proceedings had commenced each year, compared to some 500,000 criminal proceedings started in 1991 (482,674 to be precise). This means a more than four-fold increase of cases for the police to deal with. At this level of criminal proceedings both the staffing level and the level of technology made available to the police force are rendered inadequate.
- Accordingly, the clearance rate of the police force has dropped considerably in recent years, from a rate of 70-80% in the 1960's and the 1970's down to just below 40% (39.6% in fact) the previous year, while clearing up crime committed by person or persons unknown had decreased to 27%.
- These procedures of constant changes in recent years provide substantial burdens to all. The population at large is dissatisfied with the fact of high unemployment, with the high level of price inflation and with deteriorating public safety. Many openly demonstrate signs of nerve and irritation. The level of subjective feeling of public safety and security is at a critical level. Similarly, the world renouned Hungarian agriculture is at the brink of breakdown and disintegration.
- Some 30% of the population of Hungary are considered poor, while some 10% exist below the poverty line. This situation is tragic.

Perhaps it will appear to the reader that we tend to paint a rather depressing picture of present Hungarian reality. It may be so. Yet, this picture, unfortunately, represents objective facts, rather than a mere subjective assessment of the current situation in this country. The question must be posed: Is there a way out of this quandary?

It is obvious that the challenges presented by the economy, and the socio-political situation of the day are not for us to resolve. However, the following suggestions and proposals would be in order to be put with respect to the role of the police force:

- Up-dating and development of the police force has commenced, including establishing a well defined role of the police force in a legal and democratic framework. The police force has been "de-politicized" already. A modernization program had commenced that includes increased staffing levels and modernization of technology rendered to the disposal of the force. The draft Police Law, commensurate with European standards, was presented to Parliament for approval.
- Yet up-dating and modernization is not possible without scientific bases. In this respect the police force of Hungary lag behind the developed countries of Europe. In this country, basically due to political reasons, no scientific approach has ever been established that might be termed Police Sociology. Clarification of the term and development of a theory had commenced within the force some three years ago, including empirical study of the problem. In our view Police Sociology should fit the concept of Applied Sociology to investigate the following fundamental areas of concern:
-

1. The socio-organizational aspects of the police, including the internal problems associated with such a large organization, aspects of the hierarchy, its dysfunctions, features of authority and aspects of isolation.
2. Investigation of sociological and socio-psychological problems in depth associated with the individual policeman (or woman) and groups within the police force, such as, the aspects of deviant behavior by some members of the police force, or the behavior pattern of police personnel in a conflict situation.
3. Investigation of problems developed between the police force as such and the population at large, eg. the general image projected by the force as conceived by the population, investigation of the reasons and sources of prejudice directed against the police force and so on.
4. The social problems associated with law enforcement procedures.
5. Aspects of selection, training, resignation rates, rotation and promotion.

The following research is under way and relates to the above:

1. A representative sample was established to investigate and derive an ideal image of the police force and police personnel in the eyes of the population against the actual image, the aspects of various prejudices

expressed by the population and the current sense of prestige of the police force and police personnel in the eyes of the population.
2. 500 members of the police force were interviewed in order to survey the image of the police force in the eyes of the members of the force, including establishing the image of the ideal police staff person in their relationship to the man on the street and surveying the problem associated with matters of law enforcement.
3. 100 police officers and managers were interviewed to find out about various problems that might exist within the force.
4. The connection and relationship between law-enforcement efficiency against the existing settlement centers is intended in order to establish the highest possible efficiency of dislocation and stationing of police, at least in principle, that could, eventually, lead to the best utilization of the available resources of the force. To this the most efficient organization network is intended to be rendered by application of the appropriate indicators, finally the relationship of the organization network will be factor-analyzed. The ultimate aim of this factor analysis is to establish the most important variables to help establish the most efficient and most optimal organizational and command network possible in the circumstances.

It should be mentioned that current empirical surveys were preceded by several small scale trial surveys.

Further, it would be in order to say that in spite of the many difficulties and drawbacks that were experienced within the force in the past 10 years, some very important and useful surveys were, in fact, conducted also.

Based on the result of past surveys and investigations, supplemented by current investigations and surveys, some interesting and valid conclusions are possible to make already. These are:

1. The majority of the population would expect polite, but resolute and determined behavior from the police. (Yet, in practice in some instances police personnel fail to interfere even in instances when involvement would serve a good purpose and would be fully justified). The police personnel are fully aware of the existence of this problem, but tend to justify inaction on account of lack of a valid legal framework or expressing the thought that the current legal framework is full of contradictions.
2. The great majority of the population would specifically wish to see more policemen on the beat. The views expressed represent a need for proactive, rather than reactive police personnel, including the wish associated with a higher level of traffic control. The great majority of

the population think that the low traffic moral could be substantially improved by more frequent control checks performed by traffic police.
3. According to the feeling of the great majority of the population, public safety made a "nose dive" in recent years, particularly in the last three years, and this trend is continuing. A considerable segment of the population lives in constant fear, avoiding visiting certain areas of the city or township after dark all together. For many the cause and source of the problem lies with the police.
4. The majority of the population feels that the current position of the force is rather inadequate. The staffing level is low, remuneration is inadequate, and low level of technology is employed.
5. A substantial segment of the population still harbors a considerable level of prejudice against the police. The reasons and causes were outlined above. In view of current feelings and circumstances it should serve good purpose to foster a good relationship with the population at large to capture the goodwill of the population and to demonstrate the friendly nature of the police towards the population. The police, after all, are offering a service to the population, paid for by the taxpayer, to provide a service on a higher plain of public safety and comfort. In this respect the population represents the consumer while the force may be envisaged as being assigned the role of protecting the interests of the consumer. In this respect future survey work should extend to find out to what extent the police force fulfills these basic requirements. The population should and must feel that the police are there to serve their collective interests. To re-enforce these sentiments, the police could do no worse than to attempt a propaganda cum promotion exercise to gain the confidence of the population. The prejudices expressed and shown, coupled by the lack of confidence towards the police, weigh heavily against the conscience of all police staff, felt most by the man and woman on the beat.

The lack of understanding is further extenuated by the fact that the names of high ranking police personnel responsible for safety of a particular district or township are virtually kept unknown from the local population concerned. Well, it could be said as an excuse, an "almost" valid excuse, that the entire staff of the force is over-burdened and over-worked. Yet, we wish to advocate that the high ranking police personnel, including the district chief officers, should take part in public functions with increasing frequency to foster contact and good relations with the local population. It must be kept firmly in mind that until recent times any matter connected with the force and its staff was treated as a matter of overtly mystified "taboo". The population at large knew less than enough of the problems and activities of the police force. This aspect represents great dangers in

itself, what is not known or not understood is mystified, distorted and mistrusted instinctively.
6. The men and women of the force, justifiably feel that their training, by and large, was inadequate, particularly related to the proper behavior in a conflict situation. This is the very reason for the statement that drastic changes are needed and required with respect to the training of police personnel and staff as a matter of inevitability and great urgency. This represents one aspect. The other is the lack of a proper legal and regulatory framework related to the operation and regulations of the Force. In this sense any other reaction than careful approach to problems and events by police personnel would be almost miraculous to see. This unfortunate state of affairs is sensed and conceived by both the population and the police alike.

The problems touched on, in some instances rather superficially, perhaps give some indication of the most important tasks ahead to aid improvement of law enforcement in general terms in this country. It is only hoped that the majority of the problems mentioned in this essay will be solved eventually. Adopting and adapting international experiences to local conditions would help substantially.

A Note of Caution on Uncritical Cooperation in the Development of Police

by
Jorgen Jepsen

In a situation where we are all gathered in a friendly atmosphere, working jointly on "how to make police bigger and better", I feel a bit embarrassed by not being able to resist an urge to issue a note of warning. It may be out of place to warn against the dangers of policing, but nevertheless I feel strongly that this conference should not end without pointing out to our Hungarian friends the need of taking our good advice with a grain of salt.

I would like to make three *main points of reservation:*

First, I must warn that police may become too much of a success. In Western Europe we witness at the moment a growing popular demand for more police and greater powers to – as evidenced e.g. by efforts to create a Europol with powers to conduct "hot pursuits" into the territories of other member states – the establishment of large police information systems (SIS), etc.

There are understandable, but to my mind, overrated and insufficient grounds for this development. The rapid social changes we are presently experiencing, also in Western Europe, make the populations uneasy; experienced problems in social life make the search for explanations and scapegoats inviting and rewarding for politicians looking for causes with popular appeal.

Some of the elements behind the plans for increased police cooperation in Western Europe clearly indicate what the directions are of the fears or attempts to instill fear in the population. Catchwords, such as "drugs" (narcotics), "terrorism", major "invasions" of migrant populations from Northern Africa and other old colonies, not to mention the former East Bloc countries, crime in the streets, "hooliganism", and similar moral panics in Western Europe are apt to evoke stress, public unrest and demands that "something must be done". Drug addicts, terrorists and "fake" refugees are, in Bruun & Christie's terminology, *ideal enemies,* suitable targes for repressive police action, nationally and on an international basis.

The police like to present themselves as being effective regarding these things: catching terrorists, stopping foreigners with fake papers, and intercepting large quantities of illicit drugs are police events reported to the public with great statisfaction. But is it necessarily "effective" to seize 20 or 40 kilogrammes of heroin, if the annual seizures altogether amount to 5-10% of all heroin coming into the country? Or could it be, that a certain amount of police seizures are rather supporting prices on the illicit market by taking excess drugs out of the trade, thereby promoting structural rationalization, promoting one group of traffickers rather than its competitors? As suggested by Utrecht Chief of Police, J. Wiarda (Social Kritik, no. 6, 1988), it may be "effective" in promoting a positive view of drug police work, but counter-productive in limiting the long-term supply of illicit drugs by keeping up prices and thereby profit.

And is it "effective", when police forces (in e.g. Denmark) arrest and maltreat darkskinned "foreigners" on vague grounds of suspicion of intentions of illegal entry, just because they estimate that they have insufficient funds to live on during their expected tourist visit to our countries? Must not "efficiency" be measured against a set of values, of which security is just one?

In my opinion international police cooperation and the promotion of internationalization involve also an often too uncritical importation and spread of ideologies and control models from one social and cultural context to countries with different cultures, values and traditions. The upcoming EC concept of "unwanted persons" to me carries with it considerable risks of miscarriage of justice and abandonment of traditions of hospitality to persons persecuted in their home countries. Our own Danish traditions for treating the refugees from Hitler's persecutions, even before World War II, represent a frightening historical example that should instill caution today.

The belief in control as a primary value in modern societies represents a type of magic thinking which is becoming increasingly popular in our situation in Western Europe. But control is no magic solution to basic social problems of unemployment, economic under-privileged status or inhumane living conditions in modern concrete slum cities. And policing is manifestly inefficient as a solution to the drug problem. Nevertheless, in recent years social efforts directed at drug addicts have been cut in favour of increased drug police forces.

I would, therefore, suggest extreme caution in accepting Western models of reaction to problems, which place major emphasis on policing. Control is like a narcotic; with increasing use of it, tolerance develops and there is a tendency to constantly increase the dosage and to become dependent upon it, to the detriment of other aspects of social life. So, please do not repeat our mistakes out of momentary enthusiasm for Western ways.

Secondly, I would like to warn against an overly positive acceptance of new technology. In Denmark for many years we placed policemen in rather fast cars equipped with various types of communication gadgets. Soon they will also have mini-terminals for computer check of e.g. stolen vehicles and suspicious-looking persons. The number of police stations were reduced in the name of centralization and efficiency.

The lures of data technology are the core of most policemen's dreams of efficiency. But large data banks carry several risks. One of these, paradoxically, gives rise to some hope: The amount of information present may be so overwhelming that the system is self-defeating. As, e.g., when the German police searched for the Schleyer abductors and found them via the data bank, but together with so many other suspects that they disappeared in the data crowd.

On the other hand, this also means that many innocent (or less dangerous) people come into the focus of police attention. Some consider this a risk we all have to bear in order to keep up a civilized society in peace. But is this type of society with the amassing of data really so "civilized" that it is worth the price of continued and extensive surveillance? Here I think we in Western Europe could draw some lessons from the past of our Eastern European friends. The build-up of a centralized European information system deserves more public scrutiny than has characterized the debate so far. The Danes' "no" to the Maastricht Treaty on June 2nd could be seen as a sign of awareness of the democratic deficit which has so far characterized the Union plans in general, and of the secretive build-up of Europen police cooperation towards a Europol in particular. Even the Danish police says "no to Europol."

My third and final note of caution concerns the popular notion of "community policing." In my country – as in several other Western European countries – it is gaining foothold as a reaction to the above-mentioned problems of alienation and centralization. "District police," "neighbourhood watch" and similar devices are instruments for getting police back to the streets and into contact with "citizens." Another very popular development in Denmark is the cooperation between social services, schools and the police in the so-called "SSP-cooperation-scheme." The participants are very enthusiastic about it, but social workers outside the programmes are skeptical towards sharing of information in relation to individual cases (as opposed to information about general deficits in local community resources).

The idea of a "social police" is ambiguous. On the one hand, it is important that policemen have "social understanding," i.e. that they are not too far away from those they are to service and control. Neither in relation to their own social status or in relation to their self-perception. Ambitions, police subculture and relations to the power structure should not be so powerful as to set them off also from the least fortunate members of society. But on the other hand, it should be remembered that police are not social workers. A Norwegian experiment with "social police" after some time in operation showed that the "social" policemen could not themselves handle the social problems of their clientele. They became referral-persons. And their closer relation with some of their young clients made it possible for the "social police" to give discrete tips to their investigative colleagues, who then became more efficient in clearing cases. This type of role-blurring is only "effective," if certain other basic values are disregarded. In relation to neighbourhood watch, I will maintain that the citizens are not – and should not be – "the eyes and ears of police." To us in Western Europe this basic assumption is being challenged by some of the developing attempts in community policing. Rather the police should be in the eyes of the citizens, and in full view.

As important as "police control of local communities" is "control of police by the local community." But who is "the local community?" In the Danish local police control boards, manned by police (!) and local politicians, some of the politicians are supporting tough police methods, rather than being a guarantee against excessive use of force. Will local managers of businessmen be more representative? Or should the control board not (also) represent the section of the local population most subject to control?

If local police boards representing links between police and the community are not to be seen as fake legitimation of police violence and subservience to local power elites (with freedom to act as it may suit local police corps in return for seeming "community attachment") it seems necessary that the police boards also represent critics of the system – and that these are not only one or two symbolic pawns of the system, but represent a broad cross-section of the community.

The great danger is that the police become a pervasive element in local politics, providing superficial evidence that social problems are "under control."

To avoid this danger of pseudo-success I would prefer, rather than making police bigger and better, to make police smaller and better.

The Police and Stereotypes of Ethnic Minorities – the British Experience

by
Michael Rowe

Introduction

As 1993 approaches and European integration apparently proceeds ahead one might expect the salience of racial and national identity to diminish. If Europe is to become the new super-state then one might expect that national identity may become of no more importance than regional identity is at the moment. We may be forgiven for imagining that the creation of a new model European culture and identity would render the crude nationalisms of the past as redundant as the nation states themselves. On present evidence, however, this does not appear to be the likely trend. The electoral rise of far-right parties in France, Italy and Germany during the first quarter of this year suggest that immigration and national identity remain issues of importance in many Western European countries. The moves towards expanding the European Community to include countries as diverse as Greece, Sweden and perhaps eventually even Hungary, Czechoslovakia and Poland seem likely to make the issue of large-scale migration one of the most difficult and emotive of all those the EC must deal with.

The implications of this for the police are perhaps more pertinent than for many other agencies of government and society. Clearly the police may be said to be at the hard-edge' of social control and, as Lord Scarman[1] noted in the British case, may have to deal with the manifestations of problems which have their roots in areas where the police have no competence and no responsibility.

---

[1] Lord Scarman is a senior British judge. His report into the riots that occurred in Brixton, London in 1981 has become perhaps the most influential document on the debates concerning the proper role of the police in society.

This paper will examine some of the issues that have resulted in a perceived lack of consent offered to the police by much of the ethnic minority communities in British society. In his report into the Brixton disorders of 1981, Scarman (1981) described the relationship between the police and the ethnic minority community in Lambeth as a "tale of failure." In particular I shall focus on the question of police stereotyping of ethnic minorities and the implications of this for the effective policing of these communities. It is clear that there are other issues that will influence the relation between ethnic minorities and the police, but for the sake of this paper I shall concentrate on this particular phenomenon. First I will examine one of the major reasons that is often cited for this stereotyping; namely a lack of ethnic minority police officers (who could counter the preconceived notions of white officers and who would not be inclined to share these stereotypes in any case). Second I shall refer to the debate over police training that has taken place since the urban disorders of the early 1980s. Then I will discuss those aspects of police work which may contribute to the reproduction of stereotypes. Finally, I will mention the political role that the police have played and discuss the use by the police of crime figures to further their political aims.

What are the implications of large scale migration for the relationship between the police and the public? The first clarification that needs to be realized is that the police do not have a homogeneous 'public' with whom to interact. While I do not want to give the impression that this is an entirely recent phenomena, it is true to say that the population of many European countries is likely to become more diverse, rather than less, over the next ten or twenty years. If we are to assume that the police have a more straightforward role to play in a society that shares many similar demands and expectations of them, as well as sharing a common experience in their relation with other agencies, then it seems reasonable to assume that a multi-faceted population, with different demands and concerns, and, most importantly, with hugely different degrees of access to, and satisfaction from, other agencies, then the role of the police, as we have come to expect is, becomes a great deal more difficult. The question becomes: Is it possible for the police to secure legitimacy in a diverse and potentially profoundly unequal society?

One important definition needs to be made before I begin my discussion. The term 'ethnic minority' is commonly used without precision. In reality it appears to me, at least in the British context, that almost everyone technically belongs to one ethnic minority or another, thus Britain actually may contain those of a Scottish ethnic, an Irish ethnic, a Polish ethnic, a Malaysian ethnic, a Jewish ethnic, and all points in between, but to try and assert or identify a distinctly British ethnic would, I suspect, prove next to impossible. Clearly the term is generally used to refer to those who are from, or descended from, South-East Asian and African and Caribbean origin. Yet it is equally clear that the term can be used to describe those of Australasian descent or East European descent or Oriental descent. In popular and academic discussion the phrase is commonly equated simply with those who are also labeled 'black'. Any typology which is applied to human beings seems to be doomed to be inaccurate in many cases, and this area of ethnic identity seems to be more problematic than most. Despite serious reservations about the use of the term 'ethnic minority' I shall use it here, for the sake of simplicity, to refer to those who are either from or descended from Africa, the Caribbean or the Indian sub-continent. We must be aware of the limitations of the term and I feel that a fresh look is needed at this issue of identification and to consider its continued relevance in the light of these difficulties. This is not the place for such a discussion, however.

Stereotypes and Culture

My main contention is that the police (and other elements of the criminal justice system) are guilty of generalising about entire communities on the basis of their experience of certain sections of that community, i.e. those that commit crime. Gilroy (1987) cites the case of Everton Samuels who, when in court for the possession of cannabis, refused the judge's offer of a job on the grounds that it would involve him travelling for several hours each day to get to and from this proposed place of work. On hearing him turn down the offer Judge Argyle commented that his actions 'did his people no good'. After the riots in Toxteth in 1981 the Chief Constable of Merseyside, Kenneth Oxford, was quoted in the Daily Mail newspaper explaining the cause of the riot as follows: 'their fight was with us, the police, a symbol of authority and discipline which is an anathema to *these people*[2] (emphasis added)'.

It is hard to imagine a white person being held up as a representative of the entire white population. The ethnic majority community, if one can be said to exist, are not treated in this manner. Crimes committed by white people are not taken to be symptomatic of the whole white community. Rather they tend to be regarded as dysfunctions of individuals, caused perhaps by their pathological shortcomings or, more liberally, by the material circumstances in which they find themselves. For much of the black community, however, this is not the case. Whole sections of these communities have become stereotyped as criminal, often because of their supposed cultural traits. The fact that, as the Institute of Race Relations

---

[2] Cited in Murdoch, G. Reporting the Riots: images and impacts. In Beyon, I. (ed.) (1984), Scarman and After. Oxford: Pergamon Press.

(1979) have demonstrated, the police have often tended to over-police ethnic minority cultural events, and thus prioritise them as potential scenes of criminal behavior, it might be said that all those who may share this culture will also be criminalised. Even those generally considered to take a liberal approach to policing have tended to look at culture as part of the explanation. John Alderson (1984), former Chief Constable of Devon and Cornwall, has argued that the cultural propensities of ethnic minority communities are one reason why ethnic minority-police relations are often strained. Supposed cultural traits such as the smoking of marijuana, for example, thus become indicative of the behavior of all young African Caribbean men which serves to identify all young black men as criminally inclined. The fact that young black men are more likely to be stopped and searched on the streets, for example, would tend to suggest that the police are inclined to view such people as criminals. The Islington Crime Survey (1986) suggests that 52.7% of black men under the age of 25 years had been stopped by the police during the last twelve months. This compared with just 31% of young white men being stopped during the same period. In an earlier study Smith (1983) found that young black males were likely to have been stopped four times in any one year, compared to whites who could expect to be stopped just two and a half times. In a recent newspaper article John Smith, Deputy Commissioner of the Metropolitan Police, admitted that 'too many people, including police officers, were starting to think that all black youths who were out on the street were engaged in crime'.[3] The fact that so few of those stopped are subsequently arrested, let alone convicted in a court, demonstrates the fallacy of such attitudes.

How has this situation arisen? Why should the police in Britain erroneously regard certain sections of the population as more inclined to commit crime? (Incidentally the research conducted by Davis (1980) demonstrates the historical parallels in this matter.) Is this a result of a deliberate attempt to create a popular 'demon' which can serve the interests of the police vis-a-vis the rest of society to achieve improved resources and powers? Alternatively some argue, including on occasion the police themselves, that prejudices of this sort are endemic to British society as a whole and are therefore beyond the scope of the police. Poor police training in 'human awareness' is also sometimes cited as a contributory factor and the relative under-representation of these ethnic minorities in the police force compared to their proportion of the population as a whole is also often referred to. Lambert (1970) has written that the lack of ethnic minority officers exacerbates the problem caused by the lack of contact between (white) officers in contexts other than those involving alleged criminal behavior. Of course, there is no real reason why we should have to isolate one of these factors at the expense of the

---

[3] The Guardian, 27 April 1992, p. 19. Good Boy for the Job.

others. It seems likely to me that all of these factors may be involved and that it is precisely their inter-connectedness which makes this problem appear so intractable. For the sake of the ethnic minority communities involved and ultimately for the police and the public at large, it is nonetheless vital that attempts are made to oppose such stereotyping. I now propose to examine some of the issues, already outlined, which may be contributory factors in the perpetuation of the stereotype of ethnic minorities as criminal.

Police Recruitment and Training

The relatively small number of ethnic minorities in the British police force compared to the presence of ethnic minorities in the British population overall is often cited as a major obstacle for the development of good police-ethnic minority relations. In 1983 the Metropolitan Police contained some 25,000 officers, of this number only 183 were black or Asian (Boateng, 1984). By 1991 this figure had risen to some 430 ethnic minority officers in the Metropolitan Force Met (Imbert, 1991). The ethnic minority population of Britain is estimated at approximately 5 per cent of the total population; on this basis we could expect 1250 ethnic minority officers in the Met alone. Clearly, and the Metropolitan Police acknowledge this, ethnic minorities are massively under-represented amongst the ranks of British police officers. The following table indicates the number of ethnic minorities working as police officers in the whole of Great Britain and the ranks that they held in February 1992:

	Total No. of Officers	Ethnic Minority Officers
Chief Constable	48	–
Deputy Chief constable	63	–
Assistant Chief Coastable	133	–
Chief Superintendent	603	1
Superintendent	1,573	3
Chief Inspector	2,377	4
Inspector	6,939	22
Sergeant	20,540	95
Constable	95,952	1,506
TOTAL	128,228	1,631

Source: Home Office

The lack of ethnic minority officers tends to re-enforce the view of many black people that the police are a 'white' organisation who are inevitably hostile to them. Clearly white officers cannot interact with ethnic minorities with the same empathy and understanding that an ethnic minority officer could. This problem may be especially exacerbated in the reporting of racist attacks when a white officer cannot have the same appreciation of the implications of such actions as an ethnic minority officer who many have faced a similar situation in his own private life.

As I have mentioned the police force themselves have realised the importance of trying to rectify this situation by advertising for ethnic minority officers and by outreach work designed to take police recruiting officers into schools and colleges. These attempts are worthy and seem to be one practical means of trying to tackle what is an extremely difficult problem. The effects of resources aimed at encouraging ethnic minorities to join the police force may well be outweighed, however, by the negative effects of any case similar to that of Surinder Singh (the officer from the Nottinghamshire force who, in 1991, became the first officer to successfully sue the police for racial discrimination after he was repeatedly passed over for promotion to the rank of detective) receives public attention. The imprisonment, in early 1992, of several police officers from the Metropolitan Police for a physical attack of a black taxi driver can only serve to further hamper the attempts of police trainers and recruiters to attract more ethnic minority interest. There is something of a dilemma here for police managers; on the one hand they wish to attract more ethnic minorities into the job whilst, at the same time, they wish to be seen to deal publicly with complaints of racism and discrimination, the evidence of which may jeopardise these efforts.

In many respects this problem seems to be an intractable one. What is more it is clearly not a problem faced by the police alone. Employment in Britain, in both public and private spheres, remains an area of great racial discrimination (see, for example, Brown, 1984). The problem for the police is that they are unable to attract more ethnic minority recruits because the police force is not regarded as a suitable career for members of ethnic minority communities. Scharman (1981, 5.6-5.15) noted that there are no straightforward simple explanations that can explain this apparent reluctance on the behalf of ethnic minorities to join the police. He cites family and peer group pressure as well as fear of being ostracised by racially prejudiced colleagues as two common reasons for non-application. It is in this way that ethnic minority officers may be considered as 'double victims' – not only do they face prejudice from their fellow officers, but they also may face the prospect of isolation within their own community.

A variety of measures were discussed by Scharman as possible means of countering the under-representation of ethnic minorities in British police forces. The use of a strict quota system (whereby officers would have to reflect exactly the population composition of their area) and any reduction in the formal entry requirements are both rejected by Scarman as patronising and, therefore, ultimately ineffective means of improving the relations between police officers and ethnic minority communities. He did, however, recommend that the police provide additional training to bring the standards of ethnic minority applicants up to the required level and such an approach was tried in Derbyshire, for example.

So it seems clear that one way in which the stereotyping of black people as criminals by police officers may be overcome, to some extent, is by genuine attempts to make our police forces more representative of the ethnic background of the wider community. If we accept that stereotypes are bred, as much as anything, on ignorance and mystery about the real nature of individuals' lives then we may assume that greater contact with ethnic minorities in a working relationship may help to improve matters. There would also be benefits to be gained from the enhanced image for the police that would accrue from better representation. Although there will be no overnight success in such an endeavour it is imperative that processes are conceived which can at least begin to set the balance right.

One factor mentioned above was the difficulty that ethnic minority officers face with regard to racism amongst their colleagues. The case of Surinder Singh deserves mentioning once more as it was one of the more remarkable (and horrifying) of its kind. During the course of his pursuit of damages for being overlooked for promotion Singh claimed, and was supported by the evidence of others, that he had to endure a stream of racist name-calling and abuse from his fellow officers. When incidents such as this receive publicity the damage that can result to the image of the police is, not surprisingly, enormous. The extent of racism amongst police officers is impossible to predict. Extensive catalogues exist of incidents where officers have acted in racist manner. The alleged incidents range from name calling to beatings and even deaths in custody. Blake (1982) has detailed the fact that Scarman's report into the Brixton disorders ignored evidence that officers wore 'ace of spades' ties and carried an array of 'barbarous unauthorised weapons' whilst patrolling the London borough of Lambeth. The Institute of Race Relations (1979) has also documented numerous allegations of over policing of ethnic minority events and cases of individual police racism.

Of course, it is hardly suprising that racist police officers should exist, after all they are part of, and have been educated and socialised by, a society which, historically and culturally, has strong racist elements. The question should perhaps be: what action is taken to (a) prevent racists joining the force and (b) to discipline or dismiss those officers who act in a racist manner. Scarman recommended that the police should develop a scientific test for would-be applicants in order to determine which are racist and that racially discriminating behaviour should be made a specific offence under the Police Discipline Code, an offence which would normally be punishable by dismissal (1981, 5.14 and 5.41). The latter of these recommendations was rejected by Home Secretary Whitelaw in November 1982 on the grounds that the Code already contained scope to deal with such incidents (see Benyon, 1984). This may be the case, but the police seem to have failed to grasp an opportunity to make a positive stand against racism.

There has been a debate concerning the nature of investigations of complaints against the police for many years in Britain. I do not intend to dwell on the details of this debate in this context, but I shall endeavour to outline the salient features. Under the 1964 Police Act, a Police Complaints Board was established so that complaints made by the public could be investigated by the police themselves and reported and acted upon where appropriate. In general, officers from a force other than that subject to complaint would investigate the case in question. Many groups, for example, the Greater London Council, established a whole range of police monitoring groups in relation to ethnic minorities, the policing of domestic violence and the policing of gays and lesbians (see GLC, 1986). From the 1970s onwards, it was argued that this system did not offer a sufficiently impartial or public means of investigation. The 1984 Police and Criminal Evidence Act replaced the Police Complaints Board with the new Police Complaints Authority. Under this system complaints that are considered of serious enough consequence are investigated by police officers from another force but, and this is the key, the investigation is overseen by an independent team to whom reports must be made. No member of this executive body is allowed to be, or ever to have been, a police officer.

Whilst these moves were welcomed by many, it remains a concern that complaints against the police are not treated with sufficient gravity and that the police are still to some extent able to cover up their actions in the face of an inquiry.

'Cop culture'

The term 'cop culture' was coined by Reiner (1978) to describe the social and psychological features which may be associated with police work. Many critics have argued, including many police officers, that Reiner's description of the mores of policing are generalised to such an extent that they may be of no use and it is clearly important to be aware of the dangers of such generalisations. Reiner (1978) suggested that police officers tended to be 'hard boiled, pessimistic, at best tragic at worst cynical and bitter conservative in the broad moral sense, (and probably the narrow political sense too)'. Although officers may feel aggrieved at such a description, and clearly it does not apply to all officers, some of Reiner's findings seem less controversial. He suggested that the very nature of police work, with long hours of bordom and occasional exciting and dangerous periods, engenders a strong feeling of identity amongst officers. Many officers, he found, tend to socialise with one another, perhaps as a result of the vagaries of shift work, resulting in a close knit culture which tended towards social inclusion and a strong sense of values and propriety. The fact that the background of recruits suggests that this culture will tend to be white, male and lower middle class is especially important when one considers the policing of areas and events which may not be characterised in this way. Boateng (1984) noted that 80 per cent of recruits to the Metropolitan Force came from outside London and were thus unlikely to be familiar with the kinds of areas, and the problems that they face, and will be called upon to police. This is clearly another way in which officers may tend to rely on their preconceived notions of such localities and their people. If police officers have never had any significant contact with people from ethnic minority backgrounds on any level other than that of their work then it seems hardly surprising that they may become liable to fall back on the ill-informed prejudices of the media and other factors which help to generate and perpetuate stereotypes and prejudices. It is this difficulty that has led many police forces to include in their training programmes the opportunity for officers to spend a weekend living with a family from an ethnic minority in order that they may come to empathise with them as individual human beings rather than in terms of the preconceived notion of 'the Asian' or 'the African Caribbean'.

What I am identifying here, then, are the associated problems of the personnel profile of the police which enable the perpetuation of stereotypes of black people. On the one hand the lack of ethnic minority officers has been identified as a major stumbling block which the police need to overcome if they are to gain the consent of the ethnic minority communities in Britain. They may try to overcome this with specially targeted recruitment drives and campaigns and they may also offer additional support for applicants from such backgrounds. The difficulties in achieving this should be recognised but should not be an excuse for inaction.

Secondly, there appears to be a related problem in terms of some of those who are already officers. Reiner and others have suggested that the nature of much police work seems to result in a 'macho' culture which values physical ability, toughness and power above other attributes which may prove equally adept, if not superior, in the context of police work.

Thus I believe that I have shown that there are a range of structural features of policing which allow and perpetuate the stereotype of ethnic minorities as criminals. The most appropriate methods for seeking to rectify these are widely debated and some of them have been briefly mentioned already. I shall now examine another feature of this argument which draws our attention to the wider political role of the police as a pressure group seeking to advance their own interests, rather than seek simply to fulfill their role as the preventors and detectors of crime and the upholders of public order.

'Race' and crime figures: true or false?

Perhaps the most invidious of all stereotypes of black people is that of the young black male as 'mugger'. As Hall, et al, (1978) have chronicled the British scare about the phenomena of 'mugging'[4] began in the early 1970s when fears first expressed in the U.S. about the rise of street crime were echoed in Britain. Although the press did acknowledge the activities of white 'muggers' the expression soon became synonymous with vicious attacks by black youths on white elderly women. This image was propagated by many of those on the far right of the Conservative Party and by the neofascist National Front who enjoyed a limited amount of electoral success thoughout the 1970s.

The first point that needs to be made here is that the police, although involved in the creation and perpetration of this stereotype, cannot alone be held responsible for it. The press have clearly been central to this process of labelling black youths as criminal and the role of Members of Parliament,[5] and other public figures, should not be ignored.

Despite this qualification, though, the police have played an important role in the definition of black people as criminals. Nowhere has this been more apparent than in the releasing of highly selective statistics which purported to show that, in many parts of London, street crimes were committed largely by young black men. In March 1982 a press conference was held at New Scotland Yard to announce the crime figures for the previous year. Deputy Assistant Commissioner Kelland drew the attention of the press to one section of these figures that dealt with the number of cases of 'robbery and other violent theft'. These figures accounted for just three per cent of all the recorded crime for that period (no attention was drawn to any other category of crime) and apparently showed that these crimes had risen by 34% from 13,984 offences in 1980 to 18,763 in 1981.

---

[4] 'Mugging' is not actually an offence in law but it has become a by-word for street theft and robbery. This misnomer is important since the popular use of the term inevitably refers to a compilation of a variety of offences.

[5] After the outcry that occurred in 1982 over the police role in the crime figures released, the Metropolitan Police stated that they would no longer release the figures themselves. Since the figures were a matter of public record, however, the police had to release them to the Conservative M. P. Harvey Proctor in response to a Parliamentary question tabled by the right-wing Keep M. P. togethar in 1983.

Kelland also provided, for the first time, a breakdown of the racial origin of offenders and claimed that 55.4% of assailants were 'coloured' – clearly a massive over-representation for approximately 5% of the population.

Several qualifications and clarifications, not mentioned by the police officers at the time, of these figures (and crime figures in general) need to be made. Firstly there is the problem inherent to all crime figures that they do not reflect the true extent of any crime but rather the number of reported incidents. Thus a crime which receives a significant amount of publicity and discussion may tend to be reported more readily by the public. The second problem is one that I have already outlined which is that the figures released do not give any indication of the gravity of the offence or whether or not it was violent. This category can include incidences of pick-pocketing where the victim may not even be aware of their loss until after the event, as well as, crimes where the victim is threatened with serious physical violence.

The other criticisms of these figures apply to the attempt to break down the ethnic background of the perpetrators of the crimes. The figures that were released which claimed that 55.4% of offenders were black were based on the victim's perception of their assailant. The reliability of these is, therefore, open to question. Secondly the figures are not based on any records of convictions of offenders, in other words we can have no idea how many of these reported offences have actually been proven in a court of law. The third point refers to the context of these types of crime. As I mentioned the popular stereotype of the mugger was that he was young and black and that the offenders were popularly symbolised as elderly white women. The figures released by the Yard made no mention of the colour, sex or age of the victims – surely, if these details were available for the offenders the police must have been able to provide a similar profile of the victims. It has been demonstrated that Asians are fifty times more likely to be subjected to a street attack and black people 36 times more likely than are the white population (see Home Office, 1981). It is also true that ethnic minorities suffer disproportionately as victims of crime in general, although this may be caused more by the inner city areas where they live than due to their ethnicity (Tuck and Southgate, 1981).

Whatever the precise criticims concerning the reliability of these figures there can be no valid reason for their release. Even if the figures were wholly dependable what possible relation can there be between the colour of someone's skin and their propensity to commit crime? By releasing these figures the police were clearly implying the opposite. Otherwise why did they not release figures concerning the estimated height, weight or hair-colour of the offenders? Presumably these figures are not collated because they are not considered relevant or useful to the prevention and detection of crime. Why then is the ethnic origin of the alleged perpetrator seen as relevant? The inference is clear; black people commit most 'muggings' therefore, most black people are (potential) 'muggers'.

Several writers (Kettle, 1982, Sim, 1982 and Scraton, 1985) have located this series of events firmly in the aftermath of Scarman's recommendations following the Brixton riot of 1981 and the attempts by the police to divert this perceived challenge to their authority.[6] By apparently demonstrating the extent of the crime wave with which they were faced, the police were attempting to regain the initative in order to re-assert their role as the primary definers of the policing function. What better way of doing this than to conjure up the potent image of the threatening and dangerous black youth who could only be thwarted by the granting of more power to the police and by ending the Scarnsanite view that the community should be allowed to interfere with the cherished role of their police force. Kettle (1982) expressed this more succinctly than I can:

> Facts don't matter to an organisation that is fighting a dirty fight to preserve its own autonomy. What suits them are black muggers, battered white grannies and policing policies dictated by public panic rather than carefully assessed community needs.

Concluding Remarks

The process by which groups of people come to be endowed with certain characteristics or propensities is a complex and often subtle one. There is a danger that this paper may suggest that the police have been the prime mover in this process with regard to ethnic minorities in Britain. I must re-assert, therefore, that the police are but one actor amongst many on this particular stage. The role of the media has been well-documented[7] in this area and it seems clear that they must also bear a large degree of the blame for such dangerous misconceptions.

Despite this, however, the police must not be permitted to hide behind the fact that this is a phenomenon for which they alone are not responsible. The policing function is of fundamental importance to any society and it is incumbent upon the whole of society to demand that this

---

[6] Although Scarman denied that the police were institutionally racist and generally endorsed much of the work of the police he did suggest that it was 'essential that a means be devised of enabling the community to be heard not only in the development of policing policy but in the planning of many, though not all, operations against crime' (Scarman, 1981, 5.56). The idea that the community should be involved in the policing function at such a grassroots level was seen by many officers as a direct threat to their independence and integrity.

[7] See, for example, Searle (1989) and Gordon and Rosenberg (1989).

function is performed in a just and equitable manner. It is clear that any breakdown in the relation between the ethnic minority communities and the police may have damaging consequences that range beyond those directly involved. Any loss in confidence in the police that leads to non-cooperation will have a detrimental effect on the police's ability to maintain public order and prevent and detect crime.

Briefly, then, I have identified two elements to the police's contribution to the stereotyping of black people as criminals. On the one hand we have what might be described as the structural issues relating to police recruitment, training, canteen culture and the like. These are issues which the police themselves must, and in many cases are, confronted with advertising campaigns, improved training in terms of both quality and quantity, and a closer involvement of the local population (of whatever ethnic origin) in the planning and delivery of policing. All these factors will be in the long-term interests of the whole population.

The second issue I have identified is more malign. It is clear that the police, closely aided by the media, have, through the highly selective release of crime figures, contributed directly to the image of the black youth as 'mugger'. There can be no explanation for this other than that this was part of an attempt by police officers to reassert their primacy in the provision and direction of policing. It is quite possible that such events will not happen again in this form and the police leaders, if they are to remain credible in their roles, must ensure that it never does.

Notes and References

Alderson, J. (1984): *Law and Disorder*. London: Hamish Hamilton.
Benyon, J. (ed.) (1984): *Scarman and After*. Oxford: Pergamon Press.
Benyon, J. and Solomes, J. (eds.) (1987): *The Roots of Urban Unrest*. Oxford: Pergamon Press.
Blake, N. (1982): *The Police, the Law and the People*. London: The Haldane Society.
Boateng, P. (1984): *The police, the community and accountability*. In Benyon, J. (ed.) (1984.), *Scarman and After*. Oxford: Pergamon Press.
Brown, C. (1984): *Black and White Britain: the third PSI survey*. London: Heinemann Educational.
Davis, J.: *The London Garotting Panic of 1862: A moral panic and the creation of a criminal class in mid Victorian England*. In Gatrell, Lenman and Parker, (1980) *'Crime and the Law: the Social History of Crime in Western Europe since 1500'*. London: Europa.

Gilroy, P.: *The Myth of Black Criminality*. In The Socialist Register (1982). London: The Merlin Press, pp. 47-56.

Gilroy, P. (1987): *'Ain't No Block in the Union Jack – the cultural politics of only one race and nation*. London: Hutchinson.

Gordon, P. and Rosenberg, D. (1989): *Daily Racism: the press and black people in Britain*. London: Runnymede Trust. Greater London Council Police Committee (1986), *Policing London: collected reports of the GLC Police Committee*. London: Greater London Council.

Hall, S. et al. (1978): *Policing the Crisis: mugging, the state and law and order*. London: MacMillan.

Home Office (1981.), *Racial Attacks: report of a Home Office Study*. London: Home Office.

Imbert, P. (1991): *Preparing police to deal with a multi-cultured society*. In the International Contemporary Police Review, March-April 1991, pp. 2-8.

Institute of Race Relations, (1979), *Police Against Black People – evidence submitted to the Royal Commission on Criminal Procedure by the Institute of Race Relations*. London: Institute of Race Relations.

Jones, T., MacLean, B. and Young, J. (1986.): The Islington Crime Survey. Aldershot: Gower.

Kettle, M. (1982.): *Mugging Whitelaw*. London: New Society, 18 March 1982.

Lambert, J. (1970): *Crime, Police and Race Relations*. London: O.U.P. and the Institute of Race Relations.

Reiner, R. (1978): *The Blue Coated Worker: a sociological study of police unionism*. Cambridge: Cambridge University Press.

Scharman, Lord, *The Brixton Disorders 10-12 April 1981: report of an inquiry by the Rt. Hon. the Lord Scarman, O.B.E.,* London: HMSO November 1981 (Cmnd. 8427).

Scraton, P. (1985): *The State of the Police*. London: Pluto Press.

Searle, C. (1989): Your Daily Dose: Racism and the Sun. London: Campaign for Press and Broadcasting Freedom.

Sim, J. (1982): *Scarman: the Police Counter Attack*. In *the Socialist Register*. London: The Merlin Press, pp. 57-77.

Smith, D. J. (1983): *A Survey of Londoners – police and people in London*. Vol. 1. London: Policy Studies Institute.

Tuck, M. and Southgate, P. (1981): *Ethnic Minorities, Crime and Policing: a study of the experiences of West Indians and whites*. Home Office Research Study No. 70. London: HMSO.

Social Change, Police and Protection

by
Dr. Philip Rawlings and Dr. Betsy Stanko

Social change and crime panics

It is hardly surprising that the political, economic and social upheavals experienced during the last few years in Hungary have led to all sorts of concerns and fears. Nor should the reality of those fears be underestimated. As industries are closed and unemployment rises, there is worry about the uncertain future and even anger that early expectations appear not to have been fulfilled. Many sociologists have noted the way in which (during such times of upheaval) the phenomenon of the moral panic commonly emerges (Cohen 1980). Typically this takes the form of a rising concern about crime. In the case of a panic over street robbery in the United Kingdom in the early 1970s, Hall et. al (1978) argued that during an economic crisis such concern over crime enables the state to deflect criticism away from its own failure to deliver on promises, such as ensuring economic prosperity. The crime wave is presented as symptomatic of the country's problems, and the root of those problems is usually depicted as lying in a minority group. This group is presented as being atypical, and, therefore destructive of the nation's 'traditional way of life.'

What emerges is often a racist explanation of crime. The crime wave is blamed on minority groups about which little is known except that 'They' are different from 'Us' the dominant community. The crime wave is blamed on ethnic minorities, 'migrant workers', 'the underclass' or 'international criminals' – outsiders. These outsiders are regarded as having no stable, fundamental connection with the country in which they live and are, therefore, liable to create disruption. Criminal acts, which when committed by a member of the dominant community are regarded as the aberrations of individuals, when committed by a member of the minority group are seen as representative of the attitudes and behavior of the whole group. Implicit in the view that this minority community is criminogenic (even if it is not argued that all of its members are directly engaged in crime) is the horrifying, but horribly familiar idea, that in order to get rid of the crime problem there is a need not simply to eliminate the criminals, but to remove the whole community from which they are assumed to have come.

Such a crime panic coupled with the broader concerns generated by the uncertainties of social, political and economic change generally leads to calls for greater social control and discipline. There may be no desire to return to previous forms of government. So, for instance, in Eastern Europe there is no general call for the reinstatement of state socialism. However, there may be a yearning for what with hindsight, which should not be confused with perfect sight, now seems like the certainties and social order of that era. The past becomes something of a 'golden age' a time when life was more peaceful, more secure and more ordered; when doors could be left unlocked, when the streets were safe at night and when the sun always shone. Not surprisingly, the present day cannot compete with such a vision. Now jobs are difficult to obtain, the streets seem dirtier, crime seems to be rising, young people seem less polite and nowhere seems to be safe. As a result, there emerge calls for the strengthening of state institutions, such as the police, which are seen as holding the promise not just of stemming the advancing tide of disorder, but also of restoring order.

The consequence of seeing the police as having the key role in controlling crime is an acceptance of the need for more officers, more technology, more money and more legal powers. The price of defeating crime is often said to include some limitation on human rights. Yet, at the same time, there are what appear to be contradictory pressures. The desire to pursue the democratic ideal leads to suggestions which seem likely to improve the accountability of the police; hence, ideas such as community policing and encouraging greater courtesy by police officers when dealing with the public. However, in a general atmosphere which demands more law and order, the public is more concerned, or at least is represented by politicians as being more concerned, not so much with accountability as with the detection of crime. As a result the value of ideas, such as community policing, is likely to be seen in terms, not of greater democratic accountability, but of improvements in the ability of the police to detect crime by, for example, increasing the flow of information.

There is nothing uniquely Eastern European in any of this. Leaving aside the questions of whether crime and the fear of crime are actually rising, two sets of assumptions underpin the argument for more police and more police powers which is being made in the West as well as in the East. The first is that the police hold the key to crime control; that increasing the power of the police will lead to more detection and that more detection will lead to less crime. The second is that crime is almost exclusively committed by strangers in the public spaces which the police allegedly control. Crime within the private sphere of the home is not seen as a problem, except in so far as the home is invaded from outside by strangers.

Leaving aside the questionable nature of the assertion that giving the police more resources automatically leads to high detection rates (a view to which even government ministers in the United Kingdom no longer automatically subscribe), both of these assumptions are undermined by history and by victim surveys.

Historians working on the police in the United Kingdom and elsewhere take for granted the view that their field of study is defined by the police themselves. They examine police records to find out what the police did and how they did it. The focus is, in other words, on the actions of the police. But such a perspective is only part of the story. Where is the history of what the police did not do? Why is there no history of the policing of domestic violence or of racist attacks? An organization is defined not just by what it does, but also by what it does not do. We must study the silences, the refusals and the inactivities, the crimes with which the police did not deal, the gap between 'criminal law in books' and 'criminal law in action.' Neither the history of crime nor the history of the police can be written simply by an examination of what the police did.

Without this fuller history of the police, contemporary debates are likely to be distorted. For instance, if there is no history of the policing of domestic violence it may be assumed that the issue is a new one whose roots, therefore, lie in recent events, such as the rise of the women's movement since the 1960s; this would produce an entirely different perspective from a history which revealed that the reason why there is no history of the policing of domestic violence is because the police took no interest in this crime until relatively recently.

Much the same story emerges if the results of modern victim surveys are considered. These surveys show that the bulk of crime, even violent crime, is not reported to the police. Typically, this is because the victim believes that there is little the police can do. Low reporting means not just that the police are doing a fairly small proportion of the total crime work, but also that the public must be dealing with the bulk of such work.

Women, Men and the Fear of Crime

To us, therefore, one major obstacle in thinking about policing is to be found in the way the police and Western criminologists have come to define crime, and especially serious crime. This can be illustrated by examining an ever present conundrum of contemporary criminology: women report levels of fear of crime three times higher than men, but crime surveys seem to show that it is young men, not women, who are the most at risk of serious violence.

Western criminologists have tried to explain women's greater fear as something which exists outside their experiences as victims of crime. Some criminologists have characterized women as suffering from exaggerated feelings of vulnerability (at times, the words 'excessive' and 'irrational' are used to describe women's fear). Other criminologists note the importance of gender in determining fear, but attribute men's failure to report fear to their reticence over showing weakness.

In terms of police protection, this characterization of people's fear of crime has led, in Britain, to the launching of police and government sponsored safety awareness campaigns for women which focus on women's supposed fear of attack by strangers in public spaces. However, all the official data points to the danger posed to women as arising in private spaces and coming, not from strangers, but from men who are known to them, usually husbands, former husbands, boyfriends, or other relatives, friends and acquaintances.

Lessons of Protection for Policing

Our comments lead to three general conclusions. The first is that a radical re-thinking is required about the way in which we define crime and the kind of protection we wish to offer women and men in society. The second is that left to their own devices, the police will choose to focus their 'protection' efforts on identifiable groups, such as young, often ethnic minority men, and assume that women's fear is imagined rather than real. Finally, we must understand how people cope with their own protection, and when, and under what circumstances, they decide to involve the police. No matter how much the police may think that they have changed, if people do not wish to involve them in their affairs, even when a crime has been committed, they will not do so willingly. (See Rawlings and Stanko, forthcoming).

Notes and References

Cohen, S. (1980): *Folk Devils and Moral Panics,* Oxford: Martin Robertson.
Hall, S. et al (1978): *Policing the Crisis,* London: MacMillan.
Rawlings, P. & Stanko, E. (forthcoming): 'Precarious Protection'.

Topic IV.

Police Co-operation and Border Controls in a "New" Europe; an Indication of Trends for Change

by
Dr. Mike King

Introduction

Europe is composed of diverse multi-national, ethnic and cultural groupings. Nowhere is this more dramatically seen at this moment in time than in the territories that used to be Yugoslavia. However, with the move towards economic integration within many levels of a 'greater' or 'new' Europe, there are necessary consequences of standardization, harmonization and even enhancement of control. Increasing 'freedoms' of movement in goods, services, capital and people, and also incorporation for some, will have an impact of restriction and exclusion for others.

Some of these issues are addressed in this paper, which concentrates especially on change within European Border Control Policies and Police Co-operation. On the one hand we suggest (following van Reenan's (1989) conceptualization, which we elaborate later) an increasing trend towards policing system integration, both horizontally and vertically. This is taking place together with a corresponding formalization of the informal, in terms of practices which have been established already through bi- and multi-lateral cross-border control and police co-operation agreements between countries. On the other hand, there is a trend towards the 'layering' of exclusionary borders, from the internal to the external 'buffer zones'. Further, we posit an enhancement in the form of control involving networking, pro-active policing and intensification of penetration.[1] These trends can only be understood in the context of being 'necessary compensatory measures' to counteract an all-embracing notion of threat arising from an amalgam of terrorism, organized crime, drugs, clandestine immigration and asylum. The reality of that threat is questioned here.

Police Co-operation

Co-operation between the police in Europe is not a new phenomenon. Fijnaut (1991) suggests that moves towards police co-operation throughout Europe started as long ago as 1898 with a 'secret conference' held in Rome to combat 'violent anarchism' (p 104). The origins of the International Criminal Police Organization, Interpol, also date back to the International Criminal Police Commission founded in Vienna in 1923, and before that even to the international Criminal Police Conference held in Monaco in 1914.[2] Throughout the post-war period, there have also developed a large number of bi- and multi-lateral agreements among various countries in Europe for the exchange of intelligence information and, amongst other things, extradition. Some of these, for example, are the European Conventions on Extradition 1957, Mutual Assistance in Criminal Matters 1959, and Suppression of Terrorism 1977. During the 1960s there also were established the Cross Channel Conference and the Association of Airport and Seaport Police. However, developments over the last couple of decades are significantly different in that they embrace the notion of *common* internal borders and mean increasingly more than simply 'co-operation,' moving towards 'integration.' These are rooted in a number of treaties formalizing and establishing cross-border policing co-operative practices, such as that between Denmark and the Nordic Group in 1954, the Benelux countries [Belgium, Luxembourg and the Netherlands] in 1960, the Aachen Agreement between Germany and Belgium in 1969, and the Saarland Agreement between Germany and France in 1978.

Indeed, there is now a plethora of treaties and structures within the European integration domain, most of which have overlapping competence with respect to police co-operation. Some of these have been well illustrated by Reinke (1991:2) (see Figure 1.).

Figure 1.

Task-Specific Structure of Police Co-operation

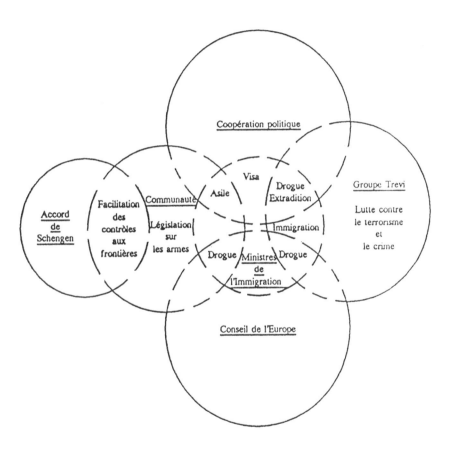

These in turn are complemented by task-specific structures, such as the *Comité Europeén de la Lutte Anti-Drog* [CELAD] and the Council of Europe Pompidou Group, against drug trafficking, the Ad Hoc Group on Immigration, *Group d'Action Financiere Internaionale* [GAFI], against money-laundering, *Unité de Co-ordination de la Lutte Anti-Fraud* [UCLAF] within the European Commission, against EC regulation fraud, and more generally by the Police Working Group on Terrorism [PWGOT][3] and the Customs & Excise Mutual Assistance Group '92 [MAG'92].

Of course, there are many problems associated with closer police co-operation or even integration. These not only involve the problem of 'sovereignty,' but also more complex practical issues from judicial harmonization, development of a European criminal code, training and technology to simple communication. We will not overly concern ourselves with these here, but will explore the indications of trends for future development.

From Schengen to Europol

The new Union Treaty [TEU] between the 12 European Community Member States, signed in Maastricht in December 1991, provides under Article K. 1. for the establishment of a European Police body, defining as a matter of 'common interest':

> Police co-operation for the purposes of preventing and combating terrorism, unlawful drug trafficking and other serious forms of international crime, including, if necessary, certain aspects of customs co-operation in connection with the organization of a Union-wide system for exchanging information within a European Police office (Europol), (Niessen, 1992:10).

This follows an agreement in principle between the European Council (Heads of State or government of the 12) at its summit in Luxembourg in June 1991 and a meeting of the TREVI Ministers in The Hague in December 1991 to adopt Chancellor Kohl's proposal made in 1988 to establish a Europol by the end of 1992. Its purpose will initially be as stated, to act as a central collection and dissemination point for information on crime generally relating to the EC area. The first stage of this will be the formation of a European Drugs Intelligence Unit [EDIU].

The basic model for police co-operaton in Europe is that of Schengen. There are two Schengen Treaties.[4] The 'Supplementary' Agreement[5] signed in June 1990 between Belgium, France, Germany (W), Luxembourg and the Netherlands is the realization of an earlier

'Basic' Treaty signed by the five in June 1985, stating their future intention of signing a document towards implementation.[6] The deadline for formal implementation of Schengen is the beginning of 1993[7] and since the signing of Schengen II, three more countries have joined, namely Italy (November 1990), Spain and Portugal (June 1991). This leaves only 4 EC member-state non-signatories, namely the UK, Denmark, Greece and the Irish Republic, although Greece was granted observer status in December 1991. Membership is not open to those outside the EC.

The Articles of Schengen are directed towards 'open' internal borders, for goods and services as well as people, immigration and asylum control and harmonization, closer police co-operation and the establishment of a Schengen Information System [SIS]. The policing and other controls are intended to be measures to compensate for the consequent loss of internal security through the reduction in border controls. We will discuss some of the problems arising from this later. Schengen II contains five main proposals for cross-border policing, which have a fundamental effect on the form of policing in those countries (although as mentioned earlier, many of the Schengen provisions are merely a formalization of the already existing informal practices). Firstly, it allows covert cross-border surveillance by other member-state police forces, including pro-active observation, in respect of persons 'under reasonable suspicion' of involvement in a (possible future) extraditable offence.[8] Secondly, it provides the right of 'hot' pursuit up to 10km within a neighbouring land territory (and unlimited within Germany), with varying powers of arrest/apprehension or 'security search,' where a 'spotted' person is suspected of either a reciprocally extraditable offence or has failed to report a serious accident or is an escapee from arrest/imprisonment. The third provision is for the exchange of 'liaison officers' through bilateral agreements. In fact this has been in force for some years, with Drugs Liaison Officers [DLOs] both between Schengen and EC countries and some in Eastern and Central Europe, too. Article 73 of the Treaty, however, also permits the 'controlled delivery' of drugs. Fourthly, the Treaty proposes the development of the SIS. This will be a computer information storage/retrieval data-base common to all Schengen member states, containing information on e.g. those wanted for arrest or under surveillance for a (suspected) extraditable offence or non-admissable aliens. The central SIS is being established in Strasbourg and is already undergoing trials *(Migration News Sheet,* May 1992:1). Finally, to compensate for the lack of formal border controls, there will be 'more selective controls' and internal 'spot checks' as a means of 'in depth defence'.

TREVI

The provisions of the Schengen model have to some extent been, and are increasingly being, taken over by the TREVI Group of Interior and Justice Ministers,[9] perhaps as a transitionary stage towards the establishment of an EC-wide Europol. TREVI, however, which was founded in 1976, is more of a non-institutional EC inter-governmental political policy-making structure. It is especially concerned with enhanced police co-operation among the 12 and establishing a common policy in areas that are thought to constitute a threat to stability, namely drugs, terrorism and immigration. In this connection too it is moving towards the establishment of a European Information System [EIS]. In addition to the Ministerial and Senior Official 'levels' it is, as was Schengen I, composed of four Working Groups. These are: I) Anti-terrorism, II) Public order, equipment & training, III) Drugs and organized crime, and IV) TREVI '92 Planning for abolition of borders including immigration. Unlike Schengen, it has no permanent secretariat, although for some years various fixed sites have been proposed including, in December 1990, the General Secretariat of the Benelux Group which also serves as that of the Schengen Group *(Migration News Sheet,* Jan. 1991:1).

To a large extent, a decision as to the location of both TREVI's permanent secretariat and the EIS will determine its future role in and the form of Europol. It is possible that the central EIS will be housed in Strasbourg, incorporating the SIS (which is there already) and the information system of MAG '92. However, it may altenatively, but unlikely we feel, be located in Wiesbaden, at the headquarters of the German *Bundeskriminalamt* and linked into their INPOL system. Lyons is another possibility with the Interpol General Secretariat or its European Secretariat as part of its current 5-year development plan.[10] Similarly, the siting of the EDIU will largely determine its future structure and orientation.[11] It may, for example, be merely an extension of respective national DIUs or Liasion Bureaus, or a structure towards a European Criminal Investigation Bureau with an eventual executive/operational role, accountable to a new EC supra-national body. The latter was implied in the Maastricht TEU, although is has been subjected to much debate. Article C provides that: 'the Union shall be served by a single institutional framework... while observing and building upon the *acquis communautaire'* (Niessen, 1992:4).

In whichever direction Europol proceeds, there is clearly a trend towards EC policing system integration. This is occurring on both distinct 'levels' of integration posited by van Reenan (1989). Firstly, horizontal integration, he suggests, is where police officers from one country operate in another. This can be seen in contemporary European police co-operation in terms of 'hot pursuit' or cross-border observation. An extension of this is also orientation-task specific operations, such as we have seen not only for drugs, but also football hooliganism and terrorism. In contrast, vertical integration is where 'a police organization is being created that can operate within the area of the EC... [presupposing] a central authority on which it depends, probably a central political power at EC level' (van Reenan, 1989:49). This may well be the form that an EDIU will take, or perhaps the UCLAF will be developed to an administrative police with the task of enforcing EC regulations.

Certainly, the dynamic of 'Europeanization' of policing systems is having an impact on national police organizational change. One can observe this in recent reorganization within the Belgian Police (de Cock, 1991) and also the Netherlands Police (den Boer, 1991b), in terms of centralization and co-ordination, as well as in England and Wales with regionalization and nationalization of Criminal Intelligence Units.

Border Controls

John Major, the Prime Minister of Britain, announced in April 1992 that 'The borders of Europe do not stop in the centre of our continent. We must not replace the iron curtain that has been torn down with a new regulatory net' (Donovan & Beavis, 29.4. 1992). In fact, developments in Europe towards integration for some are correspondingly creating multiple layers of exclusionary controls from the centre to the periphery, marginalizing also some of those caught within the net.[12]

The control of borders under Schengen are similar to those proposed for the EC and framed within the same notion of 'necessarily compensatory'. The main difference, however, is the required level of frontier deregulation, whether generally within internal borders or only controls against 'third country' nationals (or, as the UK argue, totally discretionary). As to harmonization of asylum procedures, exclusion policies, visa requirements and external border (including internal airport) strengthening to constitute a 'fortress' or 'ring of steel,' both are similar, with perhaps a 'softer' approach emanating from the EC.

'Harmonization' entails the establishment of a common list of countries whose nationals will need visas before entering the EC/Schengen area. Spencer (1990:3) has suggested that the list totals about 60 countries for the EC area under TREVI and the ad hoc Working Group on Immigration and approximately 115 for Schengen. 'Safe countries,' or rather those on the '2 x 5% rule,' are those where asylum-seekers for the preceding year constitute less than 5% of the total number and where more than 5% of whom received a favourable response *(Migration News Sheet,* March 1992:5). It also involves national introduction of visa requirements against 'refugee producing' countries. The first Commonwealth country to be controlled in this way by the UK was Sri Lanka in May 1985. Since then others have followed, including in October 1986, India, Pakistan, Nigeria, Ghana and Bangladesh, in July 1989 Turkey and in April 1990 Algeria, Morocco and Tunesia. From July 1990, Somali nationals *with* visas could no longer transit through Britain (Amnesty International 1990:26). Visa requirements were also introduced for Uganda in May 1991 *(Migration News Sheet, June 1991:4)*.

'Carrier Sanctions' introduced by most EC member-states reinforce smaller exclusionary practices by putting the regulatory onus on carriers, whether airlines, shipping or other transport companies, to ensure that any passenger intending to enter the country's 'external' border have a valid permit and other relevant documentation. Belgium passed such a law in July 1987; in October 1987 Denmark passed an amendment to its Aliens Act of 1983 imposing carrier sanctions; in January 1987 Germany (W) similarly amended its Aliens Law of 1965 and Italy passed a decree on this basis (A.3) in December 1989 (Cruz 1991:1-7). These regulations are now being questioned by some national courts. In Denmark, for example, fines imposed against Scandinavian Air Services were recently upheld by the Supreme Court *(Migration News Sheet,* March 1992:3), whereas the *Bundesververwaltungsgericht* in Berlin has condemned carrier sanctions as 'a violation' of A.16. of the Grundgesetz concerning the right to political ayslum *(Migration News Sheet,* May 1992:5).

In addition, a number of States have signed 'Readmission Agreements', which constitute *'de facto* buffer-zone[s] of immigration control' *(Migration News Sheet,* Oct. 1991:8). Austria has signed such agreements with Hungary and Romania *(Migration News Sheet,* April 1992:3), and similarly agreements were signed between the Schengen States and Poland in March 1991 *(Migration News Sheet, Oct. 1991:8).*

The borders are also changing between the EC and Czechoslovakia, Hungary and Poland. These countries, now known as the 'Visegrad Group', signed 'Association Agreements' with the EC in December 1991 and are likely to sign an agreement between themselves in Visegrad, Hungary, later this year towards the abolition of internal border controls (Niessen, 1992:13 & *Migration News Sheet,* April 1992:5). Further, the 19 EC and European Free Trade Association [EFTA] nations[13] signed an agreement for the establishment of an European Economic Area [EEA] in May 1992 providing a free-trading block with the same 'freedoms' as the EC (Commission of the European Communities, 7.5. 1992). Also, it has now been arranged that the NATO alliance is 'prepared to take on a peacekeeping role... throughout the 52 country Conference on Security and Cooperation in Europe' [CSCE] (Pick, 22.592).[14]

What we have, then, in respect of European border controls, is not one 'European' framework, at least in the short term, but many 'Europes.' These range from the inner core being perhaps Benelux, to Schengen, Trevi, EC and Visegrad, EEA, Council of Europe, CSCE, to the 'outer' being NATO[15] and thereby perhaps also incorporating the USA on the extreme periphery, but certainly within Europe as an 'observer' (Fijnaut, 1990). The impact of increasing incorporation is enhancement of internal and exclusionary external controls. Simply by examining the 'compensatory' policing strategies of Schengen II one can see a trend towards a networking and intensified penetration of control.

The notion of 'threat'

The debate of the effects of internal border control reduction and also the consequent necessity of enhancing internal and external controls is founded on two main presuppositions. Firstly, it is suggested that present border controls are effective, and therefore any reduction would need to be compensated for. Secondly, all those things which are currently controlled and thereby excluded from the internal area will, on the opening of the borders, 'flood in' thus posing a threat to security. Further, the notion of 'threat' unites individual possible 'problems' into one all-encompassing 'European internal security field,'[16] ranging from terrorism through to immigration. This has, in turn, the effect of enhancing especially pro-active controls against the possible 'threat' to a level greater than the equivalance of those currently in force or even the threats that are posed in reality.

There are a number of examples of these primary assumptions, the most basic of which would suggest that national borders are effective barriers against crime. *Bundeskriminalamt* President Boge, for example, argued in 1989 that 'organized crime will profit from the abolition of border controls' *(Bürgerrecht & Polizei,* 289-80). However, this raises the question as to the extent to which members of international criminal organizations actually recognize borders. Certainly, we are not attempting to deny the existence of organized crime, international terrorism or drug rings as problems. The 'Balkan route' is, for example, presumably an ongoing situation, now incorporating Hungary because of the 'closure' of Yugoslavia. The realities in these respects are, however, firstly that organized criminals and terrorists move relatively freely despite the existence of internal border controls and, regarding the movement of drugs, only a very small percentage of drug-seizures at borders are through 'cold' searches. To this extent, a reduction in formal and overt controls at fixed and known internal borders is unlikely to significantly alter the situation.

A large part of the 'fear' about the ineffectiveness of an external *cordon sanitaire* is the reliance on other nations. Clutterbuck, for example, has argued that:

> 'After 1992 ... any terrorist, criminal, drug trafficker or illegal immigrant, having crossed the Mediterranean and landed in a rocky inlet in Italy or Spain, will be free to move to Frankfurt or Paris or London (via the Channel Tunnel)' (1991:3).

A recent editorial in *The European* newspaper expressed similar fears, also pursuing *the 'lack* of security' continuum:

> 'Some [external] borders are still inadequately guarded. If internal frontiers also go, the EC's ability to control crime, terrorism and the scourge of drugs will be reduced; the member of illegal immigrants from North Africa and Eastern Europe ... will rise. That is no future for Europe'. (14-17.5. 1992:8).

Another illustration of this all-encompassing convergence of 'threat,' in this case the connection between mass migration, xenophobia and drug trafficking, is provided by Jamieson's suggestion that:

> The collapse of the Communist regimes has led to acute and previously unforeseeable problems of migratory movements. These affect the EC as a whole, but have particular implications for tackling the problem of drug trafficking ... Western European countries with already high unemployment risk exacerbating existing social tensions by allowing in a new tide of immigrants ... As far as the drug market is concerned, there is a risk that those who come and find no work or homes will be easy prey for traffickers (1992:13).

As we have already stressed, terrorism, organized crime, drugs, clandestine and mass immigration do collectively and individually pose problems for public order and social stability. In this sense, however, they need to be approached individually and realistically.

Conclusion

We have suggested there are three main trends in policing a new Europe. One is the process of Europeanization of policing systems towards integration on both horizontal and vertical levels. This involves enhanced co-operation, eventual harmonization of some aspects of criminal and judicial laws and procedure and the development of a central police organization with investigative powers. Secondly, there is a process of increasing 'common' border incorporation, resulting in a multi-layered system of exclusionary controls. Thirdly, there would seem to be a general enhancement of a 'control society.' All three trends are taking place within a context of an all-encompassing notion of 'internal threat continuum.'

As one submission to the House of Commons Home Affairs Committee on Practical Police Co-operation in the European Community (1990b)[17] stressed, the reduction in border controls will not entail a reduction in police controls, and 'law enforcement' such as police powers relating to 'stop and search,' terrorism, customs and immigration will remain (p 61). However, as argued by the Home Office, the existence of fixed border checks assists that policing task by providing the police with the opportunity to 'identify and examine travelling criminals and detain fugitives' (HCHAC, 1990b:21 (33)).

We feel that some compensatory measures for internal border control are necessary, as is enhanced police co-operation in Europe to combat serious crime within a changing Europe. However, such measures of compensation should not be over-protective to the extent of creating a significant increase in a 'control society' and consequent restriction in civil liberties in excess of the threat posed. Similary, the Europeanization of policing should not be conceptualized and operationalized within a notion of 'common threat.' This takes the form of, on the one hand, the embodiment of the process of universalization of crime into an 'internal security continuum.' On the other hand, that threat involves a suggested tendency that all crime is increasingly directed towards Europe, or that all migrants are attempting to 'flood' into Europe.[18] This needs to be counterbalanced with the reality of the situation.

Notes

1. cf. Cohen (1985) and Spitzer (2983)
2. For more information on the history of Interpol see: Anderson (1989) and ICPO-Interpol (1989).
3. This Group is modelled on TREVI, but is more practical and operational in orientation, having a membership of Special Branch and Security Service Officers involved in the area of anti-terrorism.
4. These are named after the town in Luxembourg in which the first Treaty was signed.
5. This Agreement is entitled the 'Convention applying the Schengen Agreement of 14 June 1985 between the governments of the states of the Benelux Economic Union, the Federal Republic of Germany, and the French Republic, on the gradual abolition of checks at their common borders.'
6. To this end, Schengen II) set-up four Working groups: I) Police & Security, with sub-groups i) drugs, ii) firearms, iii) immigration, IV) SIS; II) Movement of People; III)

Transport; IV) Movement of Goods. For a detailed account of both Schengen Treaties and their history see den Boer (1991a).

7. Although this is now unlikely before the end of March 1993, as SIS is not envisaged to be fully operational before then *(Migration News Sheet,* April 1992:1).

8. Namely murder, manslaughter, rape, arson, counterfeiting of currency, aggravated theft and receiving, extortion, abduction and hostage-taking, trade in human beings, illegal trafficking in narcotic drugs and psychotropic substances, arms and explosives, and illegal transport of toxic and harmful waste.

9. TREVI is named after a fountain in Rome, where it was first proposed that such an organization be formed, and also its first chairman, Mr. Fontayne. It is now commonly referred to as an abbreviation of 'Terrorism, Radicalism, Extremism and International Violence.'

10. Presently, about 90% of all communications traffic passing through Interpol concerns Europe (HCHAC, 1990b:3 (21)). Further, it has recently introduced a new computer facsimile transmission network, providing access-restricted 'computer encripted communications' with an 'Automated Search Facility' information system, X400. For some, this, together with 'updating' through the Interpol European Technical Committee for Co-operation initiatives, makes an attractive argument for an increased Interpol role in Europe (Birch, 17.1. 1992). However, this does not overcome the problem of Interpol primarily being an information exchange apparatus to that of undertaking an operational policing role.

11. This is also argued by le Jeune (1992)

12. For a more detailed discussion of this see King (1992)

13. Being the EC 12 plus Austria, Finland, Iceland, Norway, Sweden and Switzerland (with Liechtenstein having observer status within EFTA).

14. Presumably to counteract the current Franco-German and Belgian-Luxembourg army corps 'defence initiative.'

15. This is the sort of arrangement that was depicted by the House of Commons Home Affairs Committee (1990a:xix) as a series of widening and enveloping concentric circles.

16. This concept, together with that of 'security continuum' referred to later, is developed and clearly elaborated by Bigo (1992).

17. This submission was by the Association of Country Councils (Memorandum 6).

18. Whereas, on a world scale, the EC Member States only receive 5% of all refugees (Commission of the European Communities, 10.3. 1992).

References

Amnesty International (1990): United Kingdom: *Deficient policy & practice for the protection of Asylum seekers.*

Anderson, M. (1989): *Policing the World: Interpol and the politics of international police co-operation* (Clarendon Press).

Bigo, D. (1992): *The European Internal Security Field.* Paper presented to the European Consortium for Political Research Workshop on 'Police Co-operation in Europe after 1992' held in Limerick, Ireland, 30th March- 4th April 1992.

Birch, R. (17.1. 1992): *Why Europe Needs Interpol.* In: Police Review, pp. 120-121.

den Boer, M. (1991a): *Schengen: Intergovernmental scenario for European Police Co-operation.* Working Paper Series 'A System of European Police Co-operation after 1992', no. 5, December 1991 (Edinburgh University).

den Boer, M. (1991b): *The Police in the Netherlands and European Co-operation.* Working Paper Series 'A System of European Police Co-operation after 1992', no. 4, December 1991 (Edinburgh University).

Bürgerrechte & Polizei: Kontrollstelle Grenze: Sicherheitsverluste durch Aufhebung der EG-Binnengrenzkontrollen. In CILIP Nr. 2/1989:80.

Clutterbuck, R. (1991): *Technology and Civil Liberties.* In Counter-Terrorism in Europe; implications of 1992, pp. 3-10 (Research Institute for the Study of Conflict and Terrorism, February 1991).

de Cock, P. (1991): *The Operational Problems of Police Co-operation and Communications Between the European Police Forces.* Paper presented at a Seminar on European Police Co-operation, University of Edinburgh, September 1991.

Cohen, S. (1985): *Visions of Social Control: crime, punishment and classification* (Polity Press).

Commission of the European Communities (103. 1992): *Immigration and Asylum* Background Report (Press Briefing, ISEC/B 6/92).

Cruz, A. (1991): *Carrier Sanctions in Five Community States: incompatibilities between international civil aviation & human rights obligations* (Churches' Committee for Migrants in Europe, Briefing paper No. 4, Brussels).

Donovan, P. & Beavls, S. (1992): *Major Pledges EC Entry for Former Eastern Bloc.,* In The Guardian, 29.4.

The European: Passport to Crime, 14-17 May 1992, p. 8.

Fijnaut, C. (1990): *Europeanization or Americanization of the Police in Europe.* In Nederlandse Politic Academie: The 2nd Police Summer-Course, pp. 19-27.

Fijnaut, C. (1991): *Police Cooperation Within Western Europe.* In Heidensohn & Farell (eds): *Crime in Europe* (1991, Routledge), pp. 103-120.

House of Commons Home Affairs Committee (1990a): *Practical Police Co-operation in the European Community,* Vol. 1. (HMSO, 353-1).

House of Commons Home Affairs Committee (1990b): *Practical Police Co-operation in the European Community.* Memorandum of Evidence (HMSO, 363-i).

ICPO-Interpol (1989): *General Information* (General Documentation Service, Lyons)

Jamleson, A. (1992): *Drug Trafficking After 1992: a special report* (Research Institute for the Study of Conflict and Terrorism, April).

le Jeune, P. (1992): *Police Co-operation in Europe After 1992.* Paper presented to the European Consortium for Political Research Workshop on 'Police Co-operation in Europe after 1992' held in Limerick, Ireland, 30th March - 4th April 1992.

King, M.: *The Impact of EC Border Policies on the Policing of 'Refugees' in Eastern and Central Europe.* Paper presented to the European Consortium for Political Research Workshop on 'Police Co-operation in Europe after 1992' held in Limerick, Ireland, 30th March - 4th April 1992.

Migration News Sheet, Jan. 1991 - May 1992 (Brussels)

Niessen, J. (1992): *European Migration Policies for the Nineties After the Maastricht Summit* (Churches Committee for Migrants in Europe, Briefing per no. 7, Brussels).

Pick, H. (1992): *NATO Ready to be Europe's Peacekeeper.* In *The Guardian,* 22.5. 1992.

van Reenan, P. (1989): *Policing Europe after 1992: cooperation and competition.*, In *European Affairs,* 3 (2), Summer 1989 (Amsterdam), pp. 45-53.

Reinke, S. (1991): *The EC-Commission's Anti-Fraud Activity.* Paper presented at a Seminar on European Police Co-operation, University of Edinburgh, September 1991.

The Schengen (Supplementary) Agreement (June 1990) (Statewatch on-line database, Jan. 1992).

Spencer, M. (1990): *1992 and All That: Civil liberties in the balance* (Civil Liberties Trust).

Spitzer, S. (1983): *The Rationalization of Crime Control in Capitalist Society.* In Cohen, S. & Scull, A. (eds.): Social control & the State: historical & comparative essays (1983, Martin Robertson), pp. 312-333.

The Role of the Police and its Co-operation in Europe

by
Dr. László Salgó

First let's have a look at the police role in the society. In my opinion, the police is nothing else in the society but a firm, a special organization. If it is true, its product must be security. If security exists as a product in the society, a market must be found for this product. If the market can be found, there must be clients, buyers for this business. These clients are the citizens; this is the so-called all market policy regarding security as a business between people and police in the society.

The market is very poor in the totalitarian regimes because there is only one firm, the state, whose product is security. In democratic countries this market is very busy: there are insurance companies, security agencies, private enterprises and of course, the state too, offering their services as producers of security. A huge repertoire of security is available in this market depending on the wealth of the state (which is of course depending on the wealth of the inhabitants).

According to Max Weber: "The distinctive characteristic of a problem of social policy is indeed the fact that it cannot be resolved merely on the basis of purely technical considerations... which assume already settled ends. Normative standards of value can and must be the objects of dispute in discussion of a problem in social policy because the problem lies in the domain of general cultural values".

Undoubtedly this is the problem with crime, criminality and society concerning Hungary too. In Hungary there are and, of course, there must be general standards corresponding to all the European requirements and concepts, but in a new-born democracy which is being formed in Hungary, atavistic attitudes can be found too.

One of my starting points is the fact that security is the product of the police and a real social value at the same time with all of the characteristics of other social values.

"For Max Weber, legitimate power was the thread running through the action of a democratic political system providing its special quality, importance, coherence and order." Accepting the basic ideology and philosophy of Max Weber in Hungary the legitimate police must be one of the threads running through the action of a democratic political system, providing security for democracy and the political actions for the people. But, the police must not be either the Power itself (although it was told and interpreted in the last decades in Hungary by experts and university lectures) or one part of the Power. Following Montesquieu, the police must be taken to its theoretical position – as it is in democracies – regarding the Power as a part of the Executive.

And now, let me say a few words about the role of the Hungarian Police here, in the Carpathian Basin, in the middle of Europe.

In the early 1980s Prof. Jack Green from Michigan wrote an essay about police attitudes and behavior. Indubitably, Prof. Green characterized the U.S. conditions there, but amazingly I found many similarities to the Hungarian circumstances.

"...the police fall short on most dimensions: they lack an exclusively identifiable body of knowledge for training, education and practice; the particularistic applications of law enforcement preclude the realization of social values embodied in policing; the police cannot legitimately possess the autonomy attributed to professions due to "public trust" distinctions; operational discretion is deviant and oriented toward the protection of self interest; the police subculture acts not as a professional community but rather as a foil against organizational and public control; police motivation and commitment are individualistic and antithetical to professional service ideals; and bureaucratic rather than collegial interests guide police behaviour."

After these remarks, I think, it will be easy to understand the situation of the Hungarian Police in the late 80s, and the very beginning of the early 90s.

Figure 1.

The problems of the Hungarian Police between 1988–1991

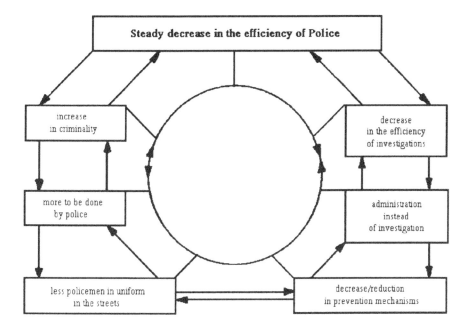

I think this figure (see Figure 1.) presents the significant problems of the Hungarian police. I know well, we have not enough time for a full explanation, that is why I do not want to comment too much about it.

Two points, however, should be mentioned.

This period was the nadir, the bottom of the hole as people harshly judged the Hungarian police because of the decreasing tendency of the efficiency of the police and the never previously experienced increase in criminal cases.

Second, several steps were, however, taken to reverse what seemed to be an irreversible trend. The first step taken by the Hungarian police towards European integration was to join Interpol. But it occured at least a decade ago. After a long silence, after the declaration of the Hungarian Republic on October 23, 1989, brand new alternatives were offered. Hungary became attractive to a wide range of different consulations and study tours to the West because of democratic developments. Such options were first initiated for the Hungarian police leaders but later for specialists as well.

Our Home Minister said once that he was convinced the only enemy will be crime in Europe instead of antithetical political views and nations in opposition to one another.

I may enumerate the numerous nations with whom we are co-operating with in and out of Europe. We need technical assistance, but also advice as to how to change the bad image of the Hungarian Police, how to change our attitudes to become more popular.

These conclusions led the management of the Hungarian police and also the Minister of Home Office in the late Autumn of 1990 to begin the reorganization and the reform of the Hungarian Police. An international manager-organizing firm, T.C. TEAM CONSULT, in close cooperation with the Dutch Police Study Center have started the program.

The last top meeting about the development and direction of the project was held on 20 March this year. Finally, I should like to present you with the provision of the future of the Hungarian police in regard to public security (see Figure 2.).

Figure 2.

Provision of the Future of the Hungarian Police in regard to Public Security.

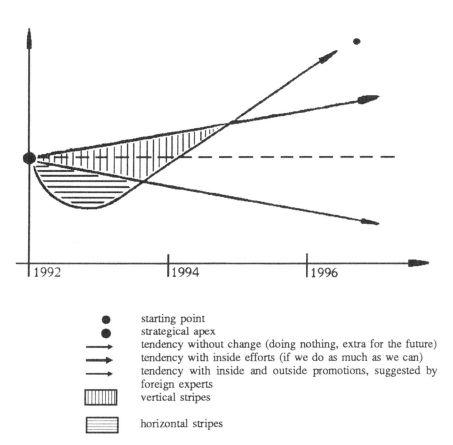

●	starting point
●	strategical apex
→	tendency without change (doing nothing, extra for the future)
→	tendency with inside efforts (if we do as much as we can)
→	tendency with inside and outside promotions, suggested by foreign experts
▦	vertical stripes
▤	horizontal stripes

There has been a small decline in public security which will continue until 1994 according to foreign experts and analysts. Can this decline, can any decline be allowed before the new elections in 1994? The answer is yes, but not without some qualifications. We cannot place the people who are residing in Hungary at unreasonable risk.

The second problem is a special police one. Have the Hungarian police enough capacity either technically or mentally to increase police (3000 police officers more for each year from 1992 until 1995) and to educate them, while transforming the police image simultaneously into a more popular one? The second answer was fortunately yes too but without help, without close cooperation and assistance from the West, it cannot be done. We are just now preparing an educational project with close assistance of our Dutch colleagues.

Notes and References

Agelink, M. T. G. & Van Gesteg, G. J. A. H. (1989): Comparative information on police systems. Report of the European Police Summer Course, 1989. Politiestudiecentrum, Warnsveld, Dec.

Van Dijk, Jan J. M., Mayhew, Pat and Killias, Martin (1990): Experiences of Crime across the World. Kluwer Law & Taxation Publishers, Deventer, Boston.

Fijnaut, D. J. F. (1989): National Police Organizations and Police Innovation in Europe. Report of the European Police Summer Course, 1989. Politie Studie Centrum, Warnsveld, Dec.

Greene, Jack R. (1982): Introduction. Managing Police Work. Issues and Analyses. Sage Publications, Beverly Hills (London) New Delhi.

Salgó László (1990): Self-government Police from the side of Practice. Home Office Review, June.

T. C. Team Consult: Introduction to the Hungarian Police. 10. 13. 1990.

T. C. Team Consult: Present analysis of the Hungarian Police, 19. June 1991. Vienna.

T. C. Team Consult: For the Efficient and Democratic Police in Hungary. Proposals. October 1991. Vienna.

T. C. Team Consult: Presentation About the Future of the Hungarian Police. 20. March 1992. Budapest.

Pintér, S., Prestel, M. and Salgó, L.: Scheme about the provisions of the future of the Hungarian Police in the aspect of public security.

Straver, M. A.: About the Dutch Police System. Presentation. 21. 10. 1991. Haarlem, The Netherlands.

Weber Max: The methodology of the Social Sciences. Trans. and ed. Edward A. Shils and Henry A. Finch. N. Y. Free Press 1949. p. 56.

Weber Max: The theory of social and economic Organizations. Trans. A. M. Henderson and Talcott Parsons. N. Y. Oxford Univ. Press 1947.

Salgó, L.: Hungary and the security. ASIS Spring Meeting Beetsterzwag 1992.

Changing the Police: Preliminary Thoughts as Eastern Europe Moves West

by
Rob I. Mawby

Introduction

Despite the large number of papers on the role of the police in modern society, this conference has been notable for the fact that contributors have avoided definitions of the police, much less the *public* police. Concentrating on the latter, I have elsewhere argued that modern police systems can be defined in terms of their legitimacy, structure and function (Mawby 1990). Legitimacy implies that the police are granted some degree of approval in society by those with the power to so authorize; structure denotes an organisation bounded by rules; and function reflects an emphasis on law, order and crime control. However, each of these dimensions allows for considerable variation between different systems. For example, the legitimacy of the police may be accorded it by the law and the population at large, or it may be granted by a powerful, unelected minority, with the police feared or despised by the majority; variations in structure allow for local, civilianized police services at one extreme and centralised 'militaristic' ones at the other; and variations in function mean that police roles may include administrative responsibilities such as tax or licensing duties, welfare tasks, overt political functions, etc.

This and similar classifications have been used in the literature to describe key policing types. For example, early this century an American police administrator, Raymond Fosdick (1969 edition), identified a continental style of policing, whilst Tobias (1977), following Jeffries (1952), distinguishes the colonial model used by the British to enforce order in Ireland and subsequently transposed throughout the Empire (Mawby 1990). Whilst these provide marked contrasts with the police of England and Wales and the USA, they clearly do not exhaust the alternatives. Bayley (1976) for example, has focused on the differences between policing in the US and Japan, and a variety of writers have distinguished the Chinese model of policing (see Mawby 1990).

In the present context, the continental system is of particular relevance. In its original form this comprised a police force legitimized and controlled by central government, perhaps answerable to a single ruler, a centralised, armed and military structure, and responsibilities which included, in addition to crime control, an emphasis on political and administrative functions. Whilst there are today considerable variations in Western Europe, in general many of these distinguishing characteristics remain (Bayley 1975; 1979; Fijnaut 1990).

However, whether or not one can talk about a distinctive Eastern European communist system is questionable. In many respects, Eastern European police in the period up to the late 1980s have much in common with the continental model described by Fosdick. For example, the distinction between the political and criminal police in Eastern Europe parallels the original French distinction between so called high and low policing (Emsley 1983; Stead 1983), and revolutionary Russia took over much of the policing apparatus of the Tsar's police (Kowalewski 1981). While contributors to this conference critically evaluate the police system of Hungary from 1945, earlier commentators were equally critical of the police system that originated in 1881 and followed the French model (Rudas 1977). This incorporated two centralized police forces, responsible to the state, and included a wide range of administrative tasks such as the regulation of boarding houses and the licensing of those keeping carrier pigeons (Rudas 1977; Ward 1984). Whilst Louise Shelley has here suggested that Eastern European systems were distinctive in the extent of control imposed from the centre across a broad spectrum of everyday activities, clearly earlier systems had this intention, even if not always its successful implementation (Chapman 1970; Emsley 1983; Raeff 1975; Stead 1983). One could, in fact, cynically suggest that one of the major changes brought about by communist European governments, though on not the same scale as China and Cuba (Mawby 1990), was to increase public participation - policing through police volunteers or neighbourhood crime control groups, changes that are currently being advocated as beneficial in Western democracies.

In the remainder of this paper I want to focus not on the past but on the future, and consider the directions in which Eastern European police systems might move. To do so I shall distinguish between the three dimensions already described; namely police legitimacy, structure and function. Two points are, however, worth stressing at this point. First, we cannot change the police without taking account of the social, political and cultural features of the society being studied, including here a historical dimension. Thus whilst some Asian societies such as China, Hong Kong and Singapore have successfully incorporated many features of Japanese policing, the latter was notably resistant to American influence in the late 1940s; and British and American attempts to recreate the German police in their own image were equally unsuccessful (Ames 1981; Bayley 1985). Second, and in contrast, it is more fruitful to look at quite separate and distinctive features of the police and how these vary between societies, and try to evaluate both the practicalities and the strengths and weaknesses of each. As a preliminary to such an attempt, I shall here focus on my original model and raise a number of questions about policing ideals.

Police Legitimacy

From where do the police derive their legitimacy? The state or government, the law, or the general public? While in democratic societies the importance of the police being answerable to the law has been stressed, equally the need for public accountability has been underlined. Indeed, it has been the subject of a number of presentations at this conference.

In general, we may see greater accountability of the police to the public as beneficial, and advocate changes in this direction. However, there are a number of problems which I would like to reiterate here. First, there is the question of how the public accredit the police with legitimacy. Is it through wider political institutions; that is, voting for politicians who are then themselves delegated to police review committees, or through specific public representation on review bodies? If the latter, how and by whom are public representatives chosen? In England and Wales, this issue is well illustrated if we consider police community consultation groups, where the atypicality and unrepresentativeness of key members has been commented upon (Morgan and Maggs 1985).

Second, there is the particular problem of public involvement in divided societies where there are distinctive communities with very different experiences of the police. Of course, in one sense, all societies are divided, but the example of Northern Ireland is a useful one to illustrate the extreme. There, until the 1970s, the police was indeed legitimized and controlled by the public, or at least the Protestant majority, but the result was hardly a system to be emulated, and more recent changes have been to improve the impartiality of the police by minimising local political and Protestant involvement and enhancing police professionalism (Brewer et. al. 1988). Given the recent increases in ethnic and regional conflict in Eastern European states, the example of Northern Ireland is of particular salience.

Third, we should be aware that many advocates of increased accountability see it as a means rather than an end. It is preferred because it will allegedly lead to a more open, service-oriented police. But there are equally persuasive arguments that the opposite might occur and that the 'public' might demand a more repressive police (as long as that 'public' is not the object of repressive tactics). Whilst there is some evidence in Britain that the public is more critical of the police than formerly (Mayhew et. al. 1989), generally the public views the police very positively and may be willing to over-credit the police with more power in the 'fight' against crime.

Fourth, and in complete contrast, many have agreed that increased public involvement in the policing process may represent a threat to freedom. There is, in fact, a fine line between a responsible citizen and a police spy. Thus the Chinese system of social control has been criticized not so much because of the power of the police as because the system of social control integrates police with local public office holders and representatives in an intricate system of social control.

The Structure of the Police

Key issues here are the extent to which there is one police organization or more than one within a country, and in the latter case whether the police is structured on a central or local level, or both. We might also consider the militaristic qualities of the police. While the image of a continental police system is of a militaristic and centralized one, as I have noted elsewhere there are enormous variations within Western and Northen Europe (Mawby 1991). Recent proposals in Hungary are to demilitarize *but* not decentralize the police; interesting, given that the Swiss experts making these suggestions come from the one militaristic decentralized police system in Europe (Mawby 1991).

Elsewhere, trends reflect the somewhat different experiences of different countries. For example in England and Wales, traditionally characterized as having a civilian and localized system, recent developments suggest a more militaristic element to policing (Jefferson 1991) and greater central control of the police (Reiner 1991). Elsewhere the Dutch, with a mixture of local and national forces, appear to be moving towards local policing, albeit within a smaller number of larger units. The French are currently discussing demilitarizing the gendarmerie, following the example set earlier this year by the Belgians (Judge 1991).

What is needed in terms of police structures is a more rigourous assessment of the benefits and disadvantages any changes might bring. For example, will a centralized police save money and improve efficiency? In a review of the situation in England and Wales, Loveday (1990) suggests that this is improbable. Similarly, Jefferson (1991) has argued persuasively that moves to militarize the police have led to an escalation of public disorder.

The issues of centralization and militaristic qualities are, of course, only two aspects of police structure. We might similarly assess the precise relations between police and public and consider what structures exist which allow for public involvement to benefit policing, or review the composition of the police in terms of gender, race and class. Alternatively, we might focus on informal police structures – cop culture or police subcultures – whereby the operation of policing is re-defined and re-ordered, and ask how far this acts to minimize the real impact of legislative changes on the police.

Police Functions

There are two major issues here: what the police do and how they do it, that is police *styles*. Reviewing the material from other countries one might ask the extent to which the police should have a political or public order role. If the police withdraw from maintaining public order, will this be done more satisfactorily by the military? Should the administrative roles of the police, common in many European countries, be given to someone else? And, should the police have a welfare role?

While the shift towards seeing policing as a *service* tends to imply a greater welfare role for the police, notably regarding police treatment of crime victims (Mawby and Walklate 1993), in Britain critics from the left and right have combined to argue that the police should refocus their role on crime and withdraw from welfare responsibilities. In this context it is important to stress that, as some speakers noted yesterday, the police *are not* social workers. But a welfare element is important in so far as the experience of both offenders and victims has to be understood in terms of the wider social environments that they inhabit.

What then of the police's role in dealing with crime? In many respects, this might be seen as the obvious major responsibility of the police. However, as Betsy Stanko said earlier in this conference, what is interpreted as real crime by the police in particular societies is a key issue. As we know from victim surveys in England and Wales, victims who experience the worst problems are precisely those harmed by incidents that the police consider 'rubbish' or not 'real' crimes (Mawby and Walklate 1993).

Finally, here, it is important to consider the ways in which the police carry out their functions: police style, and especially the distinction between a police *force* and a police *service*. As a public agency the police are public servants and should be assessed in terms of how far what they do and how they respond to their clients encourage citizens to return for help next time they have a problem! In England and Wales recently the government has been encouraging police forces to carry out surveys of their consumers in order to find out what sort of service they receive. Whether or not this initiative will succeed will depend both on how the police go about this research and how chief officers respond to the findings. It is, however, an interesting development and can be assessed alongside changes in the ways that the police respond to females.

Conclusion

I have no time here to develop these points although I have assessed the police systems of a variety of countries in more detail elsewhere (Mawby 1990; 1991). In conclusion I merely wish to re-emphasise two points.

First, while we have at this conference noted examples of where there have been improvements in the policing processes, where new policies or practices have proved beneficial, no-one has argued for a police system that they felt so proud of, so confident in, that they would advocate that we all adopted a similar system. Change in the police should not therefore be aimed at adopting the police system of another country. To do so would be to reproduce a failed system.

Second, and in contrast to this, I have attempted to define and distinguish between police systems on a number of dimensions. I hope therefore that I have asked some of the right questions if we are to improve our own police systems. Such a system might be one where the police is accountable to the public both directly and through the law, where it is organized such that is has a non-military structure that allows for local accountability, and where the focus is on providing a service with an emphasis on the control of crime. To simplify the matter, we might say that such a system is one in which, should we or our families be involved as suspects *or* victims, we should feel reassured that treatment will be both fair and humane. By those criteria, we have to date, clearly failed.

Notes and References

Ames, W. L. (1991): *Police and Community in Japan.* Berkeley, Calif: University of California Press.
Bayley, D. M. (1975): 'The police and political developments in Europe'. in C. Tilly (ed.), *The Formation of Nation States in Europe.* Princeton: Princeton University Press. pp. 1328-79.
Bayley, D. M. (1976): *Forces of Order: Police Behaviour in Japan and the United States.* Berkeley, Calif: University of California Press.

Bayley, D. M. (1979): 'Police function, structure and control in Western Europe and North America: comparative and historical studies', in N. Morris and M. Tonry (eds), *Crime and Justice: an Annual Review of Research.* Chicago: University of Chicago Press. pp. 109-44.

Bayley, D. M. (1985): *Patterns of Policing: a Comparative International Analysis.* New Brunswick: Rutgers University Press.

Brewer, J. D., Guelke, A., Hume, I., Moxon-Browne, I. and Wilford, R. (1988): in *Police, Public Order and the State.* London: Macmillan.

Chapman, B. (1970.): *Police State.* London: Pall Mall Press.

Emsley, C. (1983): *Policing and its Context, 1750-1870.* London: Macmillan.

Fijnaut, C. F. (1990): 'The Police and the public in Western Europe: a precarious comparison', *Police Review,* 63.4: 337-45.

Fosdick, R. B. (1969.): *European Police Systems.* Montclair, New Jersey: Paterson Smith. (1st edition, 1915).

Jefferson, T. (1991): *The Case against Paramilitary Policing.* Buckingham: Open University Press.

Jeffries, S. C. (1952.): *The Colonial Police.* London: Max Parrish.

Judge, T. (1991): 'Can Soldiers be Bobbies' ,*Police,* December: 24-25.

Kowalewski, D. (1981.): 'China and the Soviet Union: a Comparative Model for Analysis', *Studies in Comparative Communism* 14.4: 279-306.

Loveday, B. (1990): 'The Road to Regionalization', *Policing,* 6: 639-660.

Mawby, R. I. (1990): *Comparative Policing Issues: the British and American Experience in International Perspective.* London: Unwin Hyman/Routledge.

Mawby, R. I. (1991): 'Police Systems in the British Isles: a comparison with Continental Europe', paper to Round-table on Models of Policing in Western Europe, IHESI, Ministry of the Interior, Paris.

Mawby, R. I. and Walklate, S. (1993): *Critical Victimology.* London: Sage.

Mayhew, P. E., David Dowds, L. (1989): The 1988 *Brirish Crime Survey.* London: HMS0.

Morgan, R. and Maggs, C. (1985): Setting the P.A.C.E.; *Police Community Consultation Arrangements in England and Wales.* Bath: University of Bath.

Raeff, M. (1975): 'The Well Ordered Police State', *American Historical Review* 80(5), 122-43.

Reiner, R. (1991): *Chief Constables.* Oxford: Oxford University Press.

Rudas, G. (1977): 'The Changing Role, Responsibilities and Activities of the Police in a Developed Society', *International Review of Criminal Policy,* 33: 11-16.

Stead, P. J. (1983): *The Police of France.* London: Macmillan.

Tobias, J. J. (1977): 'The British Colonial Police: an alternative style', in P. J. Stead (ed) *Pioneers in Policing.* Maidenhead: Patterson Smith. pp. 241-61.

Ward, R. H. (1984): 'Police and Criminal Justice in Hungary', *Police Studies,* 6. 31-4.

Topic V.

Questions About Crime-Prevention and Crime Policy in a transitional Middle Europe

by
Ferenc Irk

Forums of Changes

Recent alterations in the feature of the former ruling regime have taken place in Hungary and have been labelled as, changing of the regime or more precisely, the commencement of a long procedure concerning the *changing of the regime.* Its tangible elements may be evaluated in the following dimensions:

1. A significant erosion is going on in the realm of policies. The beginning of this process dates back quite far in the past. It stands for all countries from the region though the reasons have been generated both by external (primarily the agony of the Soviet Empire, and the wish for a more updated inner and outer Soviet policy i.e. Gorbachevism) and by internal (primarily the desire of keeping up the competition with the developed West at any expense and in most cases, the extremely indebted-bankrupt countries insisting to its ideals about the command market up to its last moment) effects. It is a well-known fact though, that while the economic situation in Hungary had had better results – on the surface – than in the other East-Central European countries, it was Hungary that had accumulated the biggest amount of debt (concerning the quantity of debt per capita).

The process of changing the regime (which has still not been accomplished) varies quite broadly among the countries. After the massacres and bloodshed of 1956, Hungary has begun to shape those special significant elements of its "soft dictatorship" that were acknowledged abroad. The group nowadays called reform-communists or reform-socialists had already been preparing for modernization within barriers of power. It should be noted however that radical change of the regime had only occurred to a limited circle of the opposition. Thus there had been a last-longing coexistence – partly within, partly outside the party – of the conservative power, being ever ready for unconditional compromises with the "big neighbour", however reluctant it may have been in serving the interest of this latter group and of the oppositions endowed with strong desire for change.

2. The changes in the *economy* have been very much like those in the political realm; the erosion and the transition are going along together supporting each other.

3. The *common sense* has been overruled by three phenomena, mostly successively but eventually simultaneously: vitality, ambiguity and apathy. At this very point we can already talk about present phenomena.
The abrupt changes have triggered undigestable problems to the people of the region. Here are two Hungarian examples:

– October 23, 1956 had been evaluated as a counter-revolution until January 1989, then it varied: uprising, revolution, war of liberty. Now it is known as the national memorial day. In October 1988 the police brutally crushed down the celebrators. In 1989 the former victims of such convincing means as the truncheon or water-cannon were escorted by the police. The martyr Prime Minister Imre Nagy was labelled a traitor and counter-revolutionary for 25 years and millions of people were at his reburial in June 1989. (The policemen and their commanders were taught for quarter of a century that he was the biggest traitor of the nation).
– Janos Kadar who was the first man of the Hungarian communist system for 25 years ("the uncle") and whose burial was also attended by thousands, died a couple of weeks after the above mentioned ceremony. He is now regarded as traitor and executioner.
–

The worsening of the situation is fairly obvious including widespread criminality, the increase of violence and the declining effectiveness of the police. The benefits of democracy are barely perceived.

Certainly the lack of required historical insight it is not predictable whether or not there is a rational connection between the transition, the accelerated pauperism and social deviancy.

Malfunctions of Economic Life and Legal Regulations

The considerably increased number of loop-holes is an obvious outcome of the transition and so is the demand for stricter evaluation criteria concerning the development of the rule of law.

It is also obvious that in such an environment the abuse of the law also prevails proportionally to the unmeasurable measures of uncertainty in the executors of the laws. At the time being, but probably for a longer while too, there are going to be cases which are however unjustifiable morally, still are not or cannot be prosecuted for either legal or technical problems, deficiency of evidence. Therefore the region is a paradise for adventurers at the moment. This statement is well supported by a recently issued estimation based on Hungarian data regarding the black market. According to its figures, there are 70-80,000 people carrying out such activity in Hungary. This number though almost equals the numbers of registered private entrepreneurs. These black traders do not pay any duty on their imports, avoid social contributions to social security and what counts the most above all – especially in the eyes of those earning fixed wages – they do not even pay taxes. Certainly, the incapability or what is more the unwillingness to ameliorate this is tangible evidence of the attitude, and weakness of the prevailing power and also of the discordance of the authorities responsible for law enforcement and public order and ultimately of the vagueness of developing a rule of law system.

Hungary and its Environment

The economic-political stability and the governing style of the surrounding countries should also be taken into account in questioning the connection of social transition and criminality.

It is already a well-known fact that Hungary is a host country for a lot of refugees and residents mainly due to its policy of open boundaries and its relatively better living standard. One of its neighbours has a civil war. Several others have registered movements whose political programmes are focused on minority hatred. Some of these are based on ethnicity, others on racist grounds. The open frontiers and its liberal control allow mass incomings of even those who would have rather avoided the entire region before let alone this country itself. New forms of criminality emerge.

The new democracies of East-Central Europe are in peril by new dangers, too. One of these is the invasion of refugees, first in Central then in Western-Europe. Politicians of this latter region are still not aware of the jeopardy that it means, namely that if these people were not appealed to stay in their home countries because of fear from starving and civil wars then it would be too late to hold up the mass migration. Wealthy Europe may still lock itself up behind an iron curtain, though.

The next jeopardy conceals itself in the fact that the *mafia* of the developed countries is capable of buying up the entire public administration of East-Central Europe. The news talks only about their help in creating the convertible currency of these countries and about their alleged anticipation of this. As soon as it is going to be achieved it will not only generate completely new kinds of crimes in the region that are not likely going to be easily tackled affairs (especially considering that it causes remarkable problems to more balanced and better-off societies to cope with) but also may drift the West into troubles as well.

New tendencies in criminality

It is not more than a catch-phrase by now stating that the good old times are over. This region of Europe has also been reached by the formerly horrifyingly observed crime waves of civil societies.

Some people do believe that the game of a social regime is already up. Could it be possible though that this past regime – along with several negative effects of course – has guaranteed in its stricter sense a somewhat secured life for its citizens?

However jarring would be my response to this question, it is not meant to be either original or conclusive, since I do think that from this point of view the failed world-order had really given a sense of greater security for the citizens. Nevertheless this pleasure spoiling and some would say hostile statement of mine concerning the new regime should be supplemented with the following comments.

First of all I wish to emphasize that in the last period of the former regime the remarks of the former leaders (minister of interior affairs, general attorney) that the public safety was solid but did not comply with the reality whatsoever. To be more precise it could have been true depending upon what it was compared to. Furthermore, it is also questionable what the criteria of public safety are. For several countries from the third world, our situation is still more promising. What is more, considering terrorist activities, our region has far better results – so far at least than Great Britain which is endowed with its hundred year old civil traditions and well balanced civil society or perhaps Spain, however an ideal example it has become for several reasons.

Nevertheless contrasting our past to our present, one shall be faced with a fairly depressing picture and it cannot be eased even if we acknowledge that the seeds of devastation have already been sown. Even more its proliferation had yet begun when the official declarations still stated that everything was all right and perfect. While the speakers of the power were advocating for public safety, some – although loyal but soberly thinking officers of the Interior Ministry as well – foresaw in their prognosis an irresistibly growing wave of criminality. Certainly because its conditions – the sowing of these seeds – had already been founded by that time. It is another story indeed that the representatives of the power were not enchanted by this bitter future at all.

This process has recently been accelerated. At this point it is not wise to draw the exact line as to what extent the environment created by the former regime played, as compared with the inevitable effects of the social-economic changes. What is to be taken into account is that the Hungarian society has not been prepared for such increased criminality. Thus, neither the power nor the prosecuting machinery has developed counter-effects or maneuvers.

Also it does not seem to be doubted that the dictatorship, sweeping all deviations under the carpet and being endowed with fear as its principle, is less favourable towards unlawfulness than the dawn of democracy which is struggling with the identification of the state, the redefinition of rights and duties, the international standards of humanity, trying to cope with state deficiencies.

Inadequacy of the governing system, and deficiencies in regulations have considerably come to play in the field of the police. The police fails already manifestly to react to injuries being carried out right in their sight. (It was not rare before either, though.) The obscurity of a regulating system has (also) provoked the conviction that the policemen and their commanders believe the delay in taking measures could lead to the least troubles, whereas actions (based on former reflexes) are very likely going to be doubted owing to lack of innate legal sensitivity, clear directives and very often social consent.

Part of the problem is that ever since the last elections an Act on police based on social consent has not yet been drafted. (Therefore, presumably not only the soldiers but also the officers are unaware of the legitimate boundaries of their possibilities, rights and duties.) It is completely confusing for even the respected politicans.

Question of Crime Prevention and Crime Policy

Talking to Western European professionals, one may face a certain kind of incomprehension towards the problems of our region. They do not quite see why we are so worried about increasing crime (since we still have better statistical results than they do). They do not quite see why we are so concerned about the rapidly growing rate of unemployment (since we still have better figures sometimes than they do).

The accelerated increase of criminality demands urgent and considered interference from the advisors. Since 1992 the Criminology Department of the National Institute of Criminology and Criminalistics has been working on the elaboration of a criminal policy. Because of the short time I would like to summarize our standpoints and questions.

Prerequisites to Effective Criminal Policy

Some people draw equations between criminal policy and effective prevention of criminality. We cannot agree with that. Prevention of criminality is not merely and perhaps not even primarily an activity of the authorities. Politics - as we had seen before – is able only to orientate the state. Its execution is not a political task, although the participants might be the same organizations as those determining the policies.

Prevention of criminality has no sophisticated system for either policy (thus criminal-policy) or practical issues in Hungary. Likewise in any other realm of life the deterioration of the previous structures is more obvious than the generation of new ones.

Thus in order to create a system of implementation we should answer the following *questions:*
- which policies are to be involved in crime prevention (prevention of criminality)?
- who (which local and central organizations) is to participate in the implementation?
- what methods may the intervention apply (the limits of restrain and arbitration)?
- what circle should the intervention touch upon (according to legal intervention, when is the local, the regional or the national one due)?
- what sort of moral background should be manifested (i.e. legislating or application of law within the limits of civil liberties)?
- what measures are to be taken for achieving success (i.e. criminal policy or independent ones)?
- who are the target-groups (i.e. all the people, or just some indicated risk-groups)?
- which crimes are to be focused upon (i.e. violence, drugs, crimes due to special circumstances, crimes against properties, corruption)?

Those countries with matured development have decades to channel the reactions of changes, to experiment with adjustable new policies and to introduce the promising solutions. The results have shown however, that even the establishment of well justified new institutions may end up in failure. Certainly, it does not require detailed evidence of how likely the error of new methods is in a region where balanced evolutionary development has never been observed and where time for experiments has never been given. And what is more, this region faces a unique problem: the handling of the transition from a socialist dictatorship into capitalism.

Social Change and Crime in Italy

by
Giovanni Battista Traverso

Introduction

The enormous social changes which occurred in Italy during the last thirty years or so have deeply influenced either the theoretical frames of reference of criminologists, or the overall picture of crime, or finally our criminal policies.

The goal of the present work is to briefly describe the historical development covered by criminological sciences in my country and practices/policies within the criminal justice system, as well as to interpret at least some of the changing trends of crime and delinquency which followed the tremendous (political, social, economical, cultural, etc.) transformations which contributed to bring Italy from the destruction of the Second World War to its actual leading position among the six or seven most industrialized countries in the world.

The theoretical tradition in criminology: the primacy of the clinical approach ... with some objections

Following the Lombrosian tradition, in Italy we have historically witnessed, from a theoretical point of view, the primacy of the psychological approach for explanation of criminal behavior, an approach made successful also through the demand, coming from lawyers and jurists, for a greater use of the scientific knowledge which had been accumulating within the field of general psychology, a new science in quick progress at the beginning of the twentieth century.

In terms of Benigno Di Tullio's work, within his original theory of "criminal constitution", the psychological study of offenders and the knowledge of their personality represent the means by which "we can come to reconstruct the course of criminal action itself, and to establish how and why the idea of the crime arose, how and why it could develop and persist in the individual consciousness; finally, how and why it could translate into criminal acting out" (Di Tullio, 1945).

Just at the time of the greatest flourishing and expansion of the psychological paradigm in the Sixties, in Italy there happened important social, political, and cultural changes which deeply influenced the shift to new approaches to deviance, derived mainly from the American tradition of sociology of deviance.

The highly rapid process of neocapitalist industrialization of the Northern Italian regions, associated with a still feudal and precapitalistic structure of society in the Southern part of our country resulted in:

(a) a great social mobility linked with internal migrations, especially from the Southern countryside to the Northern big cities
(b) the strengthening of the already strong workers' movement and trade-unions, inspired by a Marxist view of social relationships
(c) the rise of pressure groups (like feminists) with the objective to protect the rights of marginalized segments of the population (the elderly, women, inmates, handicapped, mad, etc.-people characterized by a common distance from the labour market)
(d) all these (among others) elements contributed to the abandonment of the perspective of a monolithic society based on consensus toward a world view based on conflicts of value and interest.

In this context, the so-called "total institutions" (in Goffman's definition), like the psychiatric hospital and the prison, become the main target of radical criticism (Ricci Salierno, 1971; Basaglia & Basaglia Ongaro, 1971, 1975). Some English (Taylor and coll. 1975) or American (Platt, 1975) "critical" criminology books were translated into Italian; in Italy, at Impruneta (a little village near Florence), in 1973, the first meeting of a new European group ("The European group for the Study of Deviance and Social Control") was organized; some jurists coming mainly from the Law Faculty of the University of Bologna started a journal, *"La Questione Criminale"*, the first scientific magazine in Italy totally dedicated to a critical understanding of deviance and mechanisms of social control. Later on, I myself (Traverso, 1981) published, after a long sojourn in the USA, a book aimed at the systematization and a more general understanding of a great bulk of scientific material concerning the critical approaches to crime and deviance.

The central theoretical model around which everything seemed to start and move is represented – notwithstanding the peculiar, original positions of the different contributors – by the *labelling approach* (Lemert, 1951; Becker, 1963 among others), an anti-etiological approach, as we well know, by which the functioning of penal justice is interpreted within a political project of institutional reform and social change (Pitch, 1982).

I would like to add that this new theoretical paradigm is favourably accepted not only by some jurists, but also by some clinicians (very dissatisfied by their role within the criminal justice sytem) who, in different ways, are looking for new paths "toward a *new* clinical criminology" (Bandini and Gatti, 1987).

The present situation: walking backwards?

In fact, just in those years – (late Sixties and the Seventies) – many progressive legislative reforms took place in Italy, inducing big changes in the political and concrete handling of some crucial areas of social life, including the criminal justice system. Of great importance for our discussion here is to mention:

(a) the prison reform (Law n. 354/1975), which introduced very big changes in the social meaning (of) as well as in the concrete application of penal sanctions (particularly, the new legislation introduced alternative measure to imprisonment – a sort of probation was one of these – and provided prisons with professional staff (psychologist, criminologist, social worker, etc.)
(b) the mental health legislation reform (Law n. 180/1978, better known in Italy as the Legge Basaglia) which abolished the civil psychiatric hospital providing community treatment for mental patients
(c) the juvenile justice system reform (D. P. R. n. 616/1977) which let minors involved with civil or administrative court dispositions (in such instances no crime has been committed, but the juvenile is considered to behave inadequately and to have character disorders) be entrusted to local authority services
(d) the drug addiction legislation reform (Law n. 685/1975) which, by finally taking consciousness of the radically changed situation in drug addiction problems, provided a deep innovation in the criminal policy about drug matters, recognizing a differential penal treatment between persons involved in traffic/selling and persons involved in personal use of drugs (who could demonstrate a "personal non therapeutical use of a small quantity of drug" – even if it might be worth while, we cannot here comment on the controversial and much discussed upon juridical concept of "small quantity" – the law provided no punishment at all, stressing a strong therapeutic attitude toward him/her).

We could extend (but we will not) the list of fairly progressive legislative reforms passed by our Parliament mainly in that period. However, the important thing to stress here is the general failure of the "reformist dream" above mentioned.

We are witnessing a moment of great confusion, characterized, in terms of criminal policy at large, by a repressive squeeze (with a strong demand of "law and order") favoured by a long series of factors among which we can put the following:

(a) the still felt, frightful echo of the terrorism era which had alarmed Italy since the late Seventies and the first half of the Eighties: an era culminated in the assassination of Aldo Moro, Secretary of Christian Democrats, strong supporter of the so-called "historical compromise" (that is the potential political alliance between Christian Democrats and the Communisty party); an era in which we witness a deep (unexpected) transformation of the prison system: the prison loses its traditional, ideological, rehabilitative function and becomes a maximum security incapacitating institution, free from any "contractual" tie, from which one cannot get out but mad or suicidal (Pavarini, 1978).
(b) the strong growth of organized crime (particularly dangerous, it appears in the deep increase of "mafia" homicides in the Southern regions of our country, especially Sicily). At this regard I wish only to outline the very important transformations ("the great transformation" in Arlacchi terms) (Arlacchi, 1983) occurred in Sicilian society during the last thirty years and the consequent transformation process experienced by the mafia, whose leaders engage themselves in more and more lucrative activities (linked with drug trafficking and with the building market), giving birth to the so-called "financial mafia", a great machine with the goal of capital accumulation (Chinnici & Santino, 1986).
(c) the fairly high increase of juvenile delinquency (after a big decrease of this phenomenon during the Seventies and the first half of the Eighties). Since 1986 we have witnessed an increase of crimes known to the police (especially thefts, robberies, drug-related crimes, etc.) committed by juveniles. Of some interest for our discussion can be the fact that recently we had an increase in juvenile prison population of minors coming from North Africa and/or gypsies (the migratory phenomenon of people coming from North Africa has caused big problems in our country and the foreign migration as had to be controlled by a special legislation).

A final point. In this very complex situation, what about the clinician? What about the relationships between psychiatry and justice? It is a point which would deserve more space and a more adequate investigation, given its importance either from a theoretical or a pragmatic point of view. Indeed, in the last ten years many congresses, conferences, colloquia, meetings have been dedicated to the issue of the relationships between psychiatry and criminal justice, emphasizing mainly ethical and technical problems in the context of expertise (moral advocacy versus expertise; the qualification of experts; prejudicial versus probative aspects of expertise; methods and procedures of forensic evaluations; the clinical evalution of dangerousness; interaction, communication and interpretation problems among clinicians, defendants and the trier of fact; the ability of the expert to give scientifically grounded opinions on the issue of criminal responsibility; the ideological view of the mentally ill offender: that is, does he/she have anyway at least some "degree of freedom" or has he/she to be considered constrained by his/her psychopathology? And so on).

Well, also in this peculiar field the confusion is great and strong criticism on the above mentioned technical/ethical issues linking psychiatry to criminal justice (risk to become harmful) favourisg the growth of models of "justice" aimed at considering the psychiatric patient who commits criminal acts as fully responsible just like the normal. Even though these models have not been introduced in our legislation (see the project Vinci-Grossi which was not even discussed in our Parliament), the emphasis on punishment is still there and can indeed affect our criminal policy in a repressive, punitive sense.

Notes and References

Arlacchi, P. (1983.): *La mafia imprenditrice.* Bologna: Il Mulino.
Basaglia, F. & Basaglia Ongaro, F., eds. (1971.): *La maggioranza deviante.* Torino: Einaudi.
Basaglia, F. & Basaglia Ongaro, F., eds. (1975.): Crimini di pace. Riserche sugli intellettuali e sui tecnici come addetti all'oppressione. Torino: Einaudi.
Becker, H. S. (1963.): *Outsiders Studies in the Sociology of Deviance.* New York: Free Press.
Chinnici, G. & Santino, U. (1986.): *L'omicidio a Palermo eprovincia negli anni 1960-1966 e 1978-1984.* Palermo: Stass.
Di Tullio, B. (1945.): *Trattato di Antropollga Criminale.* Roma: Criminalia.
Lemert, E. M. (1951.): *Social Pathology.* New York: McGraw-Hill.
Mead, G. H. (1934.): *Mind, Self and Society.* Chicago: The University of Chicago Press.

Pavarini, M. (1978): 'Concentrazione' e 'diffusione' del penitenziario. Le tesi di Rusche e Kircheimer e la nuova strategia del controllo sociale in Italia. *La Questione Criminale*, 4, 39-61.

Pitch, T. (1982): *La devianza.* Firenze: La Nuova Italia.

Platt, A. M. (1975): *L'invenzione della delinquenza.* Rimini-Firenze: Guaraldi (Italian translation of The Child-Savers. Chicago: The University of Chicago Press, 1969).

Ricci, A. & Sallerno, G. (1973): *Il carcere in Italia.* Torino: Einaudi.

Taylor, I., Walton, P. & Young, J. (1973): *Criminologia sorto accusa. Devianza o ineguaglianza sociale?* Rimini-Firenze: Guaraldi (Italian translation of *New Criminology. For A Social Theory of Deviance.* London: Routledge & Kegan Paul, 1973).

Traverso, G. B. (1986): Il giudizio di pericolositá ed il suo accertaimento. *Rivista Italiana di Medicina Legale*, 4, 1041-1061.

Traverso, G. B. (1988.): Il trattamento del reo infermo di mente: prospettive di riforma. *Rassegna di Criminologia*, 19, 247-259.

Traverso, G. B. & Werde, A. (1981): *Criminoligia critica. Delinquenza e controllo sociale nel modo di produzione capitalistioo.* Padova: CEDAM.

Attitudes of the Czechoslovakian Public towards the Police after 1989

by
Josef Zapletal and Mikulas Tomin

Czechoslovakia was one of the countries that relieved themselves of many years of Communist rule and set off on the road leading to a free democratic and legal state. The liberation from authoritarianism in addition brought predominantly positive changes but some negative phenomena such as an enormous growth in crime occurred after the November revolution in 1989 that continues until now.

Criminality belongs among those undesirable social phenomena that today most alarms our public. It is also demontrated by the results of the public opinion polls conducted repeatedly in 1990-1991 by the Institute for the Investigation of the Public Opinion in Prague. The results of these investigations show that the citizens of Czechoslovakia placed the problems of criminality as the most urgent societal problem after the economy.

The police is one of the main organs of power concerned with the repression of criminality and the security of citizens. After November 1989 all the attributes of the police state were shaken. Organs of formal institutionalized superrvision, most notably the police, were paralyzed to a considerable extent. The processes of disorganization took place in them and addition to it here existed extraordinary public aggression toward the police as the symbol of the totalitarian power. Besides, the police was compromised due to the brutality of some of its bodies during the revolutionary events in November 1989. This had an extremely negative impact on the capacity for action by the police, because the police, with regard to the character of its activity, depends on the cooperation of the public or at least on its neutral attitude.

The crippling of the police was influenced by a number of other factors: frequent changes in managerial structures of the Federal Ministry of the Interior as well as of the Ministries of the Interior of both republics, the discreditation of police officers, the decrease of authority and the drop in confidence. The insufficient legal protection, the lengthy adoption of the Federal Act on the Police as well as the Acts on the Police of both Republics also had its part in crippling the activity of police officers.

In the course of 1990 and 1991 at the Institute for the Investigation of Public Opinion in cooperation with the Ministry of the Interior and the police of the Czech Republic, as well as in cooperation with the Institute for Criminology and Social Prevention, several investigations were carried out reflecting the changes in the attitudes of the Czech public towards the police. These investigations were implemented with the help of the standard method of the investigations of public opinion and covered about 1000-1500 respondents.

Satisfaction of the Citizens of the Czech Republic with the Activity of the Police (in %)

Question: "Are you satisfied with how the police takes care of the order and security of citizens in the place of your residence?"

Answers:

	October '90	February '91	May '91	December '91
Fully satisfied / Mostly satisfied	26	30	30	30
Mostly dissatisfied / Fully dissatisfied	68	66	58	57
Indifferent / Does not know	6	4	12	13

As sun in tables, the satisfaction of citizens with the activity of the police changed in a positive way in 1991 compared with 1990. The number of citizens satisfied with the activity of the police slightly increased and the percentage of citizens dissatisfied with its activity considerably decreased. In the course of 1991 the number of citizens satisfied with the activity of the police did not change and amounted to less than one third of the citizens; the number of fully satisfied citizens amounted to merely 3 percent. Compared with the February investigation, the number of dissatisfied markedly dropped but the number of indifferent and irresolute citizens considerably increased. The highest satisfaction with the performance of police service is in smaller municipalities (up to 2,000 inhabitants) and the lowest one in big cities (above 100,000 inhabitants).

The above mentioned results demonstrate that substantial changes that took place in the organization of the police, particularly due to its greater autonomy on the basis of the adoption of the Act on the Police of the Czech Republic have been until now reflected only to a small extent in the performance the of security service itself. One can assume that the strengthening of authority and of the overall autonomy of District Police Headquarters, the establishment of District Departments and of Police Stations, will be positively reflected already in the course of this year not only in the performance of the police in individual places, but also in the follow-up satisfaction of citizens with the activity of the police.

The Readiness to Cooperate with the Police in Detecting Criminal Activity (in %)

Question: "If you yourself became the witness of a crime, e.g. of theft, robbery or of violent criminal activity, would you cooperate with the police even if it does not concern you personally, e.g. in reporting, giving evidence, etc.?"

Answers:

	May '90	May '91	December '91
Definitely yes / More likely yes	78	82	80
More likely not / Definitely not	20	12	10
I do not know	2	6	10

The declared readiness of respondents to cooperate with the police in detecting criminal activity of these persons became witnesses of criminal activity is considerable (see Table 2.). It is gratifying that in this period the number of persons refusing a priori the cooperation with the police markedly dropped (by 50 per cent). This result demonstrates the moderate increase of the confidence of citizens in the police and the growing feeling of the necessity of the active participation of citizens in the solution of criminality as an undesirable social phenomenon.

The readiness to cooperate with the police is manifested mostly by the inhabitants of smaller municipalities (up to 2,000 inhabitants) and of medium-sized towns of 5,000 to 100,000 inhabitants.

The Confidence of the Citizens of the Czech Republic in the Police and Private Security Services (in %)

Question: "How do you look on the Police?"
"What feelings do police arouse in you?"
Answers:

	May '90	February '91	December '91
more likely confidence	30	48	50
more likely distrust	60	48	34
I do not know	10	3	15

From the comparison of the results (su Table 3.), it follows that the confidence of citizens in the police increased markedly in 1991 compared with the previous year. In the course of 1991 another positive development also took place – namely the moderate increase in the number of citizens having confidence in the police and particularly the marked decrease in the number of those citizens who manifest towards the police their distrust. Even more markedly will this positive development of the decrease of the distrust of citizens of the police stand out if we compare the results of December 1991 with the results of the investigation of May 1990. The number of the "distrustful" decreased in this period by almost half.

The markedly highest confidence in the police and the lowest distrust of the police is manifested by the inhabitants of the smallest municipalities (up to 500 inhabitants).

Question: "How do you look on the members of private security services? What feelings does the private security service arouse in you?"

Answers:

	December '91
more likely confidence	37
more likely distrust	26
I do not know	38

The question concerning the confidence of citizens in private security services was asked only in the investigation carried out in December 1991. With regard to the relatively short period of the activity of private security services in our conditions the marked prevalence of the confidence in (37 per cent) over the distrust (26 per cent) of citizens of these services can be regarded as the expression of consent to their existence. It is symptomatic that the relatively great number of respondents hiad no clean-cut relation to private security services.

The markedly highest confidence in private security services was expressed by the inhabitants of big cities (above 100,000 inhabitants) having the greatest experience with the performance of these services.

In comparing the results of answers to both last questions it is evident that currently the confidence of citizens in the police outweighs the confidence in private security services.

Conclusion

The results of the ascertainment of opinions of the citizens of the Czech Republic of the police show that the breakthrough in the barriers of distrust between the police and citizens took place and that the confidence of citizens in the police gradually increased. This fact will be doubtless reflected in the increased readiness of citizens to cooperate with the police and, therefore in more effective efforts of the police to suppress criminality.

Positive changes in the attitudes of citizens towards the police are probably the reflection of the purge of the police corps, of positive changes in the management of the Ministry of the Interior of the Czech Republic and of the police. There is evidently also the growing feeling of the menace of criminality to citizens and the deeper understanding of the role of police officers in its suppression.

Concluding Remarks

by
Louise Shelley

I want to thank Professor Jozsef Vigh both personally and on behalf of the Research Committee 29 of the International Sociological Association and the participants of this conference. He has organized this excellent meeting under the difficult conditions of the current transition. I want to thank our Hungarian hosts for their hospitality but especially for their openness. Particularly striking is their objectivity in assessing their problems and their ability to engage in probing self-examination. This is a rare and valuable quality and is particularly so in a time when individuals are themselves so involved in the process of rapid social change. I think the scholars from the approximately twenty countries who participated in these meetings have enjoyed and benefitted from the intellectual discussions on policing and crime.

The meetings have illustrated vividly that the participants from Western Europe and those from Central and Eastern Europe are coming from very different situations and analyze the problems of policing and crime patterns in very different ways. They use the same words but they denote different concepts among individuals from different social conditions. One could even say that they are not on the same intellectual wave length.

Those from western industrialized countries share a central concern – the preservation of democratic institutions and their way of life. These seem threatened now by the dramatic political changes in Europe over the past three years and the waves of refugees. The demise of the socialist system and the greater integration of Western and Eastern Europe, once highly sought objectives, now seem to hold more problems than promise. Fear of crime has replaced the more abstract desires for political change. Significant population movements from east to west, the result of the breakdown of the socialist system, represent an economic threat to these prosperous countries. The anti-foreigner movement which has its most violent manifestation in Germany is by no means confined to that society.

Citizens of former socialist countries seek greater integration with Western Europe. Their concerns are quite different from their western neighbors. The countries of Central and Eastern Europe are most concerned with the creation of democratic institutions. Many of these countries have not known democracy sinde the pre – World War II period if at all; some have always lived in authoritarian societies. Much is known about the transition from authoritarian rule when the previous country has been fascist or a military dictatorship. In these societies there usually was political and often ideological control of the society. But civil society still endured in certain economic related activities and in free markets. The socialist system provided a more encompassing control in which the institutions of civil society were suppressed and control was maintained over the political, ideological, economic and social spheres. The former socialist countries are working in a terra incognito attempting to achieve both a political, ideological and economic transformation simultaneously.

Under these conditions, the transformation that is proceeding in Central and Eastern Europe is unusually complex. There is the simultaneous demise of an encompassing ideology, an economic system based on centralized planning and a collectivist ideology. These countries are trying to move towards democratic market economies without a strong ideological base. But this transition is occurring within bankrupt societies whose authoritarian leaders handed over power only at the worst of times. As in Latin America, the transition to democracy is occurring under the most difficult situations when the non-democratic governments had nearly given up. The difficulty of the transition and, the lack of order, epitomized by skyrocketing crime rates, may prejudice citizens appraisal of democratic institutions.

Sergio Adorno, our Brazilian participant, developed a point that many participants did not really want to hear. From his country's experience, the change to a democratically elected government has not ensured change in the police. One needs to change the political system, the laws, the attitudes towards law. This does not come overnight. Even after eight years of democracy there has been no change in policing. Does this fate await the former socialist countries?

Judging by the reports of our Hungarian colleagues and the attention paid to restructuring police, law and promoting the development of a legal consciousness, their prognosis may be better. Hungary is working with a more educated population and the economic transformation, while traumatic, is not as difficult as in some other former socialist countries. In other former socialist countries, despite the best of intentions, little progress has been made in implementing successful changes in the control apparatus.

The social, political and economic conditions which now exist in all the former socialist countries are a recipe for a rise in crime. All of the participants from the former socialist countries have documented very rapid rises in crime with both increases in property crime and crimes of violence. The steep rise in crime, particularly dangerous crime, brings a concomitant desire for an increase in police and police powers. Responses that are often antithetical to a democracy.

Within these divergent social and political contexts, police and crime have different meanings. In democratic societies police are not just part of the general administrative apparatus of the state. They are expected to be accountable to the law and the citizens of the state. In contrast in authoritarian societies, the police are a central institution for the maintenance of state authority. The socialist police forces were not accountable to the citizenry, did not operate under the rule of law, could be more intrusive and could compel cooperation from the citizenry.

The successor police forces in the former socialist societies can count on none of these advantages while confronting problems of crime which are much more serious. The institutions of the state, including the police, are extremely underfinanced and deprived of the economic resources that they need to combat crime. A citizenry now liberated from the coerced cooperation with state institutions, will not provide the voluntary support which exists in some democratic societies.

Participants from almost all twenty countries represented at the conference reported on a rise in crime in their respective societies. But the reasons for this growth differed. In Western Europe, the increase in crime is attributed to the increasing affluence and changing population, often a result of immigration from less affluent and politically stable regions. The growth in crime is noted not only in street crime and certain crimes of aggression but also in areas related to high technology. In the former socialist countries, the dramatic social and political change contributes to social instability and crime.

The crime problem that has developed so rapidly in these countries is something which their law enforcement cannot contain. The social safety net has collapsed. Organized crime has expanded, in some places particularly parts of the former Soviet Union, it has replaced the collapsing state institutions. The collapse of the Marxist ideology, which predicted the withering away of crime, has been discredited. The failed ideology has been confirmed by the phenomenal growth in crime that the states cannot control, a growth that threatens not only the former socialist states but the affluent democracies of Western Europe. As the criminals look for more lucrative markets outside their collapsing economies, they naturally gravitate west. The Western European countries fear the crime originating from these newly impoverished socialist countries. Their fear is possibly out of proportion to the threat of crime but it is having repercussions that extend beyond the criminal justice system.

The comparison between the democratic societies and former socialist societies needs to be made in the following areas if one is to consider not only the trends in crime and policing but also the political, social and economic context.

1) The Economic Situation
2) Nationalist Views
3) Nature of Institutions
4) Organization of Society
5) Human Rights
6) Role of Technology

The Economic Situation

Western Europe, the United States and many advanced western societies are enjoying prosperity despite the economic difficulties of the past few years. While the problems of recession have exacerbated the problem of unemployment and of the status of migrants, they still appear to be economic havens for members of societies where the social safety net has collapsed. The societies of Western Europe are suffering from the problems of affluent youth committing delinquent acts whereas in the former socialist societies the crime problems are more often motivated by need or by anomie.

At present there is no single western country or even bodies of western countries that are affluent enough or committed to rescue the economies of Eastern Europe. With the exception of West Germany, there is no western country that has assumed responsibility for a country in the East. But in Germany, the economic redemption has had its criminogenic consequences. Violent acts against immigrants are not isolated incidents but have numbered in the hundreds in 1992. As a consequence, the police have acquired special powers to deal with the skinheads and fascist groups. There is a coupling of economic resentment of the costs of unification with that of the rising nationalism. The consequences are political, the signs are criminogenic.

In other Eastern European countries where there is not such external financial assistance, the collapse of the economy has been very strong with a limited cushion. Crime rates for property crimes have increased dramatically, some of it motivated by purely economic need. Other crimes are related to the criminalization of the second economy in the former socialist period which has developed into full scale organized crime in the post-socialist period.

The Impact of Nationalism

The growing nationalism of Western Europe is not just nation specific but appears to be setting up a barrier between East and West that in some ways is as formidable as the political barrier that existed previously. While Western European countries once feared a strategic threat from the former socialist countries and the Soviet Union, their concerns are now more on the human level. A different situation, therefore, exists in the two parts of Europe. The West fears the citizens of the East at the very moment that the former socialist states seek to be more closely tied to Western Europe. These ties were an impossiblity in the past because of political reasons, now such greater unity is prevented by economic and nationalist reasons. The once strong Western European desire for greater integration is now muted and in some cases, is actively opposed as the costs to their societies of the free movement of peoples is evaluated.

In France and Germany, as well as in some other Western European countries, there has been a significant growth in political parties which are actively hostile to foreigners. In England, as described by our participants, police-community relations are increasingly strained particularly in areas with high populations of immigrants.

In various European countries, crime and threats to order are reasons given for restricting immigration or even denying entry of Eastern European nationals. Western European countries are aware of the crime rise in Eastern and Central Europe and fear its consequences in their societies. Public opinion research in countries such as Belgium indicate that the citizens fear the crime problems brought by the Eastern immigrants and travellers as much as those from North Africans.

Nature of Institutions

The institutional structures of the affluent West and the impoverished East are very different. Western Europe is concerned about threats to its democratic institutions. This is a very real problem. In Germany, crime against foreigners has resulted in the quashing of neo-Nazi organizations as citizens worry about the reemergence of anti-democratic movements in their society. The British government, as pointed out by various speakers, is using police techniques in Northern Ireland which undermine the democratic institutions of their society. Yet the free press and the public consciousness in these societies are acutely aware of these threats to democracy. The need to preserve democratic structure is particularly important in Europe which has enjoyed an extended period of nearly unprecedented peace since World War II. Until the terrible violence in Yugoslavia, Europe seemed to have developed a means to contain nationalism to promote a larger good.

In contrast to the peace enjoyed by Western Europe since World War II, there has been neither peace nor democracy in Eastern Europe. The post-World War II period has been marked by repeated violence as Soviet troops entered Hungary and Czcechoslovakia and solidarnost was suppressed in Poland under pressure from Moscow. The threat or even the presence of violence became the norm for many citizens of these societies. The contrast between East and West has been one of state vs. individual violence. While citizens of Western Europe have feared the individual violence of the criminal, in Eastern Europe general crime rates were low and citizens worried about the political repression of the state against its citizenry or a foreign power against them. In divided democratically elected governments like Britain, only sectors of the society needed to be concerned about state violence, often in the form of a repressive police.

Organization of Society

The organizational structure of the Western and former socialist states is very different. Therefore, the same words have very different meanings in the two contexts. One example is the concept of volunteerism. For example, in Western Europe, following on the ideas of the Enlightenment there is more attention paid to the rights of the individual. By contrast, in socialist societies, there has been a collectivist ideology. Unlike democratic societies where the minority must submit voluntarily to the will of the majority, in the socialist system one was expected to sublimate one's individual will to the collective good of the entire society.

In democratic societies, volunteerism is a desired goal. It is an individual giving directly and willingly to the community. In socialists states, individuals were forced to volunteer. There was a suspicion of actions that were not within state control and regulation.

The significance of this difference can be seen most clearly in the comparative discussions of policing and of services to victims. In most western societies, the ideas of individual cooperation with the police and of citizen movements to help the victims of crime were viewed positively. They were examples of citizen initiative and were to be encouraged. In contrast, in the socialist states there was no volunteer participation within policing and no organized victim assistance programs. All needed to be controlled by the state and citizens were not allowed true volunteerism in the justice system.

Human Rights

Western and socialist societies had very different approaches to human rights. As was previously discussed, the organization of western society was based since the Enlightenment on the rights of the individual. In the law enforcement context, this meant that individuals had to be respected. There were limits to the authority of the police because the rights of the state were not automatically superior to those of the citizen.

In contrast, in socialist societies there was a commitment to collective rights. Individual welfare was protected by the state but in return individuals were subordinate to the wishes of the state. In policing, this meant that the police could use force to control order. Order was at a premium because it was for the collective good of the society. Police methods were not questioned as long as they achieved the larger societal objective.

Role of Technology

The contrasting perspectives of the socialist and capitalist countries can clearly be seen in relation to technology. While the western criminological community is increasingly concerned about the ever more potent technology with its ability to intrude into private life, Eastern European countries see this new technology as a sign of modernity. They want the advanced communication systems for their police that are known in western society and the computer records that will enable the police to provide better tracking of criminals.

Many of the Western European police are worried about the increasing intrusiveness which is possible with more advanced technology. But residents of former socialist societies, now suffering with serious crime for the first time are willing to run the risks of increased technology if it will prove effective in controlling crime.

In conclusion, the great points of difference between the Western European and Eastern European scholars made communication difficult at times. It was not a result of a language barrier but a consequence of political, economic and social differences. With such different histories, scholars from different cultures approach the problems of crime and policing from divergent perspectives. I hope that the past few days have helped explain why individuals can talk on the same subject but cannot always easily communicate.

List of Authors

Opening Speech

Dr. Péter BOROSS — Minister of Interior in Hungary

Topic I.

József VIGH — Professor, Head of Department of Criminology, Eötvös Loránd University, Budapest

Robert REINER — Professor, Law Department, London School of Economics London, United Kingdom

Knut SVERI — Professor, Emeritus Stockholm, Sweden

Topic II.

Uwe EWALD — Criminologist Humboldt University, Berlin

Kauko AROMAA — Research Director National Research Institute of Legal Policy, Helsinki

Sergio ADORNO — Professor, University of São Paolo, Brazil

Erich BUCHHOLZ — Professor, Lawyer, Berlin

Ahti LAITINEN — Associate Professor of the Sociology of Law University of Turku, Finland

Topic III.

Dr. Sándor PINTÉR — Chief Commissioner of National Police Headquarters, Hungary

Valér DÁNOS — Director, Research Institute

István TAUBER — Assistant Professor of the Budapest University

List of Authors

Jorgen JEPSEN	Assistant Professor University of Aarhus, Denmark
Michael ROWE	Research Assistant Centre for the Study of Public Order University of Leicester U.K.
Dr. Philip RAWLINGS	Department of Law, Brunel University
Dr. Betsy STANKO	Uxbridge, Middlesex, United Kingdom

Topic IV.

Dr. Mike KING	Lecturer, Centre for the Study of Public Order, University of Leicester, U.K.
Dr. László SALGÓ	Chief Constable of County Police Szeged, Hungary
Rob I. MAWBY	Principal Lecturer, Department of Applied Social Science, University of Plymouth

Topic V.

Ferenc IRK	Titular Professor Budapest
Giovanni B. TRAVERSO	Professor of Criminology, University of Siena, Italy
Josef ZAPLETAL	Institute for Criminology
Mikulaš TOMIN	Social Prevention, Prague
Louise SHELLEY	President of Research Committee for the Sociology of Deviance and Social Control, International Sociological Association, Washington

Name Index

A

Adorno, S., 72;
Agelink, M. T. G., 168;
Akers, R. L., 24;
Alderson, J., 49, 142;
Ames, W. L., 174;
Anderson, J., 24;
Anderson, M., 160;
Arlacchi, P., 186;
Aromaa, K., 62;
Ascoll, D., 35;

B

Baldwin, R., 35;
Basaliga, F., 186;
Baxter, J., 35;
Bayley, D. M., 174;
Beavls, S., 161;
Beck, U., 105;
Becker, H. S., 186;
Belyh, V., 106;
Benyon, J., 49, 71, 142;
Bigo, D., 160;
Birch, R., 160;
Blake, N., 142;
Boateng, P., 142;
Boross P., 7;
Bourn, C., 49;
Braithwaite, J., 105, 106;
Brewer, J. D., 49;
Brewer, J. D. M., 175;
Brogden, M., 35;

Broms, H., 105;
Brown, C., 142;
Bruun, K., 105;
Buchholz E., 83;

C

Cavender, G., 106;
Chapman, B., 175;
Chinnici, G., 186;
Christie, N., 105;
Clarke, R., 35;
Clinard, M. B., 105;
Clutterbuck, R., 161;
Cohen, Lawrence E., 71;
Cohen, M. A., 105;
Cohen, S., 147, 161;
Coleman, J., 105;
Cowell, D., 49;
Cox, B., 35;
Critchley, T. A., 35;
Cruz, A., 161;
Cullen, Francis T., 106;

D

Dahrendorf, R., 35;
Dános, V., 118;
David Dowds, L., 175;
Davis, J., 142;
de Cok, P., 161;
den Boer, M., 161;
Déri, P., 24;

Di Tullio, B., 186;
Donowan, P., 161;
Dowsd, L., 36;

E

Eitzen, S. D., 107;
Elliot, D., 36;
Emsley, C., 35;
Ensley, C., 175;
Ewald, U., 51;

F

Farrell, M., 71;
Felson, M., 71;
Fijnaut, C., 161;
Fijnaut, C. F., 175;
Fijnaut, D. J. F., 168;
Fisse, B., 106;
Fosdick, R. B., 175;

G

Gahrton, P., 71;
Galaway, B., 26;
Gatrell, V., 35;
Gilroy, P., 143;
Goldsmith, A., 35;
Gordon, P., 143;
Graham, J., 71;
Greene, Jack R., 168;
Guelke, A., 49, 175;

H

Hall, S., 143, 147;
Hans-Jörg, A., 70;
Heidensohn, F., 71;

Hilis, S. L., 106;
Hoogenboom, B., 24;
Hope, T., 25;
Hough, M., 35;
Hume, I., 49, 175;

I

Impert, P., 143;
Irk, F., 177;

J

Jaakkola, M., 71;
Jaap de Waard, 71;
Jamleson, A., 162;
Jefferson, T., 35, 175;
Jeffries, S. C., 175;
Jepsen, J., 126;
Jones, M., 35;
Jones, T., 49, 143;
Judge, T., 175;
le Jeune, P., 162;

K

Kettle, M., 143;
Killias, M., 24, 71;
Killias, Martin, 168;
King, M., 149, 162;
Kinsey, R., 35;
Koffmann, L., 35;
Kolozsi, T., 25;
Kowalewski, D., 175;

L

Laitinen, A., 90, 106;
Lambert, J., 143;
Lea, J. 174;
Lee, M., 35;
Lehtonen, A., 106;
Lemert, E. M., 186;

Liebl, K., 106;
Lirhanov, D., 106;
Lorenz, K., 25;
Loveday, B., 175;
Lustgarten, L., 36;

M

Maakestad, W. J., 106;
MacLean, B., 143;
Maggs, C., 175;
Magnusson, D., 106;
Marcus Felson, 71;
Marshall, T. H., 36;
Matthews, R., 25;
Mawby, R. I., 169, 175;
Mayhew, P., 24, 36, 71;
Mayhew, P. E., 175;
Mayhew, Pat, 168;
Mead, G. H., 186;
Miller, W., 36;
Milténobservedyi, K., 25;
Morgan, R., 175;
Moxon-Browe, I., 175;
Moxon-Browne, E., 49;

N

Niessen, J., 162;
Northam, G., 36;

O

Offe, C., 25;

P

Paavola, V., 105;
Patten, J., 25;
Pavarini, M., 187;
Pick, H., 162;
Pintér, S., 109, 168;
Pitch, T., 187;

Platt, A. M., 187;
Porter, B., 36;
Posio, A., 106;
Prestel, M., 168;

Q

Quetelet, A., 25;

R

Radzinowicz, Leon, 49;
Raeff, M., 175;
Rawlings, P., 144, 147;
Rease, K., 26;
Reiner, R., 25, 27, 36, 143, 175;
Reinke, S., 162;
Reith, C., 36;
Ricci, A., 187;
Rittler, E.-J., 106;
Robert, P., 25;
Rosenber, D., 143;
Rothman, M. L., 107;
Rowe, M., 130;
Rudas, G., 176;
Ryan, M., 25;

S

Salgó, L., 163, 168;
Sallerno, G., 187;
Salminen, M., 106;
Santino, U., 186;
Scharman,, 143;
Schöler, U., 107;
Scraton, P., 143;
Searle, C., 143;
Shaw, M., 25;
Shelley, L., 195;
Shipp, S., 107;
Shirley, J., 35;
Short, M., 35;

Sim, J., 143;
Simon, D. R., 107;
Simpura, J., 71;
Smith, D., 25;
Smith, D. J., 143;
Solomes, J., 142;
Soothill, K., 25;
South, N., 25;
Southgate, P., 143;
Spencer, M., 162;
Spitzer, S., 162;
Stanko, B., 144;
Stanko, E., 147;
Stead, P. J., 36, 176;
Steedman, C., 36;
Storch, R., 36;
Straver, M., 168;
Sveri, K., 37;
Szabó, A.
Szabó, D., 25;

T

Takala, H., 71;
Tauber, I., 118;
Taylor, I., 187;
Taylor, M., 26;
Thurmond, S. P., 36;
Tigersted Chr., 71;
Tobias, J. J., 176;
Tomin, M., 190;
Törnudd, P., 71;
Traverso, G. B., 184, 187;
Tuck, M., 143;

V

v. Weinhofer, K., 107;
Vähätalo, T., 106;

van Dijk, J., 24;
van Dijk, Jan, 71;
van Dijk, Jan J. M., 71, 168;
van Dijk, P., 49;
van Gesteg, G. J. A. H., 168;
van Hoof G. J. H., 49;
van Reenan, P., 162;
Vigh, J., 11, 26;

W

Waddington, P. A. J., 36;
Walklate, S., 175;
Waller, J., 26;
Walton, P., 187;
Ward, R. H., 176;
Ward, T., 25;
Weber, Max, 168;
Weiss, R. P., 26;
Werde, A., 187;
Wheeler, S., 107;
Wilford, R., 49, 175;
William, O. B., 26;
Wright, M., 26;

Y

Young, J., 26, 35, 143, 187;
Young, M., 36;
Young, T. R., 107;

Z

Zander, M., 36;
Zapletal, Josep., 190;
Zoung, J., 49;